Fandom At The Crossroads

Fandom At The Crossroads:
Celebration, Shame
and Fan/Producer Relationships

Edited by

Lynn Zubernis and Katherine Larsen

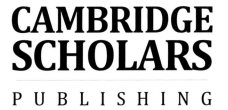

CAMBRIDGE
SCHOLARS

P U B L I S H I N G

Fandom At The Crossroads:
Celebration, Shame and Fan/Producer Relationships,
Edited by Lynn Zubernis and Katherine Larsen

This book first published 2012. The present binding first published 2012.

Cambridge Scholars Publishing

12 Back Chapman Street, Newcastle upon Tyne, NE6 2XX, UK

British Library Cataloguing in Publication Data
A catalogue record for this book is available from the British Library

ISBN (10): 1-4438-4140-4, ISBN (13): 978-1-4438-4140-5

TABLE OF CONTENTS

List of Illustrations vii

Acknowledgements ix

Introduction 1

Chapter One... 16
Lost in Space: Participatory Fandom and the Negotiation of Fan Spaces

Chapter Two 36
Taking Sides: Business or Pleasure?

Chapter Three 57
I'm Too Sexy For My Stereotype

Chapter Four.. 82
Fandom as Change Agent: Transformative Whats?

Chapter Five 116
Only Love Can Break Your Heart: Fandom Wank and Policing
the Safe Space

Chapter Six 143
And The (Fourth) Walls Come Tumbling Down

Chapter Seven.. 175
The Reciprocal Relationship: How Much is Too Much?

Bibliography 230

Index 243

List of Illustrations

Fig. I-1: The somewhat attractive Jensen Ackles
Fig. I-2: The somewhat attractive Jared Padalecki
Fig. I-3: icons (investment)
Fig. 1-1: Padalecki confers with Ackles onstage at a con
Fig. 1-2: Jensen Ackles entertains the fans
Fig. 1-3: Packed house: The space between audience and performer
Fig. 1-4: Breakfast with the boys: Jared and Jensen do stand-up
Fig. 1-5: Squee! The boys are back in town.
Fig. 1-6: Leaving an impression: Padalecki signs a fan's shirt
Fig. 1-7: The trappings of celebrity: Ackles and his arsenal of sharpies
Fig. 1-8: Plastic Winchester Theater's Sam and Dean
Fig. 2-1: Boundary violations: Padalecki with dogs Harley and Sadie
Fig. 2-2: In the closet: Sam and Dean's "Personals"
Fig. 2-3: Oh no, stalkers!
Fig. 2-4: You're writing a book about what??
Fig. 2-5: Jensen and Jared give up and pose for a photo op without Lynn
Fig. 3-1: icons (shame)
Fig. 3-2: icons (shame)
Fig. 3-3: The disturbingly attractive Ackles
Fig. 3-4: icons (shame)
Fig. 3-5: icons (shame)
Fig. 3-6: icons (shame)
Fig. 3-7: icons (objectify)
Fig. 3-8: icons (projection)
Fig. 3-9: icons (shame)
Fig. 3-10: icons (shame)
Fig. 3-11: fandom secret anonymous post
Fig. 3-12: fandom secret anonymous post
Fig. 4-1: icons (slash)
Fig. 4-2: icons (therapy)
Fig. 4-3: icons (therapy)
Fig. 4-4: fandom secret anonymous post
Fig. 4-5: fandom secret anonymous post
Fig. 4-6: fandom secret anonymous post
Fig. 5-1: icons (wank)

Fig. 5-2: icons (J2)
Fig. 5-3: icons (RPS)
Fig. 5-4: icons (tinhats)
Fig. 6-1: Breaking the first rule of fandom
Fig. 6-2: icons (subtext)
Fig. 6-3: Never dare Jim Beaver to do anything
Fig. 6-4: The creator speaks: Eric Kripke fronts his creations
Fig. 6-5: icons (fourth wall)
Fig. 6-6: icons (fourth wall)
Fig. 6-7: comic shame
Fig. 7-1: Padalecki and Ackles have each other's backs
Fig. 7-2: "I see you, you see me" – sort of.
Fig. 7-3: Paparazzi! Ackles turns the tables
Fig. 7-4: Signs of affection: Fan gifts in a con green room
Fig. 7-5: We're all in this together: Fan quilt hangs in production office
Fig. 7-6: Ackles is a Sam fan too
Fig. 7-7: Real life subtext
Fig. 7-8: Real life brothers
Fig. 7-9: Fandom is fun
Fig. 7-10: Misha Collins attempts angelic

ACKNOWLEDGEMENTS

Thank you to our colleagues at George Washington University and West Chester University, for their support and input over the five years of researching this book. Thanks also to our families, who remained supportive even under sometimes trying circumstances. Special thanks to Matt Hills for his thoughtful and comprehensive critique of the final manuscript and invaluable suggestions.

We're grateful to the two photographers who contributed so much to *Fandom at the Crossroads*, Elizabeth Sisson and Christopher Schmelke. Their talent speaks for itself in these pages. We are also indebted to Adam Malin, Gary Berman and Stephanie Pettit of Creation Entertainment for their invaluable help in facilitating interviews and understanding the intricacies of conventions, and to Betsy Morris, David Mackay, Elizabeth Yoffe, Tony Zierra, Susie Hinton, Bhavna and Night Shyamalan for the diverse perspectives about fans, creators and blurred boundaries.

This book could not have been written without the generous, insightful and candid contributions of countless *Supernatural* fans, whom we have come to know online and in person. Over the past six years, they sat down with us for dozens of interviews. They also welcomed us into their homes, shared convention hotel rooms, stood beside us in autograph lines, and joined us for squeeful episode viewings, slightly inebriated con karaokes, and treks all over the Vancouver countryside in search of filming locations. They have been there with encouragement and support, fellow fans and now friends.

Equally important to the creation of this book are the contributions of the creative side who bring *Supernatural* to life each week. The vast majority of our interviewees took time out of hectic shooting schedules to sit down with us in person, and to answer our sometimes unusual questions. We're grateful to Eric Kripke, Sera Gamble, Serge Ladouceur, Jerry Wanek, Chris Cooper, Robin Stooshnov, Carmelita Fowler, Lee-Ann Elaschuk, Mary-Ann Liu, Jason Fischer and Clif Kosterman for sharing their contributions to the making of *Supernatural*. Many of the actors and musicians associated with *Supernatural* shared their thoughts as well –

thanks to Misha Collins, Jim Beaver, Richard Speight Jr., Matt Cohen, Chad Lindberg, Gabe Tigerman, Todd Stashwick, Samantha Smith, C. Malik Whitfield, Samantha Ferris, Fred Lehne, Steve Carlson, Jason Manns, Brian Buckley and Danneel Ackles. Special thanks to Jensen Ackles and Jared Padalecki for their candor, thoughtful insights and sense of humor.

We couldn't have done it without all of you!

All celebrity interviews were personal interviews conducted between 2007 and 2011 unless otherwise noted. Fan comments included were personal interviews or online public posts collected between 2007 and 2011 unless otherwise noted.

Icons included as illustrations are all publicly posted LiveJournal avatars collected between 2007 and 2011. Fandomsecrets are all publicly posted on LiveJournal between 2007 and 2011.

Photographs are by authors except as noted below. All photographs taken for this book and used with permission.

Fig. I-1: Elizabeth Sisson
Fig. I-2: Elizabeth Sisson
Fig. 1-1: Elizabeth Sisson
Fig. 1-2: Elizabeth Sisson
Fig. 1-3: Elizabeth Sisson
Fig. 1-4: Elizabeth Sisson
Fig. 1-5: Elizabeth Sisson
Fig. 1-6: Elizabeth Sisson
Fig. 1-7: Elizabeth Sisson
Fig. 1-8: Elizabeth Sisson
Fig. 2-3: Christopher Schmelke
Fig. 2-4: Christopher Schmelke
Fig. 2-5: Christopher Schmelke

Fig. 3-3: Christopher Schmelke
Fig. 6-1: Elizabeth Sisson
Fig. 6-4: Elizabeth Sisson
Fig. 7-1: Christopher Schmelke
Fig. 7-2: Elizabeth Sisson
Fig. 7-3: Christopher Schmelke
Fig. 7-4: Elizabeth Sisson
Fig. 7-6: Elizabeth Sisson
Fig. 7-7: Christopher Schmelke
Fig. 7-8: Christopher Schmelke
Fig. 7-9: Christopher Schmelke
Fig. 7-10: Christopher Schmelke
Back cover: Christopher Schmelke

INTRODUCTION

Halfway through a celebrity Q&A at a *Supernatural* fan convention in Los Angeles, an attending fan broke the first rule of fandom ("Tell no one about fandom!") by asking what the actors onstage thought of fanfiction. A groan rolled through the mostly female crowd, followed by an awkward moment of silence as the actors groped for an appropriately diplomatic answer. The actors (Travis Wester and A.J. Buckley) seemed more amused than traumatized by the question; not so some of the gathered fandom. The dozen or so fangirls we joined for dinner that night were still talking about "the incident" several hours later, and the debate was heated. One woman asserted that questions from fans need to be moderated, lest the fan ask something "weird," going so far as to say that "an authority figure needs to step in." Presumably the authority figures in question would be the co-owners of Creation Entertainment (the company staging the event), who are both men in their fifties. The notion that a room full of adult women couldn't be trusted to ask their own questions without being vetted by two male "authority figures" was disconcerting, but it wasn't entirely surprising. It reflects some pervasive assumptions about fans—assumptions from which fans themselves often operate.

Much has been written over the last three decades about fans, often in an attempt to rehabilitate the image of the fan, to validate fan practices, to celebrate and defend fandom, to declare certain battles won. But for all the declarations about the positive force of fandom, a pervasive sense of shame permeates both fan spaces and academic approaches to the subject. There is shame about being a fan at all, shame over the extremity of "some" fans, shame over "certain" fan practices, over having those practices revealed to the rest of the world, or to the fannish objects themselves, as the fan at the convention discovered. There is also shame about studying something as "frivolous" as fandom—or worse yet, taking frivolous pleasure ourselves, "sitting too close" instead of remaining suitably detached observers.

We should know. We've been sitting too close to our television sets once a week for the past seven years. When it comes to *Supernatural*, we're anything but detached.

Supernatural (known within the fandom as "Show" or "SPN") premiered on September 13, 2005, on what was then The WB network.

Creator Eric Kripke was inspired by Kerouac's *On The Road*, sending his heroes Sam and Dean driving across an explicitly American landscape in a big black '67 Impala to investigate the urban legends that had fascinated Kripke since childhood. The show was expected to appeal to the coveted 18-49 male demographic. However, the casting of Jared Padalecki and Jensen Ackles as the show's male leads made it clear that the network was hoping to attract viewers with more than gun battles and gore. A last minute decision to make Sam and Dean brothers opened up the possibility for a closer relationship than a Luke and Han style friendship would have allowed, and turned the term "bromance" literal. The obvious chemistry between the actors, widely commented on by everyone involved with the show and anyone who has ever interviewed Ackles and Padalecki in person, also contributed to the series' evolution. Initially produced as monster-of-the-week episodes crafted to scare, *Supernatural* found its stride when it combined urban legends with a powerful and nuanced relationship drama, exploring the intense, complicated, decidedly angsty bond between the brothers.

While *Supernatural* has flown under the radar until recently, the series attracted a passionate fan base from the beginning. When Henry Jenkins put out a query on his blog in 2007 asking what show his readers thought he should be watching, the vast majority recommended *Supernatural*. Jenkins easily succumbed, writing "I more or less ended up inhaling Season One, watching the episodes in sequence and thus seeing the characters' inner lives come bubbling up again and again." Jenkins described the show as acting as a "cultural attractor," tapping into the zeitgeist of the moment (2007a). In a world concerned with the largely invisible threat of terrorism, Jenkins notes, fighting unseen evil resonates with viewers, allowing *Supernatural* to draw on our current generalized anxiety while also tapping into our more primal fears about what might be lurking under our beds, in our closets—or, most frightening of all, in our own minds.

Supernatural also tells a story of familial ties, love and loyalty. The Winchesters, father John and sons Dean and Sam, are a different sort of nuclear family. Essentially homeless nomads after the death of their mother, the boys grew up in motel rooms, criss-crossing the United States with their demon hunter father. They are far from stereotypical, yet they are what we all recognize as family. They argue, they disagree, they break apart, they come back together. But most of all they love, often to the point of literal self-sacrifice. In a political climate filled with the rhetoric of family values, *Supernatural* seems to affirm what family means while confirming that families can flourish in non-traditional ways.

In order for a media text to be a successful cultural attractor, there must also be a way in for fans, with meaningful ways to participate. *Supernatural* provides a canon open enough to invite speculation, discussion, critical evaluation, and transformative works, while at the same time sustaining a remarkably consistent mythology which has now stretched over seven seasons. Episodes continue to provide glimpses of the boys' backstory, sometimes in flashbacks to Sam and Dean's childhood, sometimes through time travel, sometimes even with a glimpse of the boys' idiosyncratic versions of heaven—enough to captivate, but never to satisfy. The show provides an intense emotional pull as well with the deep, codependent, self-sacrificing, borderline pathological relationship between Sam and Dean. Since Sam and Dean are brothers, the characters are given a pass for displays of emotion outside the cultural norms for masculinity. Thus, *Supernatural* offers fans a sort of pick-your-own love relationship between the boys, allowing fans to invest in their passionate love, either platonically or otherwise. As Jenkins writes, "We want to see men emote for each other, and the family ties allow for a narrative that can play with this instead of justifying it" (2007a).

The show is also a testament to the immediacy of fandom in the age of the internet. The first Live Journal site dedicated to *Supernatural* predated the airing of the pilot by two months, after buzz from Comic Con got fans talking. The first dedicated website went up several days after. The first fanfiction community on Live Journal was created two days before the airing of the pilot, and the first fanfiction was posted within hours of the show's debut. As we'll see later, actors and producers are often there, side by side with the fans, tweeting from the set or even during the airing of particular episodes. Fan practices are incorporated into the show itself and canon and "fanon" live side by side. Indeed the fandom surrounding *Supernatural* can be seen as an excellent example of "convergence culture, where old and new media collide, where grassroots and corporate media intersect, where the power of the media producer and the power of the media consumer interact in unpredictable ways" (Jenkins 2006, 2).

This explains what brings fans to the show. How we came to the show, and how we've negotiated the multiple roles we've occupied both in fandom and as academics investigating fandom, is a story at once parallel to and deeply entwined with our analysis of the fandom. Both of us have long fannish histories. We met via another fandom (*Velvet Goldmine*) and have shared many of the same fannish interests ever since. We did not come naturally to *Supernatural*, however, nor did we arrive there at the same time. Rather, we were lured there by a mutual friend who thought the show would be something that would appeal to us. She gifted us with DVD

Fig. I-1. The somewhat attractive Jensen Ackles

Fig. I-2. The somewhat attractive Jared Padalecki

sets, reminded us to watch on Thursday nights, and provided well- crafted
near-essays on the quality of the acting, writing and production. She
played dirty by sending us photos of the show's (somewhat attractive) lead
actors. After some initial hesitation and false starts, she prevailed—we
were both sucked headlong into the series.

We live in different states and don't get the chance to be in the same
place at the same time all that often. When we could finally arrange a "fan
weekend," we mainlined the entire first season of *Supernatural* on DVD in
what we'd later categorize as a "lost day". We sat down to watch early one
morning, and stayed there all day and into the night, stopping periodically
to ogle screencaps and close-ups and mutter appreciative curses. We slept
for a few hours and then got up with the sun to start right back in. At 6 pm
the next day, we stared at each other and Lynn asked blearily, "Did we
ever even eat anything this weekend?" The answer—alarmingly—was no.
Clearly our investment was anything but casual.

By early 2008, we were completely immersed in the *Supernatural*
fandom, but still lacking a satisfactory explanation of our own experience.
We were frustrated by media coverage that seemed to misrepresent and
pathologize fans, and by academic theorizing which seemed to give lip
service to writing as an aca-fan but to continually shy away from
confessing the actual fan side of the equation. Why, we wondered, are
fans—ourselves included—still so ashamed to admit it? The tenacity of
this uncomfortable emotion seems particularly unexpected at a time when
the economic power of fans has become an accepted (and much-courted)
force. An article by Lance Neuhauser in MediaBizBloggers posed the
provocative question, "Want to know the value of a 'fan'?" The answer to
that, according to a study by Vitrue on the LQ Digital IQ Index, is $3.60.
This value increases, however, with what Neuhauser calls the consumer's
"return on interaction"—the impetus to share experiences and knowledge.
Consumers have changed the way they communicate, with a study on the
value of Twitter followers concluding that "social media fans are two-
thirds more likely to recommend a brand they've friended to a friend, or to
buy the products themselves." The economic force of fandom alone should
garner it a more favorable place in the culture. And yet the image of the
fan remains persistently "othered" (2010).

The growing field of fan studies, into which we plunged with as much
enthusiasm and shame as we did into fandom itself, seems open to a more
immersed and emotionally focused exploration. The first wave of fan
studies assumed a dichotomy of power, following de Certeau's (1984)
description of powerful producers on one side and disempowered consumers
on the other. Second and third wave theorists moved away from an

assumed dichotomy, but continued to focus on questions of class and subversion (Fiske 1992; Thornton 1995). More recently, theorists have explored the role of fandom in constructing fans' identity, and the social and cultural significance of identity performance in distribution of power (Sandvoss 2005; Hellekson and Busse 2006; Hills 2002) and have introduced a focus on the individual and the subjective previously neglected in cultural studies, including prioritizing the emotional aspects of fanning (Lancaster 2001).

Those emotional aspects of fanning also, of course, apply to those of us who fit the definition of aca-fans. In *The Wow Climax*, Jenkins stresses the need to examine fandom from an emotional perspective, from a standpoint of immersion instead of distance:

> These aspects of popular culture are difficult to understand from a stance of contemplative distance. To understand how popular culture works on our emotions, we have to pull it close, get intimate with it, let it work its magic on us, and then write about our own engagement...capturing their own subjective responses to popular text and using them as a point of entry into understanding larger cultural processes and aesthetic issues. Unfortunately, various forms of distanciation have been built into the theoretical traditions and aesthetic categories through which we study popular culture (2007, 10).

Our decision to write from a position of immersion within *Supernatural* fandom is intended, undoubtedly with varying degrees of success, to reduce that distance. In doing so, we attempt to respond to the suggestion of Hills (2002) and others that what we write about fandom should be accessible to fans, written in a language that doesn't require an advanced degree or years of specific study to comprehend, yet without the subtle condescension that comes from underestimating fandom's collective intelligence and expertise. We also try to retain those emotional aspects of fandom that have been neglected in fan theory. After all, none of us became fans because it wasn't fun! Throughout the text, we incorporate a sampling of icons, used as both avatars for online posts in various fan spaces and as a form of creative expression. Icons are a unique language, providing everything from social criticism to biting snark to uninhibited emotional reactions, also known as "squee." Our strong investment in *Supernatural* fandom is clearly not the exception, as many SPN fan icons proclaim.

Fig. I-3

What also remains largely unexplored in the field of fan studies is the application of psychological theory which goes beyond the often pathologizing lens of psychoanalytic analysis to examine both individual and communal psychological aspects of fanning. Both Sandvoss and Hills call for such approaches to fandom, with Hills contending that it "seems impossible to take fandom seriously without taking fan psychology seriously" (Hills 2002, 22). We agree—not surprisingly, since one of us is a clinical psychologist and the other teaches from a background of literary criticism and analytical approaches to fame and celebrity. Deeply immersed in the *Supernatural* fandom ourselves, we wanted to explore fandom from the inside, looking at fannish motivation, emotion, satisfaction, and conflict. But we wanted to go further. Taking Jenkins' idea of convergence culture and the reciprocal relationship between fans and the creative side as a starting point, we wanted to cross another barrier. Having already attempted to straddle the line between academic and fan, we set out to cross an even more thickly drawn line—that between fan and creator. Juggling all three roles landed us in more uncomfortable positions than we were prepared for, but also brought to light, in an immediate and personal way, the tensions inherent in being a fan and in studying fandom.

Chapter One: Lost in Space—Participatory Fandom and the Negotiation of Fan Spaces

We begin by exploring the diverse ways in which fans participate in fandom, and the variety of fan spaces they inhabit. The most dominant constructions of fandom paint a picture of monolithic spaces in which all fans are engaging in the same behaviors. Harry Potter fans all dress up and stand in line for midnight showings, Star Wars fans all pack light sabers. In reality, the modes of fannish engagement are as diverse as the people who come to fandom. The definition of fandom has thus been hard to pin down. How can we ascribe meaning to a concept so varied and fragmented, which seems to mean something different to every individual who defines themselves as a fan? Aca-fans have categorized fans according to their degree of participation, at times leaving the less participatory fans out of the taxonomy completely. Fans differ widely in the types of participation they seek out and the fan spaces to which they are drawn.

The concept of niche-seeking is relevant to most human behavior, fandom included. We all strive to find those places—physical, psychological, social and emotional—where we feel most accepted and least different. Thus, some fans are drawn to role playing games (RPGs) and others to post fanart on Tumblr or fanvids on Youtube. Some fans feel an acute sense of being "at home" when they discover the fanfiction community for the first time on the private space of their own laptop, and others when they travel across the country to attend their first fan convention. Each fan space has its own customs, norms and expectations for participation. Different spaces meet different needs and attract different types of fans, offering validation, inclusion, artistic inspiration, escape, freedom of expression, or whatever an individual fan is (subconsciously at least) seeking. And, as we will see in later chapters, fan spaces differ widely in terms of openness, their boundaries ranging from relatively permeable to ironclad.

When a particular fan space is perceived as quite different from the non-fannish culture in which it is embedded, there is a high degree of protectiveness, with fans policing the boundaries diligently. An internalized sense of shame produced by the perception of difference is often the motivation for such protectiveness. Fans speak of finding a "safe space," but disagree on what the parameters are which would create such a place.

Chapter Two: Taking Sides—Business or Pleasure?

As we analyze fannish spaces on a continuum of open through tightly closed systems, we examine the reality of the fan closet and the forces that keep fans there. Cornel Sandvoss (2005) and others contend that fandom is now a common and ordinary aspect of everyday life in the industrialized world. Similarly, Matt Hills credits both his academic and fan lives to the "encouragement, indulgence and tacit legitimation offered by my family" (2002, 87). This comfort with fandom, however, may well be rooted in certain aspects of individual experience, including gender (male) and type of fandom (in Sandvoss's case, mostly a sports fan). Tell your colleagues that you just flew across the country to go to a *Supernatural* fan convention and you're likely to be confronted with blank stares and awkward questions. You went where? For what?

Us: "*Supernatural*."

Them: "Like the paranormal?"

Us: "Uh, no – it's a television show. On the CW."

More blank stares inevitably followed. Our responses ran the gamut from defensive intellectualizing ("The writing is great!") to denial ("It's not about the hot actors!") to saying nothing at all, which is both the easiest and most common choice. Given the cultural bias against emotion and pleasure, it is small wonder that academics should be reluctant to admit to the same behaviors they study. But as Tulloch (2000) notes, there are significant theoretical and methodological implications attached to how scholars research fandom—whether they are fans themselves, or study fandom as something that others engage in. As Hills bluntly points out, "Fans don't like academics and vice versa"(2002, 3).Thus, fans have been reluctant to allow a deep level of access to academics, limiting analysis to interviews and observations whose inherent power imbalance restricts the expression of affect in favor of the "good subject" of rational discourse. Fans' defensiveness leaves their guard up, resulting in self-censorship that compromises understanding.

Fans are not the only ones reticent to self-disclose in a public forum. Doty (2000) and Hills (2002) have questioned whether decades of hiding fan culture theorists' personal and cultural investment in their subjects have served to "squeeze much of the life out of it in many senses" (Doty 2000, 11), and call for more explicitly auto-ethnographic work. At the same time, both Hills and Doty acknowledge the danger of slipping into being "overly confessional" or appearing "embarrassingly egotistical or gee-whiz celebratory"—yet these affective states are inherent in fandom. Aca-fans attempt to occupy a space which is uncomfortably split between fan space and the perceived legitimacy of academic space. Perhaps more jarringly, aca-fans tend to be uncomfortable on both sides of the fence. Fans eye us suspiciously, reluctant to be put under a microscope and unwilling to consider us true fans. Academics are equally suspicious, questioning the legitimacy of studying something as frivolous as popular culture. The discomfort has often made aca-fans reluctant to disclose their fannish selves when theorizing fandom, downplaying the emotional, sexual and psychological investment and emphasizing the intellectual and rational. Aca-fans are doubly ashamed—not only are we defensive about studying fandom, but now we might have to acknowledge fan pilgrimages to *Supernatural* shooting locations or camping out at 3 am for Comic Con seats?

Our own strategy (occasionally embarrassing, confessional or gee-whiz celebratory) has been to immerse ourselves head over heels into our chosen fandom. The layered and nuanced understanding of the inner workings of a particular fandom and the fandom's relationship to the societal structures that support and challenge it can only, it seems, be discovered from the inside.

Chapter Three: I'm Too Sexy For My Stereotype

The pursuit of pleasure seems inextricably intertwined with the sense of shame, whether it's the evolutionary pleasure of sex or the pleasure sought in "frivolous amusement," the definition of which shifts with cultural exigency (attendance at theatrical productions and reading novels were both formerly discouraged after all). Some would go one step further and argue that the two share a second important characteristic as well—namely that we should be ashamed of ourselves for experiencing either one.

The influence of shame in negotiating fannish identity and the selection of fan spaces, as well as its impact in constraining how aca-fans study fandom, may have been underestimated in a field which likes to proclaim this "the age of the geek, baby!" In this chapter, we examine this ubiquitous and uncomfortable emotion and its role in how fans have been portrayed by both mainstream media and academic theorists. We also look at the persistence of shame and its influence on identity and psychological health, especially for women. Fandom, for many female fans, is compelling for its invitation to self-expression, including sexual expression. At the same time, the negative connotations of "fangirl" persist, leaving fans caught between the pull of a new authorized discourse and the fear of alienating subscribers to the current one. We explore here the cultural proscriptions on female sexuality which contribute to fan shame, from post-war wrestling fans and 1960s Beatlemania, to Radway's (1984) analysis of romance-reading fans and their grumbling husbands and sons, to Jenkins' (1992) and Bacon-Smith's (1992) *Star Trek* slash writers. We draw on our rich store of fan interviews and fanworks to examine the persistence of shame in contemporary *Supernatural* fandom, and its influence on the creation of boundaries, norms and censure. The "first rule of fandom" is, after all, "tell no one about fandom." Fans continue to debate the risks and benefits of its existence.

Chapter Four: Fandom as Change Agent— Transformative Whats?

One of the reasons for fans' protectiveness of their "safe space" is that it is just that—a space that offers the protection and privacy needed for genuine self-expression. In this chapter, we examine the therapeutic potential of fandom, comparing it to the safe space of the therapy room. Fandom has long been characterized as subversive on a societal level, challenging gender and relational norms and existing power structures. We suggest that fandom is often transformative on an individual level as well.

To explore fandom's potential for more individual transformation, however, it is necessary to narrow one's lens and explore beneath the surface of individual fans' motivations. This presents a significant challenge when viewing fandom from the outside. Fans, however, discuss those inner fantasies and desires with other fans on a regular basis, allowing this sort of analysis from within. We examine here the impact of the community on the individual fan, as well as the production of fanworks not merely as a form of self-projection and reflection, but as a type of therapeutic expression, carried out within that supportive community. Specifically, we discuss three well-researched routes to psychological change—narrative therapy, expressive writing, and group counseling—and locate similar modes of change through various types of participation in fandom. In the process, we challenge internalized shame in the same way fans are, explicating a more positive model of fandom.

Chapter Five: Only Love Can Break Your Heart— Fandom Wank and Policing the Safe Space

In this chapter, we examine the flip side of the supportive fandom community. As the field of fan studies has developed, there have been several large-scale shifts in how fandom is viewed. Early researchers reacted to the pervasive negative view of fans by defending fan practices as transformative and culturally subversive, seeking to rehabilitate the image of the fan. That rehabilitation has not met with much success in the mainstream media or culture, but has been widespread in academic theorizing on fandom. In the early studies that shaped the field (Bacon-Smith 1992; Jenkins 1992), academics were reluctant to recognize hierarchies in fandom, characterizing fandom as a place where diversity of opinion was uniformly welcomed; however, "wank" is also an integral part of fandom. The popularity of online communities such as Fandom Wank and ONTD (Oh No They Didn't!), the existence of 'hate memes,' and the subtle and not-so-subtle relational bullying attest to fandom's passionate disagreements.

Recognizing fandom's potential for individual transformation, we turn in this chapter to the risks inherent in seeking and finding a safe space while still struggling with internalized shame. In their efforts to maintain the privacy necessary to a sense of safety, fans diligently police their fan spaces—and other fans. We examine the impact of anonymity in online fan spaces, the use of bullying and aggression to both jockey for position and enforce norms, and the psychological motivations behind these behaviors. The intense emotional investment and therapeutic potential of fandom also creates a strong need to maintain its integrity, and to attack threats both from the outside and from within.

Chapter Six: And The (Fourth) Walls Come Tumbling Down

Perhaps surprisingly, one of the threats to the perceived privacy and safety of fan spaces comes from the other side of the boundary—the creative side who are the objects of fannish affection. Both aca-fans and mainstream media have recognized the increasingly reciprocal relationship between fans and producers, facilitated by internet technologies and social media. The assumption is that both sides benefit. However, fans do not always welcome the breaking of the First Rule of Fandom, whether it's incursion from the creative side or fans themselves doing the rule breaking.

In this chapter, we examine the destruction of the fourth wall in *Supernatural*'s recent seasons, which has intensified the sense of fan shame by allowing those outside the safe space of fandom a glimpse inside. Early theories of fandom were predicated on the necessity of distance between fan and fannish object, with that distance allowing the continued projection of fantasy that sustained the fan's adoration. Fans thus controlled the narrative text through incorporation of elements that fit with the individual's self-projection. The hapless fan who asked the Forbidden Question we witnessed at the convention revealed the lengths to which fans will go to preserve secrecy, in order to keep the boundaries between fan, creator and fannish object strictly delineated, something Thompson (1995) describes as "mediated quasi-interaction." The created distance facilitates an audience members' ability to shape a relationship with both the text's authors and the fannish objects themselves. While the fan interacts intensely with a particular text, the text does not talk back.

Or does it?

The relationship between fans and the creative side, as well as the human representations of the fannish objects themselves, are increasingly reciprocal. As media texts are more widely disseminated and fans' constructions become more visible, the division between the creative side and audience is changing. With face-to-face interaction at conventions, the hierarchical boundaries separating fans and fannish objects begin to break down. Even more strikingly, the advent of Twitter, Facebook, and instant feedback ensures that the relationship between fans and creators is no longer unidirectional. The fourth wall has essentially crumbled, and the reciprocal relationship that Jenkins first hypothesized more than a decade ago in *Convergence Culture* is a reality.

Supernatural has become the media poster child for fourth wall breaking over the past four years, its writers repeatedly demonstrating their knowledge of fandom and portraying the show's fans in "meta" episodes. The stars of the television series have also delighted in solidifying the reciprocal relationship with fans, utilizing Facebook and Twitter to interact with fans and to publicize their own projects. *Supernatural* is now the most popular subject of fan conventions, so fan/celebrity interaction occurs in face-to-face venues as well, further breaking the First Rule (and at times just about every rule) of fandom. In this chapter, we analyze the multiple ways in which *Supernatural* has taken the reciprocal relationship with fans to a new level—and fans' reactions.

Chapter Seven: The Reciprocal Relationship— How Much is Too Much?

One of the most common manifestations of internalized fan shame is the projection of fans' fears onto their fannish objects. Thus, fans continually worry that the actors, writers, directors and producers are mocking, criticizing, or otherwise pathologizing them. Although the relationship between fans and the creative side is indeed increasingly reciprocal, nevertheless the lines of communication are often indirect, filtered through third parties and prone to misinterpretation. In this chapter, we explore the reality of producers' thoughts on fans by doing something that is rarely done either in fandom or in fan studies. We ask them.

Over the course of several years of research we interviewed the showrunners, writers, and actors who make the show, to hear their thoughts on fans and fan practices. We visited the set and the production offices, where almost everyone who helps bring *Supernatural* to life—the art director, Impala wrangler, locations manager, director of photography, production assistants— shared their take on fans. We asked about things not usually covered in *Entertainment Weekly*—fanfiction, vidding, conventions, cosplay, slash. And we not only asked, we answered. As curious as fans are about what their fannish objects are thinking, the creative side is equally curious about fans. Just as fans negotiate the boundaries between various fan spaces, the creative side—actors in particular—negotiate their own boundaries with fans and make careful decisions about their constructed personas. In the course of our discussions over the past four years, we inevitably broke some boundaries too.

CHAPTER ONE

LOST IN SPACE:
PARTICIPATORY FANDOM
AND THE NEGOTIATION OF FAN SPACES

Fans have often been categorized in terms of their modes of participation, with that participation usually defined in terms of production. Most taxonomies of fandom have not defined the consumption of a fanned object or even the gathering of information about that object as participatory. We may value (transgressive) appropriation and transformation over "mere" consumption because, among other things, it provides us with texts, thus overlooking what are perceived to be more "passive" forms of engagement. However, a significant number of fans would define their participation in terms of active consumption of information about their fanned objects and the people who contribute to its creation (musicians, actors, writers, directors, players). In reality this kind of interaction with the text involves obtaining a wide ranging knowledge of the fanned object and requires a significant amount of time and effort and a specific set of technical skills. In this chapter, we use this broader definition of "participation" and then examine the varied spaces in which these practices take place, along with the differing expectations of privacy inherent in each. These expectations of privacy in turn mirror the propensity for shame and the subsequent desire for validation.

The definition of fandom has been hard to pin down, perhaps because we tend to speak of fandom as a singular entity. A fandom surrounds *Buffy the Vampire Slayer* or *Twilight* or the Boston Red Sox. But fandom is hardly monolithic, and the internet has only facilitated and accelerated the fragmentation of fandom into sometimes harmonious, sometimes fractious groups that engage in a wide array of fan practices. Fans actively consume information about their fannish "texts"; they construct wikis, write fan fiction and create fan videos and fan art; they participate in role playing games (RPG's); they find each other on Tumblr; they attend fan conventions; and increasingly they interact directly with actors, directors, writers and others from the industry side via Facebook, Twitter and blogs

Fans rarely engage in just one practice. Artists are also writers or readers or vidders. Writers might also participate on RPG sites, or they may provide commentary and analysis of episodes in forums such as Television Without Pity and the message boards at IMDB. Fans often migrate from one fan space to another as their participation in fandom grows or changes. *Supernatural* fan Mary Dominiak compared the various practices she engages in and the fan spaces she inhabits:

> I feel part of a couple of *Supernatural* communities. The first one was TVGuide.com, initially with people who were commenting on the same show-related blogs I visited…..I expanded to *Supernatural*.tv and Live Journal, and there was a definite thrill in seeing more and more people reading the things I write, both blogs and fanfiction. My correspondence with other fans has gone beyond the show, particularly with fans I've met in person at conventions or just by arranging real-world meetings. The (online) fannish *Supernatural* communities are similar in many ways to "face to face" communities structured around a common interest. The major difference is that the fan community is actually much more diverse than any of my face to face ones, encompassing a wide range of ages (as young as 13 and as old as 65) and a multiplicity of nationalities, literally all around the world.

Mary's description of her engagement with her fandom closely mirrors the range of skills and competencies that Abercrombie and Longhurst (1998) delineated (technical, analytical and interpretive). She went from being a consumer of "show related blogs" (technical skills) to a participant in various communities, eventually beginning a blog of her own (analytical skills), to writing fanfiction (interpretive skills). Her negotiation of fan spaces is also illustrative of the ways in which these skills and practices overlap.

Because fans participate in a variety of ways, they must constantly negotiate and renegotiate boundaries, stepping back and forth between public and private spaces. Some fan practices are mainstream enough to make public spaces comfortable, while others are not.

Chart 1-1

Skill	Fan Space	Fan Practices	Participation
Technical (embody an appreciation of how the textual effect is created. For television this includes evaluation of acting, conveyance of feeling, production values, script, camera work)	public spaces, may have ties to corporate entities (production companies, advertisers, special interest groups, academics)	Gathering of information through reading magazines, websites,	Consumptive
Analytic (analysis of the text from within the parameters of the text itself.)	Semi-public spaces, but with the expectation that they are fans-only spaces	Fan forum discussions, blogging.	Productive (often predicated on technical)
Interpretive (Interpretation of texts from without the text by comparing them to something else.)	Private, fans only spaces	Creation of fan works (fan fiction, videos, art, music), participation in RPG's.	Productive (often predicated on either technical or analytical skills, or a combination of both)

Fan Practices, Fan Spaces and the Expectation of Privacy

Fan spaces online occupy a middle ground, commonly perceived as private and yet in reality public and generally available to anyone with a computer. Not only can they be accessed by anyone, they are often vulnerable to outside influence, making true "fans only spaces" difficult to find. Fans, as we'll explore in later chapters, search for safe spaces in which to express themselves openly, but the threat of censorship hangs over most fan spaces in one way or another – whether this be incursion from the owners of the properties, from advertisers on the site, or from special interest groups who object to content. At times this incursion even comes from the fans themselves.

Well known sites such as FanFiction.net have offered a central space for writers from multiple fandoms. Created in 1998, FF.net remains the largest archive of fanfiction on the internet. However, there were and continue to be objections to the perceived public nature of the site, a concern given the still shameful practice to which it is devoted. The site itself attempted to validate the writing of fanfiction and reduce the threat of criticism by adopting policies that function as censorship. Real Person Fiction (RPF) and NC17 ratings were banned from the site in 2002, thus curtailing the interpretive skills and self- expression of fans who wish to write in either of these genres. Such censorship works to remove one of the primary contributors to shame by simply taking out the sex.

The Organization for Transformative Works (OTW)'s Archive Of Our Own, (known within fandom as AO3), in contrast, seeks to be inclusive and non-restrictive in its policies and explicitly excludes any outside interest groups who attempt to influence content. The Archive of Our Own:

> . . . offers a noncommercial and nonprofit central hosting place for fanfiction and (long-term) other transformative fanworks: i.e. it is free to use and does not make any money. It is multifannish and built on open-source archiving software designed and built by and for fans. It is hosted on servers owned by the OTW and therefore not vulnerable to a commercial hosting company deciding they don't like our fanworks.

AO3's twin goals, freeing writers from corporate interests and the threat of imposition of social rules inconsistent with fandom, make it attractive to fans who seek a "safe" space. However, fans have been slow to accept AO3, perhaps because it has been seen as an academic space that , no matter how open their policies, automatically carries with it an "official" imprimatur that may put some fans off.   As we'll see later, the incursion of academic spaces into fan spaces is not always welcomed. AO3 put back the sex, but the perception of judgment may remain—this time the fear of being "studied."

Live Journal and Dreamwidth present alternative spaces for fans, offering more privacy and a greater sense of community. Dreamwidth in particular feels safe for fans, as it is supported only by user fees, without ad revenue. Live Journal defines itself as "a global community of friends who share your unique passions and interests," a clear invitation to fandom to come on in and make yourself at home. However, LJ has not been as safe as fans would like to believe. Supported by ad revenue, LJ is vulnerable to outside censorship. The Live Journal purge of content and journals deemed inappropriate or obscene and the resulting fan protest, known within fandom as "StrikeThrough" in 2007, and the Fanfiction.net "RedBootton kerfluffle" in 2010 are examples of such censorship.

Some fans solve the problem of community by maintaining a journal at Dreamwidth and cross posting their fanworks in Live Journal. As we'll explore in Chapter Three, online fan spaces, despite some outside interference, nevertheless offer a greater sense of safety and privacy, which encourage self-expression. But even within the most protected spaces there is the possibility of incursion, and sometimes this threat is from other fans. Despite their shared love of a particular television show, band, or team, fans do not always easily co-mingle. For instance, the first piece of *Supernatural* fanfiction posted in Live Journal appeared within twenty-four hours of the airing of the pilot. It was "Wincest", a type of fiction that posits a romantic relationship between the two main characters of the show, brothers Sam and Dean Winchester (Winchester + incest = Wincest). This immediately sparked a response from those who vehemently opposed this budding genre, and alternate communities were formed before the second episode of the show had aired, including a now-defunct "Anti-Wincest" community. Since then communities have formed for Sam girls and Dean girls, those who want to see Dean hurt or Sam limp, those who want to indulge in male pregnancy fic (MPreg), those who want to see one or both of the boys suddenly sprout wings, or tails, or have congress with angels. Alternative Universe (AU) fanfiction is popular, putting the characters or the actors who portray them into different situations that have nothing to do with either show canon or personal reality. Jared is a troubled student and Jensen his conflicted teacher, Dean is an executive at a large corporation and Sam is an unappreciated IT person (no wait – that's not fan fiction, that's an episode of *Supernatural*!). These separate communities offer discreet spaces for all of these pieces of fandom to co-exist if not co-mingle.

Fandom Face to Face

Fans also come together in real world spaces whose variety mirrors that of online spaces, from the big, celebrity-centered events, to small fan gatherings for writers, vidders, RPGers, cosplayers and artists. As one of the most commonly utilized (and least studied) in-person fan spaces, conventions have influenced the evolution of fandom, bringing fans and creators together in a carnival atmosphere that challenges accepted boundaries between fan and producer. At conventions, fans perceive themselves as moving from the mediated world of the mass audience to the more intimate relationship afforded audiences in close proximity to performers. The perception at a fan convention is that fans are no longer in a mediated world—that fans are moving from the mediated space of a mass audience into a simple audience, face to face and all in the same place at the same time. However, while the impression is of a less mediated, more intimate space, the close contact and sense of intimacy are often illusory. Boundaries still exist, physical, psychological, and social, and mediators are still very much there—often in the form of the convention organizers themselves.

Adam Malin is the co-founder of Creation Entertainment, which started with staging comic and *Star Trek* conventions, and has expanded into the primary fan convention stager in North America. *Supernatural* is now the focus of their most popular fan conventions, with eight Creation SPN conventions in 2011.

> Malin: Gene Roddenberry was one of the first to support the whole Star Trek convention movement, and essentially for bringing the fandom community together. I still think there's no substitute for going to a live event, being with your fan community and friends right there and then seeing the stars who are also on site. I don't believe anything electronic can ever replace that. Our lives are increasingly complicated, and it's expensive, there are so many types of entertainment possibilities that we all have to be discriminatory and pick and choose. When we started doing *Supernatural* conventions, we had Jared signed and then once we had Jensen lined up, there was a collective sigh of relief from around the globe. We had people coming from all over the world, Ireland, the UK, Spain, Portugal, South American, Central America, Japan, Australia. They're coming from all over to see these guys together. People feel as passionately about these guys as they did about the Beatles!

Actor Jim Beaver (an SPN series recurring guest star), echoed this sentiment. Even though he was prepared for his first convention experience, he was nevertheless surprised by the "squee" that greeted him when he walked on stage for the first time.

> Beaver: I just thought that was a word for really liking someone. I wrote to a friend of mine afterwards and said, you're not going to believe this, but it's Beatle Mania! Way beyond anything this old cowboy was expecting.

As a self- professed "geek fanboy" himself, Malin takes a great deal of satisfaction from being the organizer and intermediary who brings fans and fannish objects together.

> Malin: To see people be happy and enjoy themselves or be fulfilled, it's great to see people be at an event and immerse themselves in entertainment and get so much reward and joy out of it. It's just a beautiful thing. It's also fun to just see people get kind of wacky, right? Somebody comes in wearing a costume and isn't afraid to walk around in it.

Malin is perhaps the ultimate BNF (Big Name Fan), setting up the convention space with certain parameters which, to some extent, reduce fan shame.   Male acceptance then becomes important to the (mostly female) fans as a means of validating female fan practices. The convention owners, who are both straight males, nevertheless explicitly validate the sexual elements of fandom, with Malin joking that Jared and Jensen are "so hunky, he'd go for them himself if he wasn't straight."
Malin is also aware of the role his organization plays in providing a middle ground—a sort of neutral safe space where fans and celebrities can come together, with the convention organizer serving as gatekeeper and boundary enforcer while at the same time facilitating closer connection than fans could otherwise gain.

> Malin: Jensen and Jared have created a world class team of representation, and they need to be a firewall for these guys, and we get that. Thankfully, we have a reputation in the industry that allows us to tear down some walls that other people might not be able to get past.

The physical space of the convention might bring the audience and performer together—performers can be spoken to and touched (during photo ops) and fans can take something of them away with them (an autograph, photos)—but the social space remains separate. Performers are protected (sometimes by convention staff and sometimes by bodyguards hired for the event) and kept in separate spaces (taking back routes through the hotels in which most conventions are held in order to avoid fan crowded hallways and lobbies) until they are presented to the fans under highly ritualized conditions. Many "green rooms" (the protected space in

Fig. 1-1: Padalecki confers with Ackles onstage at a con

Fig. 1-2: Jensen Ackles entertains the fans

which celebrities are sequestered before being escorted onstage to perform) are accessed through the back passages and kitchen freight elevators rather than public hallways. The perception may be of a closing of the gap between performer and audience, but in reality convention spaces merely reify the divide.

There are, of course, always audience members who will seek to sidestep the boundaries, setting themselves apart and outside the confines to some extent. Money can buy proximity, with fans who have the means buying top-dollar packages at conventions which get them seats at the front as well as access to certain events such as a dessert party or breakfast with the actors. Still others purchase entry to private meet and greets or backstage access. These latter attendees are often regarded by other fans with a mixture of scorn and envy, as any fan who ascends the hierarchy will be. One of the early *Supernatural* conventions made the distinction far too obvious by setting up faux velvet couches at the foot of the stage for the most privileged fans.

As we'll discuss in more detail in Chapter Seven, the celebrities on the other side of the firewall are also aware of the boundaries around the convention space, and the rules and norms that apply within it. They too must negotiate their desire for a private space, as opposed to the financial benefits of closer contact.

Fig. 1-3: Packed house: The space between audience and performer

Fig. 1-4: Breakfast with the boys: Jared and Jensen do stand-up

Fig. 1-5: Squee! The boys are back in town.

Fig. 1-6. Leaving an impression: Padalecki signs a fan's shirt.

Fig. 1-7: The trappings of celebrity: Ackles and his arsenal of sharpies.

The Search for Legitimacy:
Negotiating Fan and Non-Fan Spaces

The boundaries between fan spaces and the creative side are not the only lines to be crossed or adhered to. Fan spaces, like most human groups, tend to be hierarchical, with various routes "to the top." Accruing cultural capital in the form of knowledge, access or, best of all, a personal relationship with the object of fandom, not only allows us to navigate more easily in a mediated world, it is also a form of validation. The more cultural capital, the more admirable, since the gathering of detailed information is a skill valued both within and outside fan communities. Those fans who spend time accumulating knowledge find it easier to negotiate both spaces. The music fan's encyclopedic knowledge of discographies or the sports fan's prowess with batting statistics are two better known (and accepted) versions of this. The display of this knowledge facilitates relationships and allows us to identify kindred spirits, such as when a student walks into a class wearing a tee shirt bearing the face of *Lost*'s "Ben Linus".

Possessing cultural capital and information is one way of becoming a Big Name Fan. BNFs seek to set themselves apart in fan communities, earning privilege and status through amassing and controlling the flow of information or being able to claim entry into the other, protected realm of the performer. The Wikipedia definition of a BNF is a fan "who is particularly well-known, liked or celebrated" with the caveat that the title carries with it negative connotations and accusations of being "arrogant and self-important." In the same way that Mary Sues (self-insertion narratives) are generally hated (Chander and Sunder 2007), BNF's are often the object of scorn because they are perceived as crowding other fans out, hogging attention, or having coveted access to objects of fandom. It thus becomes difficult to balance the fan's desire for validation from both the fan community, which forms a large part of her social network and functions as a safe space for self-expression, and the object of fandom itself (performers and producers), who offer the cultural validation many fans are seeking. *Supernatural* fan Andie Masino became a Big Name Fan (BNF) through her popular online serial adaptation of *Supernatural* starring modified Ken dolls as Sam and Dean in decidedly AU adventures, known as Plastic Winchester Theater. Andie derives great pleasure and emotional support from her online fan community.

Masino: At first we were only gathering to discuss the latest episode, but now we've become a fantastic support group for each other for real life.

Fandom is what brought us together, but our friendship is what will keep us coming back long after the show has been canceled.

At the same time, she also relished being set apart from that community, the need to rise to the top outweighing the benefits of staying on equal footing within the group.

I wanted to find some way to distinguish myself in fandom. I went into fandom wanting to make my mark but not knowing how. Originally I came up with the idea for the plastic!boys because there wasn't any merchandise available for SPN. I bought the mini Impala first, then while shopping at Goodwill one day I noticed a bin full of Ken dolls and the idea sprang into my head that I could make my own Sam and Dean dolls. . . . The ability to make someone who is having a rough time or a bad day laugh is indescribable. It just fills me with joy. My biggest moment came at Comic Con last year when the woman behind me in line to ask the panel a question outed me as the PWT girl. I will   never   forget   the   cheer   that went up from the crowd, and how in that moment, I felt like a rockstar.

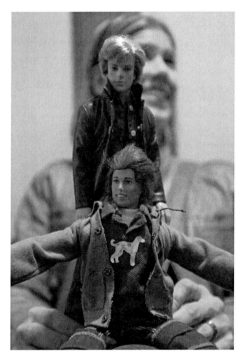

Fig. 1-8: Plastic Winchester Dean and Sam entertain fans

This validation had the added impact of taking place in a space allocated for the performers, thus moving her, at least symbolically, into a different space. This movement became literal when she was invited for a set visit to the *Supernatural* studios in Vancouver after a member of the art department saw her work. They were so impressed by it that they invited her to visit the set and compare notes, artist to artist. While Masino was thrilled, she found she also had to negotiate the transition between fan space and a legitimized creative/professional space.

> I was invited to the set because the crew enjoyed reading Plastic Winchester Theater and thought it was a really creative and original way to promote the show. I was amazed that everyone knew who I was. Jerry Wanek (production designer) walked us around and when he introduced me as Andie, people would immediately exclaim that I was the "Winchester Barbie Girl." It's a bit nerve-wracking to meet the people whose job you make fun of every week, but they were nothing but welcoming and gracious. Chris Cooper (propmaster) was studying my version of Sam's laptop and the tiny EMF reader. He couldn't believe how much detail went into my show.

Masino's experience on the set allowed her to re-define herself as more than a fan, particularly as she experienced a sense of belongingness – the same feelings fans are often looking for in fan communities.

> The moment I knew I was a part of the SPN team was when they left me and my guest unescorted on set for four hours. Occasionally a PA would come up and ask if we needed anything, but for the most part we were left alone. We were trusted to stay out of the way and to respect the actors and their jobs. Considering the bad rep fangirls usually have, that made me really proud of my ability to earn their trust.

The incursion into creative space and her felt identity as part of the team instead of a fan, however, left Masino with a complicated re-negotiation of fan space and where she fit. Masino struggled with some of the same tensions we've experienced when trying to move back and forth from entirely fannish spaces to more "legitimate" creative or academic space, as we'll discuss further in the next chapter. Andie expressed her unwillingness to go back to being "just" a fan by refusing to purchase a ticket to the next Creation *Supernatural* fan convention.

> I didn't buy a ticket for the Chicago Con because I'd already met the boys in a much more intimate setting, and to pay   money for a few moments of their time seemed wrong. I'm not saying anything against the girls who

did pay money, it was just that by the Chicago Con I had moved past being a "regular" fan.

This did not stop Masino from attending the convention, but it did keep her from being able to find space for herself once there. Feeling set apart because she had visited the set and interacted with cast and crew, she was at once fan and producer and at the same time she was neither. Her fan status was compromised by her interaction with the cast and crew; her producer status, while validated by the art department, was still not validated by the larger culture because it remained "amateur," the uncompensated work of a mere fan. Masino thus had no physical space to occupy at the convention and ended up in the liminal space of the hallway outside the ballroom where the convention activities were taking place, interacting with the fans not as a fan herself but as an object of fandom. Her Plastic Winchester Theater gave her entrée to one side, while forcing her to reposition herself in relation to the other.

How fans interact in shared spaces once they have been given non-fan access to fanned objects is connected to how they conceive of themselves as fans and to their own sense of claimed identity. Fan convention organizer Sharon Vernon remembers her early investment in fandom.

> Vernon: I followed Bryan Adams around and in 1987 I went to this thing in Toronto and I sat there and saw everybody there and I learned that we weren't the only ones doing this and it was devastating. Because up to that point the thing that I did better than most if not everybody else was being a Bryan Adams fan… There is a sense of competition. It's not even a validation thing… [If] Bryan likes me I must be special, so you need to be impressed with the fact that I saw him so many times.

A similar renegotiation of space occurred for some of the first SPN fangirls we met, who are neighbors of actor Jensen Ackles as well as fans. Thus, they have some mutual friends and occasionally run into him at non-SPN venues such as local clubs. Before *Supernatural* was popular enough to draw fans to concerts by Jason Manns and Steve Carlson, Ackles' musician friends, Jenna and Sabrina and Brenda were often the only people there who knew (or cared) who Ackles was. Their informal interactions with the actor were both euphoric and confusing for their smearing of boundaries between fan and non-fan spaces.

Unlike Masino, Sabrina made the decision to continue to pay for access at *Supernatural* conventions. She describes paying for a photo op with Ackles at a convention, after having chatted with him informally at a local club a few weeks before.

I was pleased as Punch that when I walked up to him he actually knew who I was…there is recognition, and I was like over the moon for hours. It wasn't weird either. When we see them out and about at clubs everyone is mingling, and then we get here and we thought, how weird is this going to be, because we have paid all this money to see them, but it validated the fact that he does recognize my face as one of those that support his friends. We have the privilege that they might not watch what they say around us as intensely as they might around other people. If you catch them at the right moment, they will tell you anecdotes that will not be told, and we have an unwritten agreement that we won't talk about that because we have the privilege of them letting their guard down around us. We are really privileged because they don't consider us just fans, but people they see as humans and recognize.

As much as Sabrina owns and loves her fan identity, she echoes Masino's desire to be seen as something other than a "regular fan" and relishes being set apart in the estimation of the performer. Nevertheless, Sabrina and her friends were aware that this privileged position comes with inherent risks.

When one of us went for her photo op, Jensen was like hey, and he put his arms out for a hug, but she just shook his hand. Later she was like, I can't believe I refused a fan hug, but I didn't feel comfortable getting hugged in front of this whole group of fans (who weren't getting hugs) and having that separate me. In fandom there is a fine line you have to walk, because if people know you got an extra response they are like a) how can you help me get it too or b) why the hell do YOU get that response? Nine times out of ten we don't mention it when we run into Jensen, because there is backlash, and it's a nasty kind of envy, not a "you-go-girl" kind of envy.

Bloggers and fan site moderators also struggle with their dual identities as fans and as show insiders. Rae Hanson, of the popular blog *Ramblings of a TV Whore* (2003-2011) was quite aware of both fan shame and the pull of legitimacy as an antidote.

There's less shame about being a fan with a show like Big Brother than sci fi, where people tend to raise their eyebrows more. I don't feel guilty for enjoying it, but I do feel self-conscious talking about it because I know how people feel. In my real life, I don't really have people around me that make me feel like that—understood. I think oddly it's changed from before I was a blogger, having these opportunities to visit the set, etc, and I think that has legitimized what I do.

Hanson relishes the benefits of fandom, finding a community where she feels "understood," but knows that membership in that community means that she has to renegotiate the spaces outside that safe space to make it "acceptable". Like Masino, Sabrina and Hanson, we too were faced with the dilemma of negotiating multiple positions within fandom, while attempting to maintain a level of objectivity as researchers. Straddling identities almost always necessitates losing some of what you wanted from fandom in the first place, and legitimacy sometimes reduces shame by downplaying much of what we value most in fandom – emotion, frivolity, passion, and sex.

CHAPTER TWO

TAKING SIDES:
BUSINESS OR PLEASURE?

Hanne Blank has noted the need to accept that "the process of writing a book changes both the author and the book."(2011) Similarly, the process of researching fandom in order to write this book inevitably changed us as authors and as fans. During the course of our research we wound up shifting sides innumerable times (often without initially realizing we had done so) in our quest for the type of affirmation discussed in the previous chapter. We sought affirmation as fans, as academics and as aca-fans and found that such affirmation was in many instances in short supply. In this chapter, we examine the desire for legitimacy and how it has influenced our own and other aca-fans' conceptualizing of fandom.

We discovered *Supernatural* as fans first, and in the throes of our new found love, sought out like-minded people. We opened up Live Journal accounts and joined communities like *Supernatural*.tv and Television Without Pity and tvguide.com. But it was on LJ that we felt most at home. Our choice of fan space was based on our own fan practices and prejudices. As writers ourselves, we felt this was where the real fans were, at least the ones that fit our definition of participatory fans at the time. We (narrowly) assumed that we had entered the heart of fandom and that from this vantage point we could look out and survey it in its entirety. As we soon learned, the danger for the researcher is in believing that whatever slice of fandom he or she knows best is therefore representative of the whole. (This may explain why we see so many books on English football hooliganism and so few on women who write football fan fiction.) Researchers have investigated a number of specific fan spaces, from MySpace (P. Booth 2008) to Fanfiction.Net (Black 2008) to fan pilgrimages (Couldry 2007) but none of these is or can be representative of the whole, and choice carries its own set of problems. Monaghan and Just outline the challenge:

> One problem with participant observation has been the temptation for the ethnographer to present the community in a kind of temporal isolation.

Many ethnographers, particularly in the "classic" accounts of the 1930's and 1940's employed what came to be called the ethnographic present in which communities were frozen in time, outside any historical context, and without reference to neighboring societies or encapsulating states (2000, 25).

This was a problem of which we were initially unaware, too taken with our own participation at the time.

A recent conversation between Nancy Baym, Kristina Busse and Flourish Klink hosted on Henry Jenkins' blog, Confessions of an Aca-Fan, highlights the difficulties of academics entering into and negotiating a place within fan spaces and sums up the different approaches academics have taken. Busse voices a fundamental concern immediately about privileging certain modes of fan participation and fan spaces, influenced by the researcher's desire to defend his or her own version of fannishness.

> [T]here still remains a desire to present fandom in its best guise; after all, if another scholar gets to read one story, sees one vid, I want it to conform to traditional aesthetic notions. My selections are thus restrained not only by the text's possible representativeness and accessibility, but also by my desire to not embarrass my community. There are enough shoddy journalistic pieces who point and mock, and the fan in me desires to impress the academic colleagues.
>
> The result, however, is that we as acafen are faced with not only the general problem of any qualitative scholar of popular culture on which texts to pick, but also compound the issue by having a variety of vested interests that complicate that selection. When we choose fan works that fit into our arguments, that make fandom look more creative, more political, more subversive to outsiders because that's the image we want to give to the world at large, are we ultimately misrepresenting and betraying fandom.

Nancy Baym, by contrast, does not feel these constraints, in part because her preferred mode of participation is less subversive (emotional, sexual) and more rational, which carries little shame and needs little defending.

> One reason for this may be the primary fandoms with which I've aligned myself. I was never involved in fanfic or vidding communities. I've always been involved in and studied fan communities where we talk about and critique what we're into and it seems like the dynamics are different than in communities based on fans' creative works.

Baym does not view herself as immersed; instead, she talks about being "aligned"—not inside the fan community, which is something "studied." Indeed, she consciously places herself outside of fandom,

> I stand by my sense that one thing academics ought to be doing is giving fans frameworks for at least thinking critically about the ethics of what they do, just as we are well positioned to argue to the industries about the ethics of the choices they make towards fans.

This positing is seen frequently in fan studies. Rhiannon Bury (2005), in her detailed case studies of two online fandoms for the television shows The *X-Files* and *Due South*, claims to follow the immersion strategy that we also see as useful in understanding any fan community, in that she became an active participant in both communities. However, her overt status as a researcher makes her participation markedly different than the other fans, and positions Bury as an outsider, with fans periodically questioning the ramifications of that positioning, as Bury herself also does. In fact, the term "fangirl" is a pejorative one in Bury's book, one which implies blurred boundaries and an excess of emotionality, from which the author repeatedly sets herself apart.

Our own solution to the problem of positioning ourselves was similarly imperfect—we kept our online fan spaces entirely separate from our academic presence. Our Live Journals were for fan activity only, which sometimes meant that we could not say anything about what we knew as researchers no matter how much the fan in us wanted to share these things with the fandom, including introductions to Ackles' and Padalecki's dogs and the multiple bags of salt and other Winchester essentials in the props closet.

Fig. 2-1: Boundary violations. Padalecki with Sadie and Harley

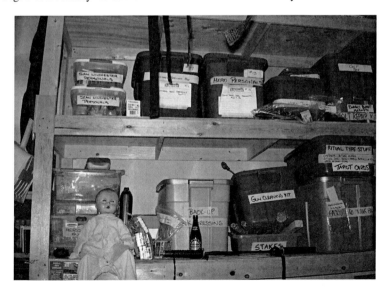

Fig. 2-2: In the closet: Sam and Dean's "Personals"

The difficulty of balancing our dual identities as researchers and fans immediately became clear on our first trip to Vancouver to attend a *Supernatural* fan convention.   We presented ourselves as researchers, interviewed fans, convention organizers, and the director of Jensen Ackles' indie film, *Ten Inch Hero*, which was screening at the convention. We were a ubiquitous presence with our recorders and note pads. On our first night there, a fan related to us how upset she was after inadvertently reading "some of that awful stuff written about Jared and Jensen"—real person slash fiction. She didn't know the term for it, but she knew she found it deeply disturbing and asked us what kind of people wrote that stuff and why, earnestly seeking our professional diagnosis.   We nodded empathically and maintained our composure until we gained the safety of our hotel room. Once there, we stared at each other with no small measure of horror. The story she read was written by one of us—and our highly emotional reaction to this fan's response to our own fan practices was indicative of our own struggle with fan shame.

Further blurring the lines between academic and fan was the fact that this trip to Vancouver was also a fan pilgrimage for us, another popular fan practice which carries a moderate degree of shame for its implication of excess emotionality and obsession. Vancouver is, as most *Supernatural* fans know, where the Show is filmed—it is SPN fandom's Mecca. On the last night of the fan convention we joined an intrepid band of fellow fans and went in search of past filming locations. We did this because we're fans and these things matter.   It was late, it was dark, but we were all on a mission to find the distinctive fence by the river, in front of which an emotional Dean confessed to his brother Sam that he would either have to save him or kill him.   We finally found the fence at just about the same time the Vancouver police found us scrambling down a muddy river bank without a flashlight at midnight, resulting in a confusing mix of fannish euphoria and sheepish embarrassment.

The following day, we were lucky (or crafty) enough to find the show's current filming location at a nearby hospital. We told ourselves and anyone who would listen that we were there as researchers, and asked if anyone from the crew would like to chat about *Supernatural*'s fans. We made it clear that we were there to ask about the fans, and that we had no interest in seeing "the boys," as everyone seems to refer to Ackles and Padalecki (because of course that would have pegged us as fans ourselves). At the time we had no clue how many rules we were breaking (rules governing both fans and researchers) and for a while, neither did the PAs, who were eager to talk with us.   When word of our presence got to The Powers That Be, however, we were unceremoniously told to leave, public property or not, and realized to our horror that we'd just been tagged as probable stalkers. Once again our researcher sides had been (temporarily) validated while our fan selves were shamed.

Fig. 2-3: Oh no, stalkers!

In the space of a three day trip we had been made to feel authoritative and validated and validating (of others' fan practices); we had also been made to feel dirty, foolish and humiliated. The final blow came as we were leaving Canada. Passing through customs, we were asked why we had been in the country. The standard query of "business or pleasure?" posed an impossible choice. Lynn chose "pleasure"; Kathy chose "business." Together we embodied the dilemma of the aca-fan.

"What kind of business?" the customs agent asked, apparently as interested in the ideas we were trafficking as any material goods we may have had to declare.

"A fan convention," Kathy replied, expecting a nod and a stamp on the passport.

"Ohhhh," the customs agent said, fixing Kathy with a less friendly stare. "You mean crazy stalker chicks."

We quickly assured him (untruthfully) that we were only there to observe and he waved us on, seemingly reassured that we posed no threat.

Aca-Shame

There is no shortage of criticism directed at fans—or at any version of popular culture. It's mass, crass and dangerous to consume. Of course this is nothing new. The culture wars have been fought since at least the late 17th Century, when Swift, and after him Pope, entered the public sphere by championing Classical learning and ridiculing the new Grub Street hacks. "The Battle of the Books" and the "Dunciad" cast writers who wrote for the entertainment of the populace, rather than for their edification, as at best dull and at worst immoral. We've been warned off popular culture by the likes of George Orwell and Neil Postman and many dystopian futures include at least some passing reference to the frightening idea of popular culture out of control.

The cautionary rhetoric and laments for the state of culture that were previously the norm have been slow to give way to the more nuanced defenses of popular culture and its study undertaken by academics since the late seventies and eighties. Acceptance is in short supply even as we are defining and defending such studies. And it is often the very people who write in its defense who undermine the enterprise. Twenty years ago Nachbar and Lause (1992) began their *Popular Culture: An Introductory Text* with an explanation of the importance of the study of popular culture. They justify what they are doing with language that exhorts us to understand and defend against precisely the culture they are examining. In the very act of embracing, they sound the same cautionary notes. Indeed they set popular culture up as the enemy from the opening epigrams onwards. The first is a paraphrase of a paraphrase – "We have seen Our Culture, and it is Us. Sort of." The original statement is of course Admiral Perry's famous "We have met the enemy and they are ours," a declaration of victory over a foe. The equally famous paraphrase of this is Walt Kelly's 1970 slogan for the first Earth Day – "We have met the enemy and he is us," in which the enemy without has been replaced by that within, asserting that our actions are hurting us and our environment. In Nachbar and Lause's paraphrase, the enemy is replaced by "culture," by which they mean popular culture, while the earlier versions resonate. Popular culture used indiscriminately will harm us and our environment, just as the overuse of natural resources has harmed us. By absorbing popular culture, we have ourselves become both victim and enemy. The second quotation undermines in a different way, by erroneously mis-attributing a Rolling Stones song. The authors quote "You Can't Always Get What you Want" but cite it as "Satisfaction". The fact that the mis-attribution stood suggests that the authors and their editors were not as familiar with the popular culture they write about as would seem necessary. Worse, it suggests that their familiarity is not reflective of deep knowledge and is not thought to rate such knowledge. Their concerns clearly lay elsewhere.

Fast forward to 2010, when one would assume that we have moved past this need to justify our endeavors and overtly or subtly take to task our academic interest in the popular. Not so. The editorial introducing the newly launched *Journal of Celebrity Studies* is at pains to explain their undertaking and to distinguish themselves from the very thing they study. Their justification, in light of the "derision" and "scorn" they've encountered in the mainstream press is understandable. However, this editorial is aimed at other academics, those who presumably are familiar with the study of popular culture in general and the study of the celebrity machine in particular. Given this, their insistence on defining themselves by what they are not (they are not a magazine, they are not Heat) seems unnecessarily strident until they observe:

> The academic study of stars, celebrity and fame . . . has increasingly become an accepted part of the academy since the publication of Richard Dyer's foundational Stars (1979) and yet it is still a topic that remains contentious – seen as residing at the most populist end of the "popular" (Holmes and Redmond 2010).

Many other areas of popular culture studies may be accepted now, but the mass market entertainment industry continues to carry with it the whiff of something unpleasant, as we discovered as soon as we turned our research lenses on something as frivolous as a science fiction genre show on the CW. We were reminded over and over again that "junk culture" is often equated with "junk food" and even more often devalued. Even the "junk culture" we so avidly consume criticizes us! An episode of the *The X-Files* (9.14 "Scary Monsters"), which concerns a young boy whose overactive imagination is literally killing people, ends with the boy undergoing "treatment" designed to deaden that imagination. The final shot of the boy shows him sitting, unblinking, in front of a bank of television screens. Similarly, in an episode of the *Doctor Who* reboot, Donna Noble's fiancé admonishes her for her junk culture diet.

> And then I was stuck with a woman who thinks the height of excitement is the new flavor Pringle. I had to sit there and   listen to all that yap, yap,

yap, all Brad and Angelina, is Posh pregnant, X-Factor, Atkins diet, feng shui, splint ends, text me, text me, text me - dear god, the never ending fountain of fat stupid trivia (Lynn 2006).

Just as we judge the people in the supermarket on line ahead of us with a shopping cart full of chips, soda and fatty convenience foods, we judge those who consume a steady diet of television shows and, to a lesser extent, mass market fiction. And if we admit to doing this ourselves, it's often in the form of a confessional. We admit our "guilty" pleasures in tones that beg indulgence.

Guilty? Pleasure?

This uneasy relationship to popular culture informs our attitudes toward those who study it as well. As Joli Jenson pointed out in 1992, there are significant similarities between fan behavior and academic behavior. In "Fandom as Pathology" she compares a Barry Manilow fan to a Joyce scholar. Both fans and scholars are passionate, acquisitive and seek as much information about their objects of interest as they can get, often down to minutiae that others might consider obsessive. This parallel has not been lost on aca-fans, who claim dual citizenship in the realms of fandom and academia. However, there are also clearly marked boundaries between the two groups. As much as the fan and the scholar resemble each other, we clearly approach and value them very differently. We are more likely to embrace the "aficionado" while distancing ourselves from the "fan"—or in this case, the Fanilow. Jenson observes:

> The division between worthy and unworthy is based in an assumed dichotomy between reason and emotion. The reason-emotion dichotomy has many aspects. It describes a presumed difference between the educated and the uneducated, as well as between the upper and lower classes. It is a deeply rooted opposition (Jenson 1992, 21).

In the years since Jenson wrote this, it's been assumed that we've gradually moved away from the image—both in academia and in the mainstream press—of fans as pathological, out of control, "other". However, we have not come as far as we would like to think. Fans are still derided in the media even as they are being embraced by media producers. Fans themselves often feel a strong sense of shame, as we will discuss in later chapters. They shy away from the stigma of being excessively emotional or excessively sexual or excessively passionate. Even if they embrace being a "total freak" it comes with the assurance that they are not as "weird" as those other fans who are even freakier. If fans aren't ashamed at what they are doing, they are ashamed at what other fans are up to. The twin cultural biases against overt displays of emotion and (for women) displays of inappropriate sexuality combine to keep fans in the closet.

Aca-fans, by contrast, seem proud to stand up and declare their inner geekdom. Cheryl Harris (1998) "dared" to confess her own fandom. Cornel Sandvoss (2005) acknowledged his love of football and alternative music and is critical of academics who attempt to look at fandom from above and never step outside the perceived safe boundaries of the academy to take an insider perspective. Henry Jenkins (1992) is a self-styled aca-fan and Matt Hills (2002) admits his affection for *Doctor Who* and Gillian Anderson. Karen Hellekson and Kristina Busse (2006) emphasize that rather than choosing fans as collaborators, they are the fans.

However, Hills also cites the profoundly uncomfortable nature of this discussion for both researcher and researched, and his "class based sense that issues of sexuality [apparently bound up with his feelings about Anderson] are not a proper topic of discussion" (2002, 87). Once they've acknowledged their position as fans themselves, it turns out that few fan theorists grant us access to their own fan lives beyond the safety of academic analysis. Harris' admission turns out not to be all that daring after all, since the site of her fannish activity, Viewers for Quality Television, seems, at least on the surface, to have more in common with the academy than with fandom Sandvoss' admissions do not put him in too much danger. After all, we encourage sports fandom on a national level. Rhiannon Bury (2005) writes an in-depth case study of fan fiction by joining a slash community, but makes it clear that she did not initially read slash—and has never been a fanfiction writer, slash or otherwise. Bob Rehak confesses his own fannish non-involvement, but it's hardly a confession at all, as he says "In terms of fandom, I'm one of those who stands on the sidelines, self-identifying as a fan even though I don't really 'do' fannish things, create fannishly, or consort with other fans" (Jenkins 2007b). Even Joli Jenson, who set out explicitly to challenge the stereotypes we apply to fans, drawing parallels between "us" and "them," cannot sustain the identification, shifting back to referring to fans as "them" by the end of her argument.

Perhaps this is because those of us engaged in the study of popular culture are forever trying to explain to those who are not why we do it, sometimes by trying to convince others that our research has implications "far beyond the realm of popular culture" (Gray, Sandvoss, and Harrington 2007, 10)—a realm that presumably matters much more. For all their championing of fandom, aca-fans have their own shame issues. Many of us have been accused of not engaging in "serious" academic research or "rigorous" methodology. As a result we theorize and politicize our pleasures in order to make them more palatable to a cultural elite that does not need any more encouragement to dismiss what we study as frivolous and meaningless. The very act of justification is of course an indication that we are uncomfortable with the position.

Fig. 2-4. You're writing a book about what?

Theorists such as Doty (2000) and Hills (2002) have questioned whether decades of hiding aca-fans' personal and cultural investment in their subjects have served to "squeeze much of the life out of it in many senses." (Doty 2000, 11) Hills calls for more explicitly auto-ethnographic work, rather than academics merely implying actual fan experiences in their writing. Both Hills and Doty, however, continue to acknowledge the danger of slipping into being "overly confessional" or appearing "embarrassingly egotistical or gee-whiz celebratory".

The necessity of maintaining distance between us and the objects of popular culture that we study is an additional dilemma for aca-fans. The traditional concern with aesthetic distance which has long shaped acceptance of high art and literature, thought necessary for legitimate art, has influenced the perception of necessary distance. Hills and Jenkins (2001) take issue with this, noting that Bourdieu's (1984) idea of holding art at a distance is antithetical to fandom, where holding the fannish object close is integral to the pleasure.

Much of what is referred to as proper distance is in reality a caution against excessive emotional intimacy. While Hills and Jenkins have cautioned against distance, aca-fans at times contribute to the pathologizing of fannish emotion and behavior. Many prominent fan studies theorists weighed in as part of a 2010 online discussion in Ian Bogost's blog, which warned aca-fans about being emotionally invested in their objects of study/fandom (and thus unable to remain at a distance and appropriately critical). In the extensive comments which followed, Bogost set himself apart from certain fans, labeling them as 'obsessive', and confessed that he found some of them to "verge on perversity", prompting a response by Jenkins in recognition of the very real consequences of such labels on fans.

Both the objects of fandom and the emotion surrounding those objects continue to be deeply problematic areas. In a discussion about aca-fans on Jenkins' online blog, Flourish Klink, Nancy Baym and Kristina Busse debated the ethics of the fannish practice of writing fanfiction about real people ("real person fiction" or RPF)—in this case, band members interviewed in Baym's research. Klink compared this to the ethical dilemma of studying fandom when you also define yourself as a part of it.

> Klink: Your story about the band member makes me think about fans' reactions to the academic articles they themselves are in. That's a productive comparison, I think - "fans are to acafen the way that band members are to RPF writers" - because I think it opens the door to discussing the competing ethical responsibilities we have. Part of defining oneself as an 'acafan,' I think, is about making an ethical commitment to the fan community, yes? So that when they read your academic work, they don't feel like that band member - misrepresented and kind of miserable. Obviously, there's some important differences—an academic is making truth claims, whereas a fan is not; academics have cultural power, whereas fans rarely do; fans do not (usually) put themselves forward as public figures, whereas musicians and actors must by the nature of their work.

But ultimately, academics and fan fiction writers both mine preexisting texts and come up with narratives that make arguments about our world, right? They aren't the same, but they are similar.

Tulloch (2000) points out that there are significant theoretical and methodological implications attached to how scholars research fandom – whether they are fans themselves, or study fandom as something that others engage in. Sandvoss sets out the methodological and ethical difficulties in asking fans to articulate their inner fantasies and desires, and notes that only a few empirical studies have done so. Vermorel and Vermorel (1992) interview several fans who discuss their fantasies, but remain firmly in academic mode as they do so, investigating from the outside. In contrast, studying fandom from a position of immersion provides access to open discussion of the unconscious motivations of fans, both individually and collectively. Studying fandom from within, however, also puts the researcher at risk for bias. As Baym notes, researchers studying fandom from the outside were often overly pathologizing; those of us who look at fandom from an insider position are at risk of being overly applauding.

> Baym: When I first started studying fandom and read much of the textual analytic work on soap opera fans I was mortified by the willingness to make claims about what fans got out of the genre without ever actually looking at what fans did or talking with them about it. Not surprisingly, these textual analyses often led to analyses of fans as deeply screwed up people living vicariously through texts. I was also struck by the fact that so much of that work was written in language that was borderline incomprehensible without a Ph.D. in the area. In response, from the start, my core obligation has been to write about fans in a way that honors their perspectives and in a way which they can read easily.... But 'honoring' does not mean 'fawning.' .....We are often eager to criticize previous research in order to situate the value of our own, we need to be willing to criticize the fandoms we study too. Similarly, there are temptations to paint fans as good guys and industry professionals as bad guys, which is just as intellectually sloppy......I see my role as an academic as doing systematic and rich analysis that provides a basis for understanding social phenomena. All of the relevant identities we experience as researchers can be mined for their contribution to understanding if we are reflexive throughout the research process (Jenkins 2011).

"I don't trust those academics."

We might argue that aca-fans actually reify the gap that continues to exist between fans and the scholars who claim to be just like them. After all, why do we define ourselves as aca-fans if not to "maintain ideological authority" (Jenkins 2006, 27)? If the study of what is variously defined as elite or high culture (or just culture, with the assumption that we are not talking about mass culture) confers on us some cultural advantage, then studying popular culture levels the playing field. What happens to our role as mediators of artistic understanding if the people we would mediate on behalf of know more, or have a differently valued knowledge?

Several recent examples illustrate the mutual marginalization of fans and academics. As Hills (2002) bluntly points out, "fans don't like academics and vice versa." A glaring example of what became known as "How NOT to research an online community" blew up in late 2009 when two academics who were outsiders to fandom decided that an easy way to collect a large quantity of (questionably obtained) data about female sexuality would be to create a Live Journal for the sole purpose of surveying online fandom. Without any research into fandom itself, the researchers developed a survey which asked a variety of poorly formulated questions about drug use, real-life sexual behavior, personal kinks, masturbation habits, and rape fantasies. Unfortunately for researchers Ogas and Gaddam, who held themselves out as cognitive neuroscientists, their stereotype of fans seemed to produce some serious miscalculations. Fans are a smart, savvy, literate group—as blogger Alison MacLeod (2009) writes in her coverage of the resulting wank, "stuff like feminist analysis of television casting decisions is a walk in the part for many of them." Many of the fans who ran across the survey were professors, social researchers, feminist academics, lawyers, psychologists—and neuroscientists. They soon figured out that Ogas and Gaddam held PhDs in the rather irrelevant fields of visual processing and artificial intelligence. They had also failed to mention the lucrative book deal that prompted their research on "what netporn teaches us about the brain" (now sold as *A Billion Wicked Thoughts*).

The fandom community came together to boycott the survey, calling it "ignorant, casually homophobic, patronizing, misogynistic, profoundly privileged claptrap." The moderators of the kinkbingo community, thingswithwings and eruthros, whose members were solicited for participation, warned fellow fans:

> They are outsiders to fandom. They are outsiders to fanfiction. They are outsiders to slash. And they haven't tried to learn, or to understand, or to think about fannish communities. Instead, they have made assumptions about who we are, about what we read, about what we find hot; they plan to use those to explain what makes women tick, what our brains make us do.

They also penned a response to the researchers, making clear their refusal to be studied by outsiders:

> We don't know how aware you are of your subject, but there have been multiple studies on fanfiction done over the last thirty years, and few if any of them have represented the community in an accurate or complex manner. Studies of fans, particularly female fans, tend to follow in the long history of pathologizing women's behaviour and women's desire...the history of othering and shaming the weirdos as a form of boundary-policing.
>
> We have become convinced, after years of reading horrifying interviews and studies that purport to know something about our communities.... that the only way for these communities to be fairly represented is for them to represent themselves. We trust the folks at fanlore.org and we trust the folks at the OTW and we trust acafans like Alexis Lothian, who participate in the community as fans. We trust our fellow fans who are anthropologists and our fellow fans who are IT specialists and our fellow fans who are historians and our fellow fans who are literary critics—we trust these people with the chronicling of our history, because they are part of our community. We do not know you, and we do not trust you; we have good reason not to trust you...Why should you be the one writing a book on us? You know nothing about us. We're not interested in being part of yet another inept, inexpert, hastily-researched study that tells the world how utterly fascinating we are, or how our patterns of desire prove your bullshit pet theory about desire and the brain. You seem to think that the promise of a "positive mention" in your book will thrill and convince us, but such thinking is based on the assumption that we care about our image in the popular media, or that we care about explaining ourselves to the wider world, or that we long for fame, or something. The last thing we want is more cognitive scientists breathing down our necks while we try to form a safe space for kinky fannish expression.

When the book itself was listed for sale on Amazon, fans tagged it with terms like "complete crap", "pseudoscience", "written in crayon", "wrong on the internet", and "raise your hand if they tried to get you."

Similarly, though not nearly as dramatic, fan response to a special *Supernatural* issue of *Transformative Works and Cultures*, the journal for the Organization for Transformative Works (OTW) was not universally enthusiastic, despite the explicit "we trust the OTW" sentiment contained in the Survey!Fail response, and even though a non-academic fan had contributed to the issue. One fan, who was contacted in December of 2009 by TWC editors to let her know that her work was being cited in the journal responded: "WTF is Transformative Works and Cultures?" And later, after she had checked out the journal's website, she says:

> Considering this is apparently a fan run thing I feel slightly better about it. Not good though. Pretty far from good.

In the space of three short sentences she's moved from a readiness to embrace back to a guarded position of distrust. The comments to this writer's post echo her concern. Some try to explain what OTW does, assuring the writer that it's not "shady" and saying "these are the aca-fans you've heard so much about."

What this reassurance suggests, however, is that the OTW and aca-fans in general linger on the margins of fandom, almost mythical beasts. This is even more surprising when one considers how many aca-fans there are in the *Supernatural* fandom. We are there, but we don't interact in the same ways or in the same spaces—or if we do, we don't admit it—and therefore the fans don't know who we are. As far as the fans are concerned, aca-fans are clearly "other."

Another commenter observes that when looking at the OTW website "it's not obvious they're in fandom." (Of course, making this more obvious sometimes leads to criticism of another sort. Posters to our blog, *Fangasm*, have accused us of being "too fangirly" and "stalkerish" when we attempt to combine fannish squee with aca-fannish theorizing. The criticism is that we're either too academic or we're too "fangirly".) Meanwhile, the OTW aca-fans were also voicing their own WTF's over what seemed to them inexplicable fan behavior. In response to a post from one upset fan whose work had also been quoted, one of the OTW editors had this to say:

> When I first saw it [the post], I was trying to figure out how to respond. And then I saw reasonable response after reasonable comment get dismissed. And I realized that the OP didn't actually want to raise awareness or address a real issue. I'm not sure what she wanted.

The editor wants a reasonable response, the type expected in academic circles. But the OP [original poster] is responding as a fan—she's concerned with being identified and she's concerned that her fannish practices might come into the harsh and judgmental light of the "real" world. The editor's response suggests that she does not understand fan shame or the anxiety this fan was feeling. The fan was not concerned with raising awareness, she was concerned with her own position, and understandably distraught (from a fan perspective). The editor's approach is the academic one in which emotion must give way to reason. Neither understands the response of the other.

Again, this response subtly positions the respondent as outside, as the editor expresses her frustration.

And yet I can't help feel hurt....About the misrepresentation...and the demands that we not only live up to an ethics higher than all academics but also higher than all fans.

The problem here is that the rules and "ethical standards'" are completely different, and perhaps mutually exclusive. This may be why attempts to integrate academic and fan sides ultimately fail—hence our own (imperfect) decision to keep our fan and academic sides separate for the most part

The language of the official rebuttal to the post and to the general reaction in fandom takes on a defensive tone, as the researchers attempt to convince fandom that it's better to be studied from within than from the outside, as we also believe.

> We (as in Karen and Kristina, but also as the entire TWC staff, as well as the OTW supporting us) consider ourselves fans first. We don't think we're academic interlopers who think it's neat to add to the *Lord of the Rings* debate by looking at those crazy women slashing the hobbits. We are fans, we create fan works, and we participate in the community – a community we think is important and worthy of study. We'd rather fandom be studied not by some random outsider, but by people who know fandom's nuances – who know that fandom is always more complex and more complicated than we may believe or see.

Giving their real first names when outing themselves as fans seems like a bold move –especially in light of the fan shame we will discuss in the next chapter. However, they reveal little about their own fan practices and the move to validate fandom might well been seen by the offended fan as more condescending than legitimizing. Unfortunately, the editors never had the chance to communicate with the original poster, because her post was f-locked (locked to all but friends) shortly after it was put up, a move that reinforced the split between "us" and "them" from the fan's side. Later, the researchers position themselves differently, again attempting to explain their efforts to study fandom ethically.

> We are an academic publication, drawing from a myriad of different disciplines and fandoms. We have created an ethics guideline that forces scholars to seriously consider the potential costs of citing, referencing, and linking even publically posted material. We are doing our best to meld together academic and fannish requirements.

The difficulty of maintaining a largely untenable position emerges here. Their very identity is challenged as they shift from the "we" above (Karen and Kristina) to the closing "we" where they have given up all

personal identity to become an "academic publication." First names are
lost. What might be read by fans as a lack of empathy, can also be
understood as genuine surprise by the academics.

Most aca-fans, ourselves included, encounter a similar struggle as we
attempt to simultaneously uphold fannish ethics and academic rigor. Even
Jenkins' implementation of the term "aca-fan" is somewhat muddied. At
times he's an Aca-Fan, with the hyphen acting more as a reification of the
divide between those two identities. At other times he's an Aca/Fan with
the backslash between the words functioning to suggest a far more
intimate relationship between his two halves, even if this relationship is
never borne out. As much as we would like to believe otherwise, being an
academic is often fundamentally at odds with being a fan and vice versa.

Finding a Voice

The first version of this book was far from an intellectual, rational, and
unemotional academic text. Instead, we penned a giddy, euphoric,
rollercoaster of a roadtrip through the *Supernatural* fandom, carried out on
midnight forays to filming locations, in online fanfic communities, and at
a succession of fan conventions all over the world. We were fans first and
foremost, shelling out hundreds of dollars for flights and tickets and photo
ops, writing fanfiction, and sharing in the online and in person fannish
squee.

But we were also academics, increasingly utilizing our professional
credentials to gain access to the other side of the fan/famous wall in order
to interview the creative side of *Supernatural*. We quickly found that
doors were opened to us as academics that would not have been open to us
if we presented ourselves as fans. Showing up at a filming location as
"just" fans resulted in threats to call security. Leading with our
professional titles, we were able to secure the interviews we sought. Our
attempt to be both enthusiastic emotional fangirls and rational academic
researchers proved a difficult fence to straddle. And despite our best
intentions, we found that the hybrid text we wanted to write could not be
written. Clearly writing as academics to an audience of fans would not
work, and writing as fans to an audience of academics was an equally
untenable position—as the following episode, written for our original
roadtrip novel in fan mode, makes clear.

*One of our first interviews was with actress Danneel Harris, who at
the time was the girlfriend (now wife) of Supernatural star Jensen Ackles.
The interview was set to take place sometime during the fan convention we*

were attending in Los Angeles, though the details had not been thoroughly ironed out. While we waited for Danneel's phone call, Lynn discovered she had no reception in the cavernous basement of the hotel where the con was taking place.   We were reasonably certain there is cell phone reception in the Arctic Circle, but there was not a bar to be had in a hotel in LA, of all places, where everyone's people are calling everyone else's people, and where a missed call can ruin a career.

Normally being out of phone contact would not have upset us all that much, but when a sought interview was riding on a phone call, things look different. Lynn first ran around trying desperately to get a few bars on her phone. We then tried to get word to Danneel through everyone from the con photographer to Creation co-owner Adam Malin (who responded with a polite but exasperated reminder that he was in fact "kinda running a convention here, ladies.")

Lynn, however, did not give up easily. She had paid for photo ops with the actors, like most of the fans at the con (unlike Kathy, who resists being photographed under any circumstances with Amish determination) and so during the photo with Mr. Ackles she attempted to enlist his help directly by explaining the planned interview and unforeseen impediments. Sounds simple unless you know that photo ops last about ten seconds, during which time you say "Hello" to the celebrity, smile, perhaps get an arm around your back, and then move the hell out of the way and let the next person crowd in for her picture. The photo ops are relentlessly organized, and allow no room for deviation. So when deviation happens, no one is very happy. The photographer isn't happy. The other fans aren't happy. And the security detail, not-so-affectionately known as the Men With No Necks ('MWNN'), look ready to move into swift and potentially lethal action. Not that any of this stops an intrepid researcher—or a fangirl. Jensen, who apparently knew about the interview, was in the middle of helpfully brainstorming ways of putting Danneel in touch with us when Lynn was grabbed none-too-gently by the MWNN and "escorted" from the photo op room. She had clearly been pegged as one of "those" fans, and was definitely in trouble. Kathy, wisely, had decided to cower in a corner during all of this, too tongue tied still to talk to any of the actors and preferring to fade into the background.

Undaunted, Lynn politely thanked the MWNN for their assistance, and got right back in line for her next photo op, the "sandwich" photo (as in sandwiched between the boys, which is vaguely dirty and thus very popular). When her turn came, she walked up and Jensen immediately tried to continue their conversation, which Lynn pretended to discourage (mostly for the benefit of the MWNN). "Shhh, I'm not talking to you, I totally got in trouble for it before!" A hasty exchange of email information ensued and we resigned ourselves to rescheduling the interview. We were disappointed, but settled back into our seats to enjoy the rest of the convention, and easily slipped back into fan mode. Suddenly, the convention photographer appeared and pulled us out of our squeeful place with an exasperated look and a whispered "Come with me" order.

We hustled out of our seats, dutifully followed the photographer down an empty hallway to a side door and the "secret" backstage entrance. Danneel appeared with a smile, and we found ourselves being ushered backstage by the very same security guard who, minutes before, had unceremoniously kicked Lynn out of the photo-ops room when she dared to speak to the talent. Now he holds back the curtain separating the backstage area from the autograph line and solicitously helps us and Danneel step over the various cables, then closes the curtain behind us to seal our crossover. The irony wasn't lost on us, nor were the stares of our fellow fangirls.

The Squeeful Fangirl, as described above, has no place in an academic text, and yet it is precisely that fangirl who informs everything we write about. How do we go about banishing our subject from our text? We have attempted throughout our research to remain mindful of our co-existing identities, and the impact they have on both the lens we use to study fandom and the conclusions we draw. What we learned is that "co-existence is futile."

Fig. 2-5. Jared and Jensen give up and pose without Lynn

CHAPTER THREE

I'M TOO SEXY FOR MY STEREOTYPE

In May of 2007, actor and object-of-our-affection Jensen Ackles traveled to England to appear at his first fan convention, 'Asylum.' We, unfortunately, did not. Instead we glumly sat around in Starbuck's puzzling over its odd name.

"Why Asylum?" Kathy asked over coffee and chai.

Lynn, the psychologist, pondered. "Place of refuge? Fans coming together, feeling safe?"

"Or place to house the crazies," Kathy countered.

Shame. We've encountered the uncomfortable emotion repeatedly in our fannish lives. Shame that we're hooked on a sci fi show. Shame that we're reading fanfiction. Shame that we're ogling actors on television. Shame that we're spending our hard-earned wages flying across the country to ogle them in person. Shame that we're investing time, energy and emotion on something so frivolous. Few media fans are unfamiliar with the experience.

In fall 2010, an online blog ran an article identifying the "Top 7 Scariest Fandoms" (Armbruster 2010), warning the rest of the world about fandom with derisive comments about fans of everything from *Harry Potter* to John Lennon. Not only did they toss around the derogatory words fans have (unfortunately) come to expect, like obsessive and crazy, they also linked to fanworks which were included for the sole purpose of ridicule. "Remember, you can't bleach your eyes," was included as a cautionary statement. At the same time the *Citypages* blog was running, we were—fittingly enough—at a fan convention in Vancouver. The *Supernatural* fandom was miraculously not included in *Citypages*' list of infamy, but has garnered "scariest", "most obsessive," "batshit craziest," and a variety of other colorful titles in the past. The accusations may seem benign, even silly, but they are hurled at fans often enough that fandom has internalized a significant degree of shame about being a fan.

Fig. 3-1

In a packed auditorium full of enthusiasm and excitement that day at the convention, it was fans and not the media who went to the microphone with the question: "Before you got the part on *Supernatural*, did anyone warn you about the fans?"

There is no lack of love for the fans from the actors themselves. As actor Matt Cohen (young John Winchester on *Supernatural*) aptly answered, "It's because of you guys that I get to work. And I don't need a warning, you guys aren't nearly as crazy as me!" He went on to say, "I feel like the luckiest guy ever, I have no career, no job, without you guys, so thank you," bowing to the fans before he left the stage.

Padalecki and Ackles also got the "fan shame" question that day— what's the worst thing a fan has ever done? Ackles answered, "I gotta be honest, I think the fans of *Supernatural* are pretty cool.... they have some self-respect and they respect the show and the guys that work hard on the show, and so I think we're lucky in that aspect that we've got really cool fans."

At times, the celebrities appear to be more positive about fandom than the fans themselves. Have we just been called obsessed, crazy, sick or accused of being stalkers too often? Name-calling, after all, has consequences. Aca-fans seem as contradictory in their opinions of fandom as fans. When he took issue with fellow media scholar Ian Bogost's characterization of some fans as obsessive and verging on perversity, Jenkins noted that there are real things at stake for fans who are called "obsessive" or gamers who get called "sick and twisted," and potential consequences when pathologizing words are deployed by people in positions of power (2010).

Bogost was criticizing fanboys and fangirls, and both have been targeted for shaming. The experience plays out differently, however, depending on gender. Some of this difference is related to sexual stereotypes. Male media fans may fear that being a fanboy evokes images of the 40-year-old virgin still living in his mother's basement and collecting Star Wars light sabers. In other words, the fear is of being perceived as sexually unsuccessful. Scott Bukatman references this fear in his autoethnography when he confesses to being "worried about my dick" in language which recalls Freud's castration anxiety and suggests discomfort about fanboy behavior as developmentally fixated (Bukatman 1993, 93).

For female fans, the site of fan shame may be different, and perhaps more persistent in a decade when Comic Con fanboys are reclaiming the word "geek" with revolutionary fervor. While male media fans fear being perceived as not sexual enough, female fans fear being categorized as too sexual, or at the very least too emotional. *Supernatural* as aphrodisiac may be acceptable when curled up on the couch at home with one's partner, but picspams devoted to Jared Padalecki's abs may be a bit more problematic in the culture at large. We turn now to the link between shame, emotion and sexuality for women, especially as it plays out in *Supernatural* fandom.

Fans and the Spectre of Female Desire: Do These Women Have No Shame?

A 2010 discussion on *In Media Res* focused on a Youtube clip of a very young fan named Cody "Crying for Justin Bieber" and insisting she wants to marry him (Garrison 2010). At first, the clip seems an exception to prohibitions against excess emotionality and sexuality for females. While such affective fan performance is often pathologized, in this instance the young girl's display of emotion and her fantasy of marrying the singer are presented as cute and amusing. Why is Cody's reaction viewed as normal, instead of as a worrisome break with reality or evidence of imminent stalker behavior? Why isn't the derision that has been leveled at "hysterical" female fans since the days of Beatlemania evident here? Because Cody is three years old.

The discussion brings into focus the cultural fear of female sexuality which sometimes lies beneath criticism of female fan behavior. Because Cody is still a child, her intention to marry Bieber can be easily dismissed as harmless childhood fantasy without any concern about breaks with reality or potential stalker behavior. The distinction can be seen as the difference between "desiring up" (the young fan wanting things that are above her maturity level, which is considered a developmentally appropriate striving) and "desiring down" (grown women wanting things, including cultural objects like *Twilight* or younger male celebrities, which are below their expected maturity level). The emphasis here, however, is less on expected timetables of human development and more about what defines "mature sexuality" for women—and why that might be threatening. Lindsay Garrison, of the University of Wisconsin Madison, suggests that the girl's "extreme youth displaces the threat of any active female sexuality (a key element in the moral panic and othering of Beatlemania, *Twilight* fandom, and Bieber Fever) or physical harm." Desiring down, and perhaps any sort of outside-the-box desire, is viewed as pathological. As aca-fan Helen Anne Peterson puts it, "not only sad, but wrong and weird….read as pitiful."

The language used to describe the "wrong" kind of desire is powerful in dismissing those aspects of female sexuality that are threatening, and is an integral part of the cultural containment of female desire in general. In the same blog conversation, Kristen Warner notes that the conceptualization of young Cody's desire as safely within a discourse of innocence and naiveté contributes to that containment. The young girl's emotional reactions are framed as cute and funny, avoiding what Teresa Stern calls "the spectre of adolescent female desire." The video also literally avoids any focus on Cody's older sister, also a fan but already at an age when her desire is perceived as unsettling rather than innocent. As Kristina Busse adds to the online conversation, "There's something about women desiring—and especially when turning (younger) men into lust objects— that unsettles and needs to be controlled." Even female fans themselves are apparently unsettled, as the fans who wanted only moderated questions at the LA *Supernatural* convention demonstrated.

At the same time, TPTB are marketing commodities like Bieber, *Twilight*'s Robert Pattinson, and *Supernatural*'s own Jared Padelecki and Jensen Ackles to appeal not only to young girls but to their mothers, attempting to create intergenerational appeal in order to gain the widest possible audience. Still, when grown women succumb, they may face social proscription. In stark contrast to the reactions to the young Bieber fan, the celebrity website ROFLRAZZI posted a photograph in 2010 of a group of "Twilight Moms" tearfully awaiting the arrival of one of their objects of affection, presumably actors Robert Pattison and/or Taylor Lautner (Pattinson was, at the time, in his early 20s and Lautner on the cusp of eighteen). The article was provocatively titled, "Boo! For Pedophilia Double Standards" and insisted "You know, if this was men cheering for 17 year old girls, someone would call the cops." Fans of young women from Brooke Shields to Britney Spears to Miley Cyrus would presumably also be subject to incarceration. Nevertheless, posters referred to the women as creepy, ridiculous, and unattractive, and called the Twilight Moms phenomenon "messed up." "Most of the Twilight moms," one poster insisted, "Want to sleep with every member of the cast." One went so far as to accuse the women of being "above the law" and another to disparage their inadequacy as parents, seeming to imply that they should be tending home and hearth. "These women are still in adolescence, instead of raising their own children, they support this stupidity. Do these women have no shame??" (ROLF RAZZI).

If they don't, they are the exception.

Freud himself considered shame a feminine characteristic; one of his initial insights was the explanation of "hysteria" among women in the late nineteenth century as related to sexual repression. Many authors have asserted links between shame and femininity, with women more shame prone than men. Bartky (1990) goes so far as to say shame is the female emotion in a patriarchal society. Since women take on an identity that is under constant surveillance by self and others, they often feel pulled to construct a façade to protect the true self underneath, which is experienced as shameful and inadequate. Shame acts as a boundary between private and public aspects of the self, attempting to protect against intrusion. A public self is constructed to shield the vulnerable imperfect real self, and anything that might tear away the public self and expose the inadequate identity underneath is experienced as a serious threat, as we'll revisit in Chapter Six.

Seu (2006) conducted a discursive analysis of women and their experiences of shame. The women she interviewed spoke of a constant, underlying anxiety about being exposed, of people seeing "who they really are." The women saw this split as a protective strategy, but were also aware that it prevented something from developing fully—perhaps a sense of self that is experienced as coherent and not split off. This helps women feel competent and less vulnerable; unfortunately, it also prevents the positive, hidden qualities from developing or being validated. Even positive feedback given to the façade self isn't meaningful, since the person is fully aware that the outside input isn't applicable to who they really are. One woman interviewed in Seu's study admitted that she tuned into what people expected from her in order to "gain acceptance," reminiscent of Gilligan's (1993) ideas about women playing a series of roles and adapting themselves to others' needs. Walkerdine (1990) relates some women's inability to identify with their own successes as the result of role playing to cover up a repressed self, which is inhibited by social conditioning. What the inadequate position does not allow women to do is to make a statement of their own value. We need the mirror of other people's validation and acceptance to believe in our own worth, which hiding ourselves precludes. Shame can thus be destructive. Bartky writes:

> Better people are not made in this way, only people who are weaker, more timid, less confident, less demanding, and hence more easily dominated... In all these ways, shame is profoundly disempowering. The need for secrecy and concealment that figures so largely in the shame experience is disempowering as well, for it isolates the oppressed from one another (1990, 97).

Such an understanding of shame provides an explanation for fans' stringent policing of the First Rule of Fandom. Telling no one about fandom both preserves the safe space in which female fans come together to share their authentic experience, and simultaneously contributes to the continued covering up of that experience in "real life."

As the public shaming of the Twihard moms for their display of desire illustrates, one of the sources of shame for women is the culture's containment of and discomfort with female sexuality. The cultural context within which one grows up necessarily influences the development of sexuality; this context differs for males and females. Women continue to struggle to create a healthy sexual identity for themselves in a society still filled with mixed messages, double standards, fear and exploitation. Their experience as objects of desire—instead of subjects of their own desire— complicates their ability to connect with their own bodies and their own sexuality. Discomfort with impossible standards of physical attractiveness can leave women divorced from any positive feelings about their bodies and disconnected from their own sexual desire. Open discussion, acceptance and valuing of female sexuality are necessary in order for healthy development to occur, yet this often doesn't happen, either in families or the culture at large. Young women are not encouraged to get in touch with their desires, but to concentrate on their desirable appearance instead—to be objects of desire instead of subjects.

Fig. 3-2

Benjamin (1988) describes the same two choices of madonna or whore which have been cited for decades as limiting women's acceptable roles. A comforting asexual nature is ascribed to a mother whose power is restricted to serving her children's or partner's needs, but not in having free will to do whatever she chooses, as the poster criticizing the TwiHard mom for not being home taking care of her children inferred. Or a woman can be sexy, but as an object, not a subject, expressing not her own desire, but her pleasure in being desired.

While undoubtedly macrosystem norms have evolved in the last few decades, nevertheless the roles articulated by Benjamin continue to exert an influence, perhaps more difficult to challenge in their current less overt forms. In addition, the emphasis on appearance as all-important, encouraging both women and men to focus on females as objects, threatens to replace a consideration of "what I want" with "what they want" when it comes to sexuality. Karp and Stoller (1999) described the "new girl order," which continues to resonate two decades later.

> We are given the not-so-subtle message that sexual attractiveness and sexual satisfaction are one and the same. If we can just cut all the fat from our diets, go to the gym three times a week, and wear the right lingerie, we'll be able to attain sexual nirvana. Of course, that's not how it works.

The thing we women are never encouraged to do is to focus on what
actually makes us feel good.

Fandom is, for some of us, the exception to that rule. Fandom is
something to be indulged in. Something that makes us feel good. Therein
lies both the appeal and the problem.

The shaming of women for open expression of sexuality is nothing
new, both within fandom and outside. Female wrestling fans in the 1960's
were strongly criticized for their overt appreciation and blatant objectifying
of male wrestlers, with mainstream news coverage questioning the
women's normalcy and sympathizing with their husbands' dissatisfaction
(Dell 1998). Radway (1984) described female romance reading fans and
their grumbling husbands and sons. The entire world was grumbling when
so-called Beatlemania swept the sixties. The phenomenon was headline
news not for the significant musical talents of the foursome, but for the
reactions of their female fans, whose swooning and crying constituted a
rare open expression of emotion and sexual feelings which has been
described as revolutionary (Ehrenreich, Barbara, Hess, and Jacobs 1992).

Conflating sexual fantasy with sexual behavior is part of the problem.
In Rhiannon Bury's ethnographic case study of two mailing list based
female fandoms, members complained that people think nothing of it
when men talk about lusting after women, but if women talk openly about
the sexual attractiveness of men, they are viewed as "sluts" (Bury 2005,
11). Despite such periodic protests, shame about being a fangirl persists.
Kristina Busse has written about this internalized sense of fan shame,
noting that stereotypically female fan interests are more regularly mocked,
and that fans themselves maintain their boundaries within fandom by
buying into the same feminizing and infantilizing bias that often goes
along with such mockable fan practices, particularly for females who don't
"outgrow" their interest in pop stars, tv shows, or boy bands. Accusations
of being too attached, too emotional, too invested—too obsessed—
continue to be thrown around both in academic discussions and within
fandom (2010).

Fangirls are not the only women dismissed for what are perceived as
overly emotional or overtly sexual reactions. A successful scriptwriter for
shows like *House*, *Smallville*, *Tru Calling*, and *Dark Angel* posted in her
LiveJournal the story of her creation of the character of Ben on *Dark
Angel* and the casting of *Supernatural* actor Jensen Ackles in the role.
Apparently Ackles blew everyone away with his audition – almost.

Fig. 3-3: The disturbingly attractive Ackles

This was exactly the character I'd envisioned. It was clear to me that if anybody else got this role, I would have to commit ritual suicide. Fortunately everyone else wanted him -- except one highly placed producer. He was upset by the fact that the people in casting that night had been mostly women; that we all liked Jensen Ackles; and that he was a good-looking actor. Because, clearly, that must be what was influencing us. "Something very disturbing was going on in that room," he insisted.

Leaving his opinion of our emotionality aside, I asked what his issues were with Ackles -- hadn't that been a terrific reading? He admitted the reading was fine, but -- "He doesn't have muscles." "What?" "He doesn't have muscles, he doesn't look like a soldier. If he was genetically designed to be a soldier, wouldn't they make him strong?" My head spun for a moment. I said, "Our heroine is Jessica Alba" (tightropegirl 2005).

Amusingly, that same producer hired Ackles as a regular for the following season after seeing his work, but his initial reaction was to dismiss the opinions of any females when it comes to an attractive male— and, even more tellingly, to find it "disturbing."

The Authorized Discourse

Heather Meggers has analyzed the challenges that women continue to confront when considering their own sexualities (2012).   Culturally, Meggers asserts, women are socialized to view sex in terms of relational intimacy, romanticism, commitment, and above all, privacy.   We are certainly not encouraged to be kinky, our own desires policed by the constant threat of "slut-shaming" or other types of relational aggression. Yet in practice, women often experience interest in less conventional sexual interactions and activities (Leiblum 2001), including the more "kinky" fantasies of erotic force (Bivona and Critelli 2009) or consensual dominance and submission (Zurbriggen and Yost 2004). Fantasies involving voyeurism, exhibitionism, and engaging in other "taboo" or forbidden acts have also been documented to occur relatively frequently in women (Arndt and Goldenberg 2004; Hariton and Singer 1974).   The disconnect between what is acceptable in terms of behavior—and even fantasy—and the reality of women's fantasy lives, especially regarding non-romantic or unconventional fantasies, can have very real consequences. Researchers have identified reduced frequency of fantasy, reduced arousal and reduced subjective reports of sexual desire as sequellae of increased guilt (Leitenberg and Henning 1995).
Researcher Michelle Fine (1988) emphasized the importance of the "authorized discourse" on sexuality to determine whether women connect with their own desires or dissociate, as suggested by Meggers, with harmful results. The authorized discourse defines what is safe, what is taboo, what will be silenced.   Fine and Meggers identify harmful consequences when the discourse is limited. If the only discourse of sexuality is one where males are in search of desire but females are only in search of protection, then women are cut off from their own exploration of desire.   Fine calls for more discussion of the risk-free, nonvictimizing

pleasures of fantasy and masturbation, an authentic discourse around what feels desirable and undesirable to each individual woman, and a forum for women to openly discuss the realities of their sexual lives – to redress the missing discourse of female desire.

That fandom can provide some of that missing discourse is suggested by the interaction and fanworks in various communities of *Supernatural* fans, which allow women a forum in which to get in touch with their own authentic desires and openly express their genuine experience, including their sexual selves.

Fig. 3-4

At the same time, fans struggle to shrug off both the internalized shame and the external attempts at censure. The fans who Jenkins interviewed for his early article on slash writers almost twenty years ago expressed frustration with both fannish and academic accounts of slash that "dismiss or fail to address its erotic and bodily pleasures" (1988, 30). How much has changed in the last two decades? Judging by the icons, fanfiction, and vids peppered throughout the *Supernatural* communities, one would at first think the answer is quite a bit.

The research on shame and the authorized discourse thus seems applicable to the fandom community. The perceived safety and anonymity of online fandom encourage the lifting of constructed "socially acceptable" facades, thus providing a medium for expression and validation. At least within the fannish space, the need for concealment disappears. Fans openly proclaim their appreciation of sexually explicit fanworks created for the enjoyment of other women in a way that rarely happens in "real life" social interaction. The message is clear, as well as the challenge to the authorized discourse.

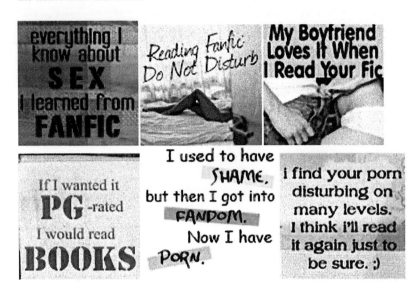

Fig. 3-5

Some segments of fandom have certainly grown more comfortable with the objectification inherent in celebrity culture—for women as well as men. Women who "look" have historically been constructed not as desiring subjects capable of objectification, but instead as "silly girls who are in love" with a male celebrity, and therefore unable to separate fantasy from reality (Bury 2005). We are accustomed to the male gaze turned on women; fandom turns the female gaze on men (and sometimes on other women as well), thus reconstructing the discourse of desire for women. In fanfiction, icons, vids and fanart, fangirls address their awareness of the cultural expectations for shame and the push towards internalizing it—and push back against such imposed expectations, as the playful use of the term "porn" in SPN icons implies.

Fig. 3-6

Yet female fans continue to grapple with their own desires when these fall outside the authorized discourse. Within the *Supernatural* fandom, there's plenty of evidence for the continued existence of internalized shame. Fandom itself buys into the stereotype of the overly emotional, crazy fangirl on a regular basis. In fact, fans have internalized such a strong sense of shame that they've projected it onto the objects of their affection, expressing their fear that the celebrities are either terrified or disgusted by their own female fans.

Fig. 3-7

Fig. 3-8

Supernatural fan Andie Masino describes a real life incident that seems to illustrate the same projection and shame. Masino had travelled to Texas to see actor Jensen Ackles in a community theater production of A Few Good Men (we had made the same trip, for the same reason). She had her Plastic Winchester dolls in her purse, enjoying the fannish squee with friends, when she ran into actress Danneel Harris, at the time Ackles' girlfriend, in the rest room. Andie describes her reaction:

> We were in each other's space for less than three seconds, but that's all it took to begin the deflation of my previously shiny attitude. She gave me a look—a dismissive, fangirls-are-so-STUPID kind of look. In three seconds I went from Cinderella at the ball to Cinderella cleaning the chimneys. I felt ashamed of being a fangirl. Danneel Harris wouldn't fly to Texas to watch an actor in a play. Danneel Harris wouldn't write about it later in her LJ. Danneel Harris wouldn't carry around Ken dolls in her purse. I felt stupid. I felt embarrassed. In that moment I swore I was done being a fangirl. I was done with PWT, done with LJ, done with anything that could give me the stigma of a fan.

Masino was able to quickly shrug off the shame, perhaps because she was surrounded quite literally by fellow fangirls.

> Being with my people helped. I was able to share their squee and realize that I could never look down on any of them. By the end of the night, I had no shame putting Plastic!Sam on Real!Jared's seat in full view of Danneel, Jensen's parents, and anyone else….It didn't bother me because this was me, take it or leave it. I was never going to have this opportunity again, and hell if I was going to blow it because I was too embarrassed/self-conscious/hesitant.

Fans also continually police the boundaries of their own fannishness, negotiating what is acceptable and what is "over the line" so they can defend against fears of being criticized or judged themselves. When it comes to fan practices, how extreme is too extreme? It's always the fan just on the other side of that line. *That* is not me, fans proclaim. I'm not delusional. Other fans may be crazy stalkers, but me, I just watch for the plot.

Fans' recognition of their own defensiveness is humorously rendered in the above icons, but the pull to deny the perfectly understandable desire to simply stare at Dean Winchester's assets is nevertheless clear. When female fans do express their genuine desires, they often do so with preemptive apologies.

Fig. 3-9

Fig. 3-10

Of course, both men and women participate in fandom for a multitude of different reasons, not all of them having to do with sex. Fans role play and dress up and collect autographs and die cast Impalas. (We may have one or two on our coffee tables). They engage in extended discussions of characters, research the show's myths and monsters, argue theology and history, and post thoughtful meta. In other words, they do watch for the plot. This does not mean some fans don't also watch for the rare glimpse of Jared Padalecki's abs.

Internalized shame is a frequent topic of intellectual conversation and various forms of meta within fandom. A 2010 fanvid by sisabet and sweetestdrain explored the popular but shame-wrought fannish genres of hurt/comfort and slash, including their own individual investment, in a powerful video format. The vidders used the explicitly anti-shame song "OnThe Prowl" (which begins with a woman singing the provocative lyrics "I was thinking about picking up some….young boys") to present powerfully sexualized images of attractive young men taking off their clothes, roughing each other up, and eventually being graphically tortured. The vidders caption the fanwork (titled "Self Portrait") as "where is our line?" Their criterion for inclusion of a clip is that "it really got to me." That both the vidders and many of the commenters are in agreement as to what "gets to me" allows both expression of genuine desire and the opportunity for validation, which is an important component of reducing shame. In fact, fans repeatedly note that they recognize the moments depicted in the vid as ones which moved them as well—we confess that we recognized all the clips from *Supernatural*, which was, not surprisingly, well represented (sweetestdrain 2010).

"On The Prowl" is explicitly objectifying, which prompted fan discussion of the morality of turning the tables on males, even within a culture where sexualized violence against females is much more pervasive. (Compare this to the "Women's Work" vid by Luminosity and Sisabet, which takes a critical stance on the horror genre's depiction of eroticized violence against women). Fans who commented on "On The Prowl" expressed their discomfort at being "fascinated and attracted by male suffering." One fan describes the vid as "hot, cringe-inducing, thought-provoking." Another fears that she doesn't seem to have "a line" in some cases, confessing "Yeah, I am disturbing." The vidder responds with normalizing and encouragement: "Own that shit!"

> Rusty_halo: We live in a world where violence by men against women is omnipresent and systemic, while violence by women against men is comparatively rare. So I do tend to think that media portraying sexualized violence against women is more offensive, because it's perpetuating an existing oppression, whereas media containing sexualized violence against men is less offensive because it's a reversal of the dominant paradigm.

Bagheera_san: I felt perfectly justified in an eye-for-an-eye way. Because for me what this vid says is, "We can objectify you just as well as you can objectify us." This… is brutal and honest female desire. It may not give fangirls any moral high ground (the opposite) but then, being morally superior has never been a tool of emancipation.

The Persistence of Shame: Don't Ask Don't Tell

James, one of the few male *Supernatural* fans we interviewed, jokingly called sex the elephant in the room the first time he met up with fellow fans in real life (including the two of us) at Ackles' community theater production of *A Few Good Men*.

James: Online communities are a whole lot more sexual. There is an underlying sense of sexuality that revolves around the show, that doesn't get discussed that much. For example, when we all met up in Dallas, we all thought Jensen was incredible looking, yet we were hesitant to talk about it there at the table until I brought it up. Almost like we were looking for a way to legitimize our travelling across the country to see him SOLELY based on his looks. Which I don't think anyone did, but there is that mystique to try to justify our fannishness on something more than looks and sex, which people are more comfortable doing online. We all seemed a bit hesitant to squee in real life, I suppose.

Tellingly, as we all sat around the big table at the Pancake House in Fort Worth, a dozen fans who had flown across the country to watch a community theater production starring Mr. Ackles—eleven women and one gay man—it was the sole man at the gathering who dared to bring up sex. The emphasis on secrecy and concealment which Bartky references is quite evident, then, in media fandom.

Female fan behavior is often associated with fan fiction, especially slash, which has been a magnet for cultural proscriptions on female sexuality, and thus an additional source of internalized fan shame. Joanna Russ' groundbreaking book *How To Suppress Women's Writing* (1983), tied the suppression of women's writing to the suppression of female sexuality, examining the ways in which women's writing has been made invisible for hundreds of years. Russ identifies the formal and informal prohibitions that make it difficult for female writers, including vilification as either lesbians, or "loose women." What Russ calls "pollution of agency" also contributes to suppressing women's writing—if indeed a woman wrote something about sex, she shouldn't have. (And if she knew enough about it to write it well, she must be a slut).

Two anonymous posts in the fandomsecrets LJ community, a popular (all anonymous) forum for expressing fans' shame about everything from who they ship to what they fantasize about, confess fans' shame about liking two of the most controversial genres in fanfiction, which we'll consider in more detail in the next chapter: slash and hurt/comfort.

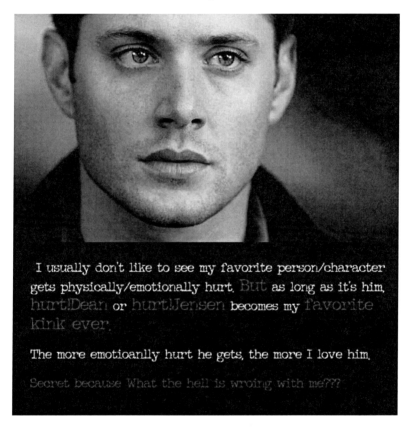

Fig. 3-11: Anonymous posts in fandomsecrets on LiveJournal

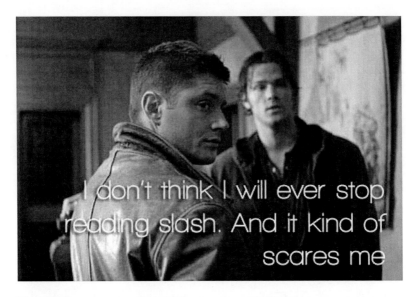

Fig. 3-12: Anonymous posts in fandomsecrets on LiveJournal

The term "out" is often used by fans, and especially fanfiction readers and writers, to describe the fraught decision of whether or not to tell those outside fandom about being a fan, drawing a conscious parallel to the coming out process for GLBT individuals. Fanfic enthusiasts run the gamut of the Kinsey scale, but many self-define as "other" regardless of their sexuality. This is more pronounced when the fanfiction in question is slash or includes any kind of explicit sexual themes, but the sense of being different is also noted by readers and writers of hurt/comfort, sub-genres such as MPreg or various kinks (wing!fic, tail!fic, tentacleporn, knotting, bloodplay, watersports—you name it, and there's fanfiction about it) and even by writers and readers of "gen" fanfiction, which contains no romantic pairings. Just the admission of liking any kind of fanfiction can be a source of shaming.

The question of being out is a loaded one for most fans—including us. In fact, while we've just consciously outed ourselves as slash readers and writers in writing this book, we've kept the lines of demarcation between our academic selves and our slash-writing fangirl selves rather boldly painted in "real life." Fans who know us online by our LJ names read our fanfiction and engage in conversation by posting in our journals or through our posts in theirs. Those fans know some of our social and political views, but mostly they know that we can tell a story of Sam and Dean or

Jared and Jensen and keep them entertained—sometimes with humor, sometimes with angst, sometimes with sex. We're proud of all those abilities, at least in the safe space of online fandom. The discomfort, for us and many other fans, comes when the lines of demarcation get smudged. In our "real life", we are academics, professors, partners, mothers. We live in the suburbs and work at major universities. Our fan lives were spent online, at conventions, and fan meet-ups, As our research progressed, we found ourselves flipping dizzily back and forth between our slashwriting fangirl and intellectualized academic identities. Boundaries blurred, with sometimes embarrassing results.

There was a telling moment at a large *Supernatural* fan convention when we were about to admit our fannish identities to some of the people who know us only as our academic selves. Another slashwriter, hearing what we were about to do, warned us not to. She'd learned the hard way that there can be serious consequences to being outed. We kept quiet, succumbing to shame and feeling as duplicitous as the woman behind us in line, who confided that she lied to her husband about where she was sneaking off to that weekend.

A Live Journal post in 2010 asked fans whether they let their real life friends and family read their fanfiction, asking "Are you out to your real life friends?" In answer, fans expressed fear of being judged and misjudged, or of being thought weird or abnormal, especially when it comes to the personally revealing content of fanfiction. One fan said, "I don't let my family or friends read my stuff. They'd think I was weird, and probably call the funny farm men in white coats to take me away!" To which the original poster replied:

> I know I shouldn't be ashamed of my tastes (H/C, a little smut/slash once in a while), but it seems like this is a common occurrence for a lot of people. And I don't really know how to rectify it. On the one hand, I know I will be judged for what I write, it is something that other people wouldn't understand. On the flip side, I KNOW I shouldn't have to hide this stuff, but it's easier, and in the end, it lets me write what I want. At least for me, that's the most important thing to maintain, my ability to write what I want and not fear that someone I know is going to read it, judge me, and confront me about it in my real life. If that means I have to separate my fan fiction involvement from my real life, I will, because to have to self-censor, if I couldn't write/read H/C, I don't think I would have any fan fiction involvement (2010).

A similar discussion took place in the LJ community *the_slash_pile* as fans weighed the risks and benefits of continuing to hide their fanfiction writing, discussing the risk of being "exposed" when it comes to sexual desires/fantasies, and fears of being shunned by family or friends.

> Anon: I don't want my family to know : it's much too tiresome to explain why exactly a girl reads/watches two men going at it. Besides, if they ever see any of the stuff I write, particularly in my one on one RPs where ALL my numerous kinks and fetishes are exposed... I dunno XD but I don't think it'd be good.
> Anon: I would be shunned if they read my stuff.
> (the_slash_pile 2010).

The First Rule of Fandom: Protection or Repression?

A discussion in the LJ community *metafandom* titled "In Defense of Fan Fiction" included this apologetic paragraph from an anonymous fan on LJ, which was tellingly unsuccessful in actually coming up with much of a defense:

> Some people think that fan-fiction is purely voyeuristic [sic] in that people like to imagine their favourite fictional couples together, and that's the end of that one... and on some levels, yes; I agree. A lot of it is voyeuristic. But, to counter that, a lot of it isn't. True, "romance" is probably the most popular genre on fanfiction.net... Sadly, I fall firmly into this category—teenage girls who can't really help themselves but let their daydreams carry them away.

Other fans responded, challenging the equating of the pleasures of voyeuristic fanworks or fantasy with something sad or wrong, again hypothesizing a gender divide in acceptability and expressing the concern that women have a history of men policing their desires for appropriateness.

> Deadparrot: This paragraph makes me flinch, because I believe that we should not be ashamed of writing fanfic. Yeah, I write romance. Yeah, I even write porn. Yeah, I did this as a teenage girl. And yeah, I sometimes daydream about characters. None of this should mean that my writing—our writing—is automatically worth less than that of some fanboy who daydreams about being Paul Atreides and about things blowing up and writes a script about his daydreams and then gets it turned into a movie. I am looking at you, James Cameron. [sic] I love fandom, you guys. I love what we do. No shame.
> Oracle dreams - There is no law or moral high ground to govern fantasy. And, in a perfect world, people would rise up in unison and rebel against such a thing. Sexual provocation is an extremely individual but also, sometimes, irrational thing. Things that stimulate the mind are not always stimulating in real life situations.

Annesible: Someone asked for tips about coming out as a slash fan. I talk about how most representations of women's sexuality are filtered through the straight male gaze and that writing about men invests me and other women with our own sexual gaze. I'm reclaiming my sexuality by appropriating male cultural entitlement and using it for my own purposes. You get the idea. I happen to think all of that is true, but it's also a great way to put the pressure on the other person to accept what I'm doing.

Fans have often debated the continued existence of the "first rule of fandom," contrasting the desire for privacy to ensure freedom of expression, with the awareness that secrecy perpetuates shame.

Oconel: Why are we so intent to "keep the slash secret"? If we want the producers to know that fans like it, that slash sells, why make them think that we prefer het couples when the male leads or female leads (ha!) have more chemistry between them? Why is it ok to ask at a con about a het couple and not about a slash one?

She was talking about slash in particular, but could have been speaking about any fan practice. Other fans weighed in, expressing their ambivalence about the benefits of privacy and the costs of secrecy.

Itichitachi: I don't know where to draw the line. It's something that I want to see on tv all the time like it's normal, but it's also something I want to keep private, to myself, where it can't be ruined and where no one can judge me. This leads to --> I feel it is something that people will judge me about --> it is something to look down on.

Missyjack: Subcultures like fandom form because a group of people are engaged in customs and behaviors which are considered unacceptable in wider society. Within the subculture these activities become normalized, but when the mainstream discovers them its invariable condemnation reminds people of their outsider status. Some people feel shame when their behavior is pointed out as deviant, but for others being an outsider can be a thrill.

Tmzcori: It's like, when we're in fandom we talk and discuss and do silly things all over, mostly without caring who sees what. But as soon as someone 'official' might see us, we hide and people feel embarrassed.

Elspethdixon - Why do we keep the slash secret? Because when we don't it is mocked, and misrepresented. But maybe we still shouldn't….. because it doesn't make sense. Because it is okay to talk about slash, and why shouldn't it be? With not talking about slash we put ourselves into the shadows and make it seem like it's something shifty, like something even we're embarrassed to admit to.

Another fan identifies the gender-based double standard, and the pressure women feel to remain within the bounds of convention.

> Starwatcher307: In visual porn, so many men are enamored of two (or more) women together that it's not even worthy of surprise. Two women together = "hot." So why shouldn't women view two men together as "hot"? ... To ask the question plays into the stereotype that men and women are "different" and that it's not quite "seemly" for a woman to express her sexuality in other than conventional ways.

These fans are echoing Fine's research on the importance of the authorized discourse, as well as Bartky's emphasis on the disempowering nature of the felt need for secrecy and concealment that's created by shame, which isolates and prevents validation or normalizing. Shame about sexuality is also seen in the constant questioning of why women (straight or otherwise) like slash. Fans are beginning to take on shaming by outsiders, though, at least occasionally. A 2010 TV.com poll declared that *Supernatural* had the "Craziest Fans". SPN fans were mocked for loving the show to "almost clinical levels" and called "perverse enough to make someone want to claw their eyes out." Some fans responded with the familiar cries of "that's not me, I'm perfectly normal," but others instead took the writer to task for his shaming. One fan explicitly challenged the conflating of sexual desire and behavior, as well as the lingering double standard for males and females.

> TeaLes: There is a huge difference between thinking and doing. Everybody's mind is a "messed up" place in one way or another. It is what you actually do that is important and it's the ability to differentiate between thoughts and reality that separates the sane from the insane. You do not have to think about it if you don't want to, but don't judge those that do. Women have too much guilt over their sexual fantasies as it is. Live and let live ;) Men have been able to openly fantasize about two women (and even real twins) together for a long time without getting looked down on. It is about time we give women the same liberty I think. And for the incest part, is there anyone out there who actually thinks that the boys are brothers for real? I'm not a big Wincest fan myself but to you who are— cred, you have every right to have just as dirty fantasies as men do! And cred to the *Supernatural* cast/crew for being mature about it and seeing it for what it is—fantasies, just like the show (and every other show) is, it's all just fantasies and fantasies are a good thing.

Professional and fanfic writer Alex Beecroft has also protested shaming, questioning why the idea of women getting off on slash is so "disgusting".

Are straight women not allowed to have a sexuality? Are women supposed to have such tight control over our sexual fantasy life that we can decide not to find something sexy even though by nature we do? Are we, in short, supposed to stifle our sexuality because it makes men uncomfortable?

Beecroft goes on to note that such an expectation sounds like a very old form of oppression.

Men have put women in chastity belts and insane asylums in the past because they were uncomfortable with the fact that we too are sexual beings. Stifling our writing is likely to be taken as one more attempt along the same lines. And really, people get off on all kinds of things..... Just as many men enjoy the thought of two women together, many women enjoy the thought of two men together. Why not? Men are sexy. If you're reading a story in which they are both viewpoint characters you have the treat of being able to identify with whichever hero you find it easiest to empathise with and still be able to admire the other one through his eyes. Rationalizing the appeal of two men together can probably be done, but why should we have to? Too many people have tried to tell women in the past what their sexuality should be. To them I say 'tough'. I find this sexy. Whatever guilt trip you try to impose on me to try and 'correct' this kink, I'm not buying it. Why shouldn't I write stories celebrating and enjoying something that I find very lovely

Good question. In the next chapter, we explore the benefits of doing just that.

CHAPTER FOUR

FANDOM AS AGENT OF CHANGE:
TRANSFORMATIVE WHATS?

"The search for self-worth begins by finding what is indestructible inside, then letting it be."
—Prudence Kohl

In the fall of 2008, we went to a different kind of Supernatural fan convention – WinCon, short for Winchester Writers Convention. Unlike most cons we've attended, there were no celebrity guests, no photo ops, no autograph sessions, no actor Q & A's. Wincon was just for fangirls. Fangirls who were, it seemed, just like us. These were participatory fans. Fans who make fanvids, create fanart, and write fanfiction. Many of the attendees we already knew as their online avatars. We had been happily reading their fanfiction for years, and they had been reading ours. Through exchanges in comments to each other's fiction, art and autobiographical posts, in some ways we knew each other at a deeper, more genuine level, than many of our real life friends knew us. With these women, we didn't hold back. We talked about all those things we rarely dared to in real life. Stigma, prejudice, misogyny, homophobia. And of course, sex.

At Wincon we all came together, most of us allowing our online and real-life selves to merge for the first time. The feeling of wholeness was exhilarating, as fans happily crowded into contests for the best videos, attended lively panels on the pros and cons of RPS (real person slash) and why we all want to hurt Dean Winchester, and scribbled down tips for writing better sex scenes. There were variations on the arts and crafts lessons that might be stereotypically considered "women's work," which brought the familiar parlance of online fandom into the real world in often hysterical ways. For example, a play on fandom's term for an avatar created to ensure anonymity—and frequently start wank—known as a "sockpuppet," was translated into a sockpuppet-making lesson (bring your own socks) This activity culminated in the most irreverent and adult version of "sockpuppet theater" imaginable.

We're used to fans wearing their "tinhats" online—fandom's term for fantasizing two ostensibly straight real people in a decidedly not-straight relationship—with a mix of shame and glee. At WinCon, fans took the description literally, grabbing aluminum foil, glue guns, sequins and sparkles in a make-your-own-tinhat contest. Neither of us won, but the very idea was so exhilarating that we grinned our way through the entire event, cheering on the contestants as they paraded through the hotel conference room, tinhats gleaming.

One fan brought her very own plastic Winchester dolls, Sam and Dean as variations on Ken (with no Barbie in sight), who quickly ended up in an impressive variety of compromising positions. Dean lost a gun; Sam lost a leg. Fandom, as always, was there to fix them.

There was appropriately drunken karaoke and a vidding contest with breathtakingly well done meta vids commenting on serious subjects like homophobia and misogyny on television and crack vids celebrating the epic love story of Sam and Dean in subtext. There was a raffle whose proceeds went to charity, and a Badfic Idol contest that had people groaning and trying to cover their ears to the read-aloud tales of tentacles, mpreg and detachable sex organs. There happened to be a WWII veterans convention at the hotel the same weekend, resulting in many raised eyebrows and questions as to what all these women of varying ages and nationalities were doing wandering around in their pajamas carrying laptops, and why there weren't any "gentleman companions." One bewildered man asked if we were with an aluminum foil convention. Obviously the tinhat parade was a success.

There was a chance to dress up with impunity at WinProm, sing "Back in Black" and "Carry On My Wayward Son" with fifty other fangirls, and have long conversations about John Winchester's parenting skills with someone you never thought you'd get the chance to meet face to face. WinCon was a place to fangirl other fangirls instead of celebrities. To tell a writer in person that her fanfiction impacted you, changed you, affected you. To hear people tell you the same.

At the end of the weekend, physical hugs replaced the virtual hugs we're all used to giving each other online, and there were more than a few real tears. The experience was powerful, both for the lack of shame we've examined in the previous chapter, and the sense of community we will turn to next. In short, WinCon was therapeutic. It was like our online fandom community had been magically brought to life in the real world, without a shred of shame. "I felt like myself for the first time," one fangirl said.

In this chapter, we examine the therapeutic potential of fandom, from supportive gatherings like Wincon to the online communities in which fans come together. Fandom has long been characterized as transformative and subversive on a societal level, challenging gender and relational norms and existing power structures (de Certeau 1984; Fiske 1992; Thornton 1995). Jenkins has discussed the transformative potential of fandom on a similar level, building on the ideas he first expressed in *Convergence Culture* about the function of popular culture as a civic playground, enabling people to play with power on a micro-level and leading to greater civic engagement (Jenkins, 2010). There is little doubt that fandom can be transformative on this level -- fan communities are often connected with social change and activism. In the *Supernatural* fandom alone, the charitable organization Support Supernatural has organized fans to contribute to animal rescue organizations for nearly the entire time the show has been on the air. Actor Misha Collins utilized his substantial Twitter following to found the nonprofit Random Acts in 2010, which organized a trip to Haiti where fans helped to build an orphanage and has continued to bring fans together to make a difference.

Viewing fandom primarily as transformative on a societal level, however, can obscure the potential for transformation on a more individual basis. Recently, theorists have explored the role of fandom in constructing identity, and the social and cultural significance of identity development and performance   (Hellekson and Busse 2006; Hills 2002; Sandvoss 2005). These studies focus on the individual and the subjective previously neglected in cultural studies, but tend to utilize a psychoanalytic lens which can be subtly pathologizing. What remains largely unexplored is the application of psychological theory to fandom which goes beyond psychoanalytic analysis to examine both individual and communal aspects of fanning. Sandvoss and Hills have called for such approaches to fandom, with Hills contending that it "seems impossible to take fandom seriously without taking fan psychology seriously" (Hills 2002, 22).

Sandvoss (2005) rightly notes the methodological and ethical difficulties of asking fans to articulate their inner fantasies and desires. To date, only a few studies have done so. Vermorel and Vermorel (1992) interview fans who discuss their fantasies, but the researchers remain firmly in academic mode as they do so, investigating from the outside. Hinerman (1992) also analyzes fans' Elvis fantasies from the outside, and perhaps relatedly, seems to include a disproportionate number of more extreme examples. Hills (2002) points out the difficulty inherent in ethnographic studies of fandom, which have taken fan accounts as "knowledge" without recognizing the defensiveness with which fans interact with academic researchers as they seek to justify their own practices. He accuses academic theorizing of fandom of emptying it of the very dimensions which define it—affect, attachment, passion—by observing from a detached outsider position, and by relying on ethnographic studies which place fans in a defensive position as they try to convince the researcher that they aren't irrational, crazymadwrong stalkers. In adopting such a defensive position, even the fans themselves end up over-emphasizing the rational attributes of the particular fannish text instead of celebrating its emotional appeal.

Thus, investigating from an outsider position necessarily impacts not only the investigator's lens, but the fans' response, since fans are fearful of being (mis)judged and mistrustful of academics in general. As we saw in Chapter Two, researcher Ogi Ogas found this out firsthand in 2010's Survey!fail, as fans swiftly pegged him as an outsider and boycotted his survey. Mirna Cicioni, in her theorizing of slash fans, recognized fannish mistrust as an impediment to research, writing that "slash fans would probably be even less prepared to discuss their personal problems than to reveal their identities" (1998, 174). This is likely true, if fans are talking to academics or outsiders. Fans, however, discuss their inner fantasies and desires with other fans on a regular basis. Despite sharing some of the discomfort noted by other researchers, we believe that being genuinely immersed in fandom provides greater access to open discussion of the motivations of fans, both individually and collectively.

Cicioni (1998) suggests, as we will here, that rather than being a stimulus for social change, participating in fandom, including writing fanfiction, provides a safety valve for the stress women feel in their daily lives and relationships. Fandom is not only, as is often theorized, about subversive and societal change—but also about pleasurable and individual change, with challenges to existing norms and power relations more a by-product than the source of fans' motivation and satisfaction. Sandvoss (2005) took a similarly individual focus when he addressed the role of fandom in identity performance, but his analysis of fan psychology through an object relations perspective relied heavily on identification and introjection,. In this chapter, we expand on Sandvoss' discussion of identity performance by looking at textual production of fanworks not merely as a form of self projection and reflection, but as a type of expressive writing, carried out within a supportive community. We also broaden Hinerman's understanding of the healing potential of fantasy inherent in fandom. Hinerman understands fantasy as "a way the individual sutures his or her own identity back together (bonding the ego to the unconscious) when it is most vulnerable" (1992, 116). His analysis of fans' Elvis fantasies, however, is limited to experiences of trauma with a capital "T", exploring the use of fantasy in more extreme situations which engender fluid boundaries between the real and imagined. We explore here the broader therapeutic potential of fandom in facilitating identity development and in confronting the sorts of challenges most of us experience in everyday life.

We also emphasize the communal context of fandom, especially for female fans, building on Penley's contention that in fantasy, the "subject participates in and restages a scenario in which crucial questions about desire, knowledge, and identity can be posed, and in which the subject can hold a number of identificatory positions" (1997, 480). The psychological distance created in fictional stories allows a broader freedom to express and rework themes and perform identities, as Penley suggests. However, as Driscoll (2006) also notes, Penley's application of a psychoanalytic lens neglects the communal dimension of fandom within which the reading and writing of fanfiction and the sharing of other fanworks is carried out. Many of the therapeutic benefits of group counseling are reiterated within the fandom community: catharsis, a sense of universality as fans discover a common sense of difference and subsequent belongingess, and group cohesion as the fandom comes together around a shared passion. From Tankel and Murphy's (1998) study of male comic book fans to Steven Classen's (1998) analysis of couponers, the importance of community in fandom as a way of negotiating identity and finding support is clear.

In order to expand the existing theory, we pull from three bodies of psychological literature which have not yet been widely applied to fandom—the established research on narrative therapy, the newer field of therapeutic expressive writing, and the healing components of group counseling. At the same time, we want to explicitly state our belief that reducing fanworks to solely therapeutic, or mostly transgressive, or mostly anything is missing an important point. Fandom is as diverse as any other community, and individual motivations are just that. Fans participate in fandom, and vid and draw and meta and write fanfiction for a wide variety of reasons. Henry Jenkins has identified at least ten categories of fanfiction, with goals as diverse as fixing plot holes and extending timelines, to playfully making fun of characters and storylines, to turning up the ratings of a PG television show to NC17 and having a fabulous time doing it. (1992, 162) Slash writers themselves describe a variety of motivations, and have expressed frustration at academic accounts which are overtly or covertly reductionist. Fans' own voices have been subsumed beneath an artificially totalizing discourse which has too often been hostile; we are aware that while our attempt to allow fans to tell their own stories uses a more positive lens, we are nevertheless at risk of layering a different kind of totalizing discourse above their words. Sometimes, as Jenkins and colleagues have memorably stated, slash is merely "normal female interest in men bonking" (Green, S., C. Jenkins and Jenkins 1998).

With this in mind, we attempt here to add to the existing theory on fannish motivation by examining a more phenomenological explanation for fanworks in general and fanfiction in particular, keeping in mind that the therapeutic potential of fandom exists alongside the propensity for shame which was the focus of the previous chapter.

In Their Own "F" Words: Fans Talk About Fandom, Fanfiction and Fantasy

A 2011 online survey conducted by Teresa Stern revealed three predominant and overlapping ways that fandom can be transformative: fandom builds confidence and self-esteem, offers a support system, and creates a space where people can explore and grow more comfortable with their identity. Some respondents said that fandom had "saved their lives" through lonely times when they'd considered suicide, or offered hope when in despair over coming to terms with their sexual identity. Those who felt "different" had finally found in fandom a place of inclusion and support. Many respondents said they were more confident and comfortable with exploring and expressing their sexuality. Several who identified as autistic said that fandom taught them more about interacting with other people than years of groups and classes. "I learned," one participant said, "that who I am is not only okay, but has value" (2011).

Stern's survey was a small self-selected sample, but fans answered candidly because Stern, while an academic (a graduate student at Hunter College School of Social Work), was also the mother of a fangirl well known in the fandom community, who coordinated the survey and verified the good intentions of the researcher. Fans frequently discuss openly among themselves their participation in fandom and its perceived benefits and intermittent frustrations. A great deal of discussion revolves around the production and consumption of various fanworks, through which many fans interact with each other and participate in fandom. There is often a layer of defensiveness blanketing these discussions, since the non-fannish world can be at best confused and at worst critical of fannish behavior. Anyone who writes fanfiction has been challenged by spouses, siblings, parents and friends. "You're so talented, why don't you write original fiction?" "Don't waste your ability writing crappy fanfic." "Don't you want to write something that can be published and make money?" We have certainly heard these same questions ourselves.

There are both pros and cons of a market economy versus a gift economy, especially for females, but some of the reluctance to move the fanfiction community away from a "pure" gift culture is the fear that one of the important motivations for this form of writing might be contaminated; that is, the need to tell the stories that the individual wants to tell, without the constraints of courting readers or pleasing publishers or submitting to the whims of editors. While fanfiction writers are almost as excited by comment counts as any professional writer is by book sales, and most incorporate the input of a beta (editor), nevertheless the freedom to write "just for me" remains at the forefront, fulfilling a different need than the prestige or monetary rewards offered by publication.

> Joyful – I tell the stories I feel the need to tell. The ones that are inside me, and need to come out.
> Diorama23 – For me that is the reward—the emotional satisfaction of playing more in a world you love. A lot of people don't get that (fanficrants 2010).

The fanfiction community—not just of *Supernatural*, but in general— is largely a community of women. In recognition of the gendered nature of fanfiction writing, LJ user cupidsbow posted the provocative question "Does fanfiction make us (women) poor?" A discussion of why women write fanfiction, including a debate about whether the non-capitalist aspect of fanfiction culture is a good thing or a bad thing, ensued, with literally hundreds of fans weighing in. Many responses alluded to gender bias against women's writing in general (citing the prohibitions against women's writing identified by Joanna Russ in 1983 in *How to Suppress Women's Writing*), while also analyzing the specific motivations and benefits of writing fanfiction. Specifically, fans emphasized the freedom of expression offered by fanfiction as a source of play, experimentation and identity exploration.

> Into_desire: I am only now recovering a sense of myself as female, beginning consciously to "write from the body" as many feminist rhetoricians describe. And you know one of the most effective ways I can do this? Fanfiction.
> Pennypaperbrain: Once there is a commercial market for a genre, it begins to have rules. People who are savvy about publication…. begin to write according to those rules. I'd hate to see that happen to the splurging, splooging, creatively volcanic mass of fanfic. My own experience of fanfic is of writing and reading it for its own sake but also of using it as a safe

space to explore difficult themes which are now emerging in my other writing.

Threerings: Fanfiction is something we do because we enjoy it, it's fun, it gives us community and allows us a freedom of expression that is truly rare in the mainstream culture. It also helps us to become empowered as writers, as creative beings, as women comfortable with sexuality (cupidsbow 2007).

Fans wrote about the joy inherent in a freedom of expression rarely found elsewhere, a place for open experimentation and self discovery. Fans also recognized the social aspect of the fanfiction community, drawing analogies to historic female communities such as quilting, farming, and cooking. Cassiphone suggested that the writing and sharing of fanfiction was more a form of roleplaying than writing, with the end result being to participate in a social activity, not just to create a story. Her analogy rang true across fannish gender lines as she compared the social process to RPGers (female and male), who invest a great deal of intellectual and creative energy into roleplaying campaigns and also get nothing tangible in return, but "lots of delicious intangibles." In other words, the process of writing and sharing fanfiction is separate from the story itself.

Astolat: Fanfic does not have to be paid to not make us poor. I find (and love) that fanfic is turning into the basis for a giant sprawling feminist community that acts as an "old girls network" kind of like men's clubs and golfing—If fanfic and our connections through it can serve us as a kind of connective supporting tissue where we can teach one another useful skills (writing, editing, web skills, programming, video editing, etc) and even give a helping hand now and then, that is helping to make us rich, without commercialization.

Lookfar: The fanfiction community is the most amazing women's art culture I've ever experienced, and quite possibly the most amazing there has ever been, just in terms of sheer numbers and output. I see it as part of a long history of women's "secret" art—quilts, pies and hats being some of the others. Remember how quilts were suddenly elevated to the status of Art? I suppose it was an outgrowth of feminism and the civil rights movement. I've often thought that, just as women supported, competed with, and communicated with each other in the venue of the 4-H tent and the quilting frame, they are creating art together in the fanfiction realm. It certainly seems to be a characteristically female way of art-making— intimately, dialogically and communally.

Elz - I tend to think that the derivative aspect enables the communal aspect, which is the primary appeal of fandom: working from the same sources allows us to build up a shared language and culture, it gives writers a built-in audience and readers a built-in draw, it allows people to comment and expand on each other's work and do a whole host of things that wouldn't be possible if everyone in the community was writing original stories. It really does seem to me that women aren't just taking the subservient role in a traditional game, but have instead kicked over the tables and started playing by their own rules. Which I really enjoy.

Kicking over the tables is an apt metaphor for what many women are doing within the perceived safe space of fandom—constrained by shame and limiting life narratives, fans are attempting to get up and get out from behind these defensive structures to explore and express their genuine emotional experience. In the next section, we examine the use of two specific fanwork genres through which fans accomplish this change—hurt/comfort and slash.

Telling the Stories that Need to be Told:
Hurt/comfort and Slash

A popular genre in fanfiction and fanworks is "hurt/comfort", in which pain, injury or disability is inflicted on a character and another character provides some sort of comfort or healing. (See the discussion of the "On the Prowl" fanvid in the previous chapter).

For example, a request on the LJ community *spnstoryfinders* asked for "any stories where Jensen/Dean is really lonely and sad, where he doesn't have any family, or they treat him badly, he's abused, bullied, invisible, has no one to care about him. I'd love ones set in high school, but that's not a must." Another that same day requested "serious Wincest or J2 fics where one of them has a disorder/illness/sickness that they have to deal with. Example: Epilepsy, Tourette's, OCD, ADD, ADHD, Diabetes, Phobia etc…. speech impediments or stuttering too. I would like as many as possible."

Because of the popularity of the genre, in the spring of 2010, there was a "Hurt/comfort Bingo" fandom challenge hosted on the dreamwidth site, in which writers were invited to create H/C fanworks (fic, vids, art, icons, podfic, picspam, meta) in a commonly used fannish format that requires them to fill squares on a virtual bingo card. Prompts ranged from abandonment issues to assault, body dysmorphic disorder to bullying, child abuse to counseling, eating disorders to exhaustion, self- harm to sex pollen, with several hundred prompts in all. The rules clearly required warning for potentially triggering content, and the mods also offered cards which would not include any reference to sexual abuse or assault, or custom designed cards which would avoid other triggers. Nevertheless, the format was seen by some as dismissive of real life issues which cannot actually be neatly and easily "cured" or criticized for mis-defining as "hurt" some conditions not defined in such a way by people who actually have them. The disagreement was indicative of the difficulty those outside fandom—and many fans as well—have in understanding why someone would want to read or write about such topics. Such misunderstandings sometimes occur when readers perceive the hurt in the story but miss the potential for healing.

Fandom responded with thoughtful meta about the Hurt/comfort genre and its importance to fans who consume or create H/C fanworks, citing the therapeutic potential of reading and/or writing fanction which addresses, either directly or indirectly, posters' real life challenges. The discussion took place in the LJ community *metafandom*, and in public posts on dreamwidth.

> Anon: Hurt/comfort is a staple of fandom for a good reason - because many people find h/c therapeutic [sic] comforting or reassuring, who have suffered the kinds of things that are on the h/c bingo cards - cancer, paralysis, blindness, loss of limb, chronic illness, sexual abuse - and that many of those people, as well as others, may want to read stories about healing cock, or write them. And those people are not wrong, or in denial, or stupid, nor should they be made to feel ashamed. Fantasy is what we're here for.

> Anon: h/c is absolutely my kink when it comes to things I've experienced. I may not write it much in my public stories, but my private RP is full of people who magically say the right thing, and healing that comes from external forces, and solutions for things that don't have solutions in real life. It's cathartic, and it's comforting.

> Anon: A fic you could call romantic, unrealistic and appropriative of real experiences of trauma, I might also call the h/c fic that calmed me down after I was triggered by something else (or it might even be the one I wrote after I was triggered).

> Anon: I write H/C fic in some ways to help deal with my own issues and my own needs. I think everyone writes fic to deal with their own issues and their own needs. ....Would I find a story about someone with a chronic breathing problem easy to read/write? Not after last year. Not even after my condition is finally controlled by medication. Would I write one? I might, yes, to help me cope with all the experiences I had. ... I can't help but feel that the conversation overall ... has tended to simply villainize people who write H/C as "writing fic about disability to get their kicks from it" and I feel that is an oversimplification and unfair to the writers.

> Anon: You can work through your issues from the safety of your own home. I often find myself making my characters live through situations so that I don't have to. I doubt I would be half as obsessed ... if I didn't face a long history of addiction and mental illness in my own family (toft 2010).

Another commenter expressed the difficulty of writing something therapeutic by reconceptualizing the "hurt" experience and reworking it into something that has meaning in the individual's life narrative, yet not dismissing the hurtfulness of the original experience. Her comment highlights the highly individualistic nature of the practice.

> Dirty Diana: I think that the structure/wording of the challenge had major problems, which is very different from saying no one should write hurt/comfort. It's like the difference between one person's therapy through non-con and a challenge called "rape-yay!" or something.

Fans who read and write one of the other most popular genres of fanfiction—slash—feel similarly about fandom as a therapeutic place. At the same time, as we'll explore in the next chapter, there are also frequent disagreements within fandom about what topics should and should not be talked about, portrayed in vids or art, or written about in fanfiction, including both hurt/comfort and slash. Fans remain ashamed, and continue to shame other fans, as they struggle with the boundaries between fantasy and reality. Nevertheless, the fanfiction community is seen as a safe place by many fans, especially the slash community.

There are almost as many discussions within the fannish community as within the academy attempting to figure out "why women write slash," and an exhaustive list is beyond the scope of this chapter. Two broad themes we have already identified as relevant to our discussion of the individual transformative nature of fandom are commonly noted by fans as their answer to that question—freedom from shame, especially shame about sexuality, and the disconfirmation of otherness which comes from finding a like-minded community. In an open post on the *metafandom* community, fans engaged in a discussion similar to the one prompted by the Hurt/comfort bingo wank, on why the slash community is important to them as readers and writers of slash fanfic.

> Anonymous: Part of the appeal of the community of slash fandom is that it's a community of "others" and not just that, but a community of people who embrace their otherness and bond together and take power from that status. There are days when I really NEED to know that space is out there, that I'm part of this place where being "other" is something to be proud of, not just a danger and a difficulty to endure. Same goes for fanfic. It's stuff I just don't get elsewhere because mainstream entertainment, even mainstream erotica, doesn't' dare go THERE—with there being anything from queerness to dark!fic to "the awesome and ass kicking but older, not conventionally pretty woman gets the hot stud in fic, whereas the producers of the canon wrote the woman out of the show stating how they need more young T&A 'chicks' [reference to Warner Brothers' misguided

attempts to add "T & A" to *Supernatural* in its third season by introducing two female regulars who were universally despised by the fandom].

Fig. 4-1

The perception of outside criticism or incursion is often what prompts a defensive response from fandom, and some of the most thoughtful meta by fans. In 2007, new LiveJournal owners Six Apart responded to a complaint from a conservative organization about fanart with possible underage sexual content by (seemingly randomly) shutting down individual accounts and communities, sending the LJ community into an even more fearful and self-protective state than usual. LJ poster Egelantier responded with a passionate defense of hurt/comfort fic and slash in an open post that was widely read throughout fandom:

Egelantier: I was born and grew up in....very old-fashioned, puritan and intolerant place .... (a) patriarchal, hypocritical, male-dominated and strictly-controlled space, and so not the place where you want to get your sex-ed or your body image or your sexual self-esteem. It was fandom where I started to get it right. it set me free me from shame. you see, my kink is hurt/comfort. if I remember fantasies I had since I was seven, or books/cartoons/shows I liked in my childhood, I realise that I had this kink long before I knew what sex was. and I was horribly ashamed and terrified of it all my life, and never ever talked about it with anyone; actually believed myself sick and wrong and deranged for getting this fantasies and such pleasure from certain fictional things. ... fandom cured me of it in

five minute flat. I discovered hurt/comfort genre, learned that there were
people out there who enjoyed it as much as I did, weren't feeling guilty for
it, wrote it and read it and discussed it cheerfully. and that was pretty much
enough. I can talk freely about it now, I know what is in my fascination
with h/c for me and can use this information, and I can enjoy it without
guilt or fear. ...I'm still immensely thankful for this fandom education ...
exploring and questioning and working through in maximally safe and
harmless way ... I'm mostly a gen reader, I rarely read or watch anything
higher that 'r' rating, and there're corners of fandom I never visit - but if
one day, say, mpreg fanfiction will disappear, or incest, or chan, or
anything else, I'll be gravely disturbed. because until then fandom's
message, from old 'there's porn for everything' joke to sexualized feedback,
would be: exploring your sexuality is okay. enjoying your sexuality is
okay. accepting and meeting darker parts of your sexuality is okay. in fact,
being you is okay.

Other fans responded to her post in a discussion in the LJ metafandom
community, sharing their own experience of fandom as healing.

Guiltyred: I grew up in Oklahoma.... and one just didn't acknowledge
the possibility of being gay or otherwise different (this during the late 60's
and 70's). Not having the outlet of fandom, I buried a lot of feelings and
kept a lot of self-loathing deep inside, where it festered for far too long.
Now, I've unchained my creativity and my imagination in all things, not
just sexual imagery, and fandom has given me a fantastic way to do
this....And what you said about "being you is okay" is so right, and yet that
seems to be exactly the message that those in charge don't want people
(women in particular) to figure out. I'd love to see that become the battle
cry for women in the 21st century when they decide that they won't be
owned any longer.
Timeofchange: Fandom is a gift in so many ways, and that is definitely
one of them for me, too. My background is different from yours, but
shaming women for their sexuality seems to be universal. It was fan fiction
that opened my eyes and heart to the wide range of "normal," and fandom
that freed me to know myself as a sexual adult.
Smilla02: A few days ago, a few friends were reflecting on how
wonderful it is that a community of women exists where women feel
SAFE to express their sexual fantasies. I agree. It's revolutionary. It has no
precedents, it's beautiful and wonderful, even with all its imperfection. We
like it, we thrive in it. For some of us it's an eye-opening experience, a
journey toward self-discovery. I would like to underline that a SAFE
environment is what makes this possible. We are "virtually" close. We
write and publish on the net and talk about stuff that maybe we wouldn't
talk about in real life with the same ease. I'd say that under certain aspects
we are even more close than with real life friends (metafandom post,
5/11/2010).

Anon: Fandom sets your fantasies free and gives you a place and a peer group that you can talk freely about them without feeling the shame that the rest of the world would bring down on you for them. Sex is celebrated, and the more the merrier. And in fandom, almost everybody's into it. Those who aren't can just scroll on by.

For these fans, the freedom fandom provides to read and write and say what you want—and what you genuinely feel—is cherished as an antidote to the shame we explored in the previous chapter.

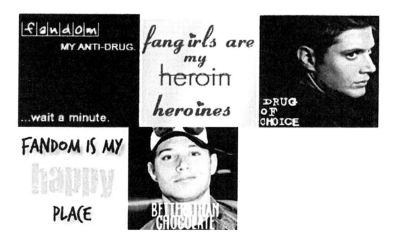

Fig. 4-2

Fans refer to their most "guilty pleasure" fics as Id!fic or drawerfic—fanfic that pushes the boundaries of believable far enough to feel like it's tapping directly into one's unconscious drives. The fannish terms acknowledge both the fans' awareness that they're plundering deep and possibly repressed psychological territory, and the simultaneous shame that makes them want to hide it away. Dreamwidth user strina draws a clear distinction between the literary value of "good writing" and the therapeutic value of id!fic, regardless of whether or not it's well written, in a post titled "Terrible, Horrible, Motherfucking Amazing Stories I Have Loved":

That's idfic/drawerfic. Winged hermaphroditic super-abused superpowered Harry falls in love with his middle-aged professor (who likes to call him "little one" in a vaguely fetish-y way). …That is not a story with scads of literary merit... Because "good" stories often have to temporize, to maintain reality and your suspension of disbelief and the dynamics of the canon. But idfic says fuck that, let's turn this shit up to ELEVEN and SEE WHERE IT GOES.... Fanfic is, at its purest, an expression of love. So, you know, dear writers of idfic: Don't be ashamed. Take them out of the drawers and set them free. I guarantee someone out there is going to MOTHERFUCKING LOVE them (strina 2010).

Fig. 4-3

LJ user ellen-fremedon also recognizes the healing inherent in universality, and the value of the community in shaping fans' approaches to the id and the reconstruction of their life stories:

> I think it's because of .... the utter shamelessness of fanfic. Because the scenario cuts pretty close to the id, you know? And it's just one of a large number of similarly... charged storylines (soul bonds, every fuck-or-die scenario ever written...) that you see very very often in fanfic, and from time to time in profic as well. And the profic? Almost uniformly sucks. Because pro writers either have some shame, and relegate the purest, most cracklicious iterations of those stories to drawerfic that their workshop buddies will never see, or else .... their versions are written so solitarily that they don't have any voice of restraint, to pull them back from the Event Horizon of the Id Vortex when it starts warping their story mechanics. But in fandom, we've all got this agreement to just suspend shame. ...And so we've got all these shameless fantasies being thrown out

into the fannish ether, being read and discussed… There is a way to write close to the id, and MFA workshops don't teach it (ellen_fremedon 2004).

Instead, fans teach each other. There is a long history in fandom of women mentoring other women, whether it's how to write a believable sex scene, the rules of grammar and punctuation, or the norms of goodfic, badfic, Mary Sues and crackfic, as we experienced firsthand at WinCon. Often the mentoring is less about writing and more about acceptance and normalizing, as fans attempt to break down the barriers of shame and claim a piece of that alternative discourse. The therapeutic potential of fandom appears to be largely confined to the boundaries of the fannish community, within which it's considered appropriate and desirable to kick over a few tables and take down some defenses. There remains a pervasive fear of being outed to anyone in real life, who might respond with shaming or censure, prompting fans to want them sequestered from outside criticism.

In the open meta discussion on letting real life friends/family read fanfiction, one fan expressed her doubt that anyone outside fandom could understand—or accept—her preferred forms of fanfiction, Hurt/comfort and slash. She is especially critical of psychologists' misunderstanding of writers' motivations.

> Here on the internet, I am not afraid to say that I read and write hurt/comfort, that I like my characters whumped in ways that in real life would be horrific scenarios…..It's not the suffering that I am interested in, it's the characters around that suffering person who interact with the character, help them through the situation, that make something so special. But experience has shown that people outside fandom really suck at interpreting what all of this means to us…. I am not here to be judged or put into a box that clearly wasn't made for me and doesn't describe who I am or why I do this….Here, we are a community, we understand and respect for the most part that people have unique interests and it's not something we have to hide, it's something to embrace and celebrate and share with other people with similar interests.

Other posters also cited the therapeutic value of writing fanfiction as allowing expression of experiences which are outside the boundaries of real life.

> Anon: I also struggle with the fact that I have specific lines I won't cross in my own life, and in my fic, the characters I'm writing don't necessarily share those boundaries…. I started writing fanfic as a therapeutic tool and it's turned into something I do for the fun of it. Still,

the possibility of being outed casts a bit of a pallor over the whole endeavor.

Anon: [E]verything I write reveals something about me because I only write about characters I truly "get" and I truly can identify with in one way or the other. Because of that, it's pretty damn impossible for me to be able to tell anyone in RL what I'm doing, and more to the point, why I am doing it. I don't write smut, h/c, slash, or anything that would be difficult to explain to a non-fandom person, but still, it's such a personal process that the thought of sharing it with someone who won't understand is just plain terrifying

Anon: Writing is always such a personal process which reveals my ideals, my likes and dislikes, my secrets, sometimes even my ambitions, that it's terrifying to reveal so much to RL people who are not into fandom when I'm not ready to reveal such information. When it's internet!people in fandom who I don't know in RL, somehow it's okay because they share the same space I do. They either like the same pairing, or the same genre, or whatever it is that gives us one common link to understand why one another would like that space.

These fans speak eloquently about the ways in which fandom is personally important and therapeutic for each of them, citing the opportunity to express themselves (including their sexual self) in an uncensored way, the validation found in acceptance, and the safe space of the community to express fantasies, issues and needs. The need for such a safe space is deeply felt, as these anonymous fans in the LJ community *fandomsecrets* confess:

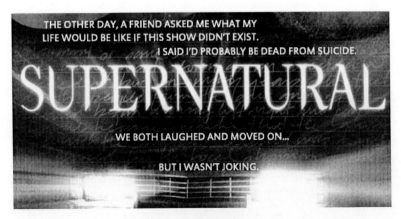

Fig. 4-4: Anonymous post in fandomsecrets on LiveJournal

it should be
obvious why
this is a secret

I have a hard time talking without crying when
I'm at my therapist's office. I sit shoved into
the corner of her couch and I realised, that if I
imagine that he's there, behind me, arms almost
around me, whispering encouragement into my
ear, well, I can get the words out without
sobbing and it's a much better day.

Fig. 4-5: Anonymous post in fandomsecrets on LiveJournal

Over the past few years, I have gone through a lot of stuff, especially
with my family. It's been hard and depressing. Fandom is my escape. For
the few hours I can get on the computer everyday, my fandom cheers
me up and helps me forget about everything else. From the show itself
to the amazing fans with the gifs, icons, macros, jokes and amazing

fanfiction. This community in particular: You have helped me realize I
am not alone in a lot ways and that I am not crazy. I could sit here and
cry with relief at some of the secrets I have read on here because I see
so much of myself in other people. And it gives me hope that I'll be okay.

Secret because not one soul in real life has any idea I even HAVE a
fandom, let alone any idea as to how it has saved me.

Fig. 4-6: Anonymous post in fandomsecrets on LiveJournal

What are the theoretical mechanisms that allow fandom to function in such a powerfully transformative way for some fans?

Narrowing the Lens: Theoretical Underpinnings

The writing of fanfiction is one of the most researched modes of fan participation; much of the research has focused on the subgenre of slash. In her essay "Slashing the Romance Narrative", Krustritz (2003) suggests that fanfiction, and especially slash, is intended to "fix" the canon narrative, an idea also put forth by Jenkins. Certainly that's one reason fans write fanfic—the overwhelming amount of fanfiction written in the *Supernatural* fandom to fix season finales that left one of the Winchesters dead (or even worse, skewered and bleeding in hell, calling desperately for his brother) attest to the evidence in support of this explanation. Many theorists have suggested that women writing slash is about empowerment, including Camille Bacon-Smith's argument, based on her research with *Star Trek* fans, that "women write about men together because men, holding power, can relate to each other as powerful equals" (1992, 249). Jenkins and Sedgwick have suggested that writing about two males is an attempt to right the gender-based cultural power imbalance, to allow males the freedom to express vulnerability or remove the barriers to homosocial intimacy (Sedgwick 1985). These explanations ring true, but seem to be only a part of the picture. The men who make up the most popular slash pairings—such as *Supernatural*'s Sam and Dean Winchester—are often powerful and equal. But they also frequently take turns being the stereotypical "damsel in distress" in fanfiction, saved again and again by the self-sacrificing hero—in this case, his brother. Slashing such a pair is a conscious choice to embrace both elements of masculinity and femininity, of vulnerability and power, not merely a pairing of equals. The characterizations in fanfiction may be less about who Dean and Sam are, and more about who the writer is.

The fans whose voices we've heard here seem to be writing and reading and commenting for a different reason than those suggested by Bacon-Smith, Sedgwick or Jenkins. Changing the narrative, yes; but not necessarily to make female characters more heroic or male characters less stereotypically male, or to flesh out the canon characterization or change an episode ending. Instead some fans are using the familiar characters with whom they identify to play out whatever the writer (and readers) want and need to express. Sometimes that means breaking the characters down even more, sometimes that means throwing them into bed with an unlikely partner, sometimes that means putting them up against impossible challenges and then making them fail or succeed according to what the writer wants to explore. It's not the canon narrative that's being fixed—it's the writer's narrative. Fanfiction writing seems to be as much about individual empowerment as about throwing off societal norms related to gender, class, or ability.

When women write slash, the displacement inherent in writing male characters may allow not only an exploration of male emotionality and reality, as Jenkins and others have suggested—but a less defended exploration of female reality. The equality in (potential) power which exists simply because the characters are men, endowed with the assumed power our culture ascribes to all males, allows the slash writer to play with power dynamics the way we (as females) never would or comfortably could if we were writing a man and a woman. Krustritz (2003) suggests that fanfiction exists because there is something faulty and inadequate about the socially approved texts out there. We suggest that fan fiction also exists because humans are creative, and are pushed to work and rework their "stuff" until they get it right. There may well be something faulty or inadequate about the socially approved texts, but the metatext isn't always the subversion of that. The metatext is sometimes "I am emotional, intellectual AND sexual and that's okay"—which may be equally subversive.

What are the mechanisms by which emotional disclosure and self-understanding occur within the fandom community? We turn now to the literature on written emotional expression and narrative therapy to explore some possible routes of individual transformation.

Writing and Healing—Emotional Expression through Written Expression

Writers have long attempted to examine and relive their own injuries in their fiction; Hemingway attempted to cope with his wounds by writing characters who were rugged heroes, triumphing over impairment—his version of hurt/comfort fic. Over the past twenty years, a growing body of research has demonstrated the therapeutic effects of writing about stressful life events and trauma, emphasizing the value of emotional expression in healing (Sloane and Marx 2004). Pennebaker and colleagues have shown repeatedly that individuals who express emotions through writing about a stressful event show improved physical health and a greater sense of psychological wellbeing (Francis, M.E. and Pennebaker 1992; Klein and Boals 2001; Park, C.L. and Bloomberg 2002; Pennebaker, J.W. and Beall 1986; Pennebaker, J.W. and Graybeal 2001). In the expressive writing paradigm, the writer is encouraged to explore repressed emotions, talk about past traumas, and use imagined scenarios to increase a sense of safety through displacement. We suggest that fanfiction may offer some of the same benefits, allowing individuals to write about the same themes of trauma, relationship, identity and emotional expression in a displaced manner.

Greenberg, Wortman, & Stone (1996), studied female college students with a history of trauma, examining the efficacy of writing about one's own experience directly as well as in a displaced manner, and found that both methods improved coping and reduced stress. This study suggests that there is therapeutic potential in writing fiction as a coping strategy. Other studies found beneficial results of expressive writing when used as a self-help activity (Pennebaker, 2004), and in internet based modalities (Lange, A., J. Van de Ven and Schrieken 2000; Sheese, B.E., E. L. Brown and Graziano 2004), moving the paradigm even closer to the expressive writing of fanfiction. The mechanisms through which expressive writing improve mental and physical health are not fully understood; current studies suggest that expressive writing affects people on multiple levels—cognitive, emotional, social and biological. Beneficial effects are believed to result from confronting previously repressed emotions, which may reduce the physiological stress that results from emotional inhibition. Pennebaker proposed that actively inhibiting thoughts and emotions about trauma requires a great deal of effort, creating cumulative physical stress. Writing or talking about the trauma and associated emotions reduces the need for inhibition, thus reducing the stress (Pennebaker 1985).

Catharsis theory (Scheff 1979) may also provide an explanation. Scheff suggested that "optimal distance" is necessary from the distressing emotions expressed, so the person can feel safe and in control, and can terminate the distress before it becomes overwhelming, increasing self-efficacy. Expressive writing itself provides some of this distance; the distance inherent in crafting a fictional story, as in fanfiction, may be even more optimal. In fact, in Greenberg's study, the real-trauma participants (who wrote about their own experience directly) reported more fatigue and greater avoidance at follow up than the imagined trauma participants (who wrote fictionalized stories). Greenberg suggests that the real-trauma participants may have received too strong a dose of exposure, resulting in avoidance. Imagining fictional stories instead fostered self-empathy by moving the person from participant to observer, so they could then reorganize and reinterpret their emotional pain from the outside, uncontaminated by shame or guilt (Greenberg, M.A. and Stone 1996). Thus, catharsis and written emotional expression displaced through fiction, fanfic or otherwise, may offer a greater sense of safety and control, and facilitate development of a more resilient sense of self. Following Markus and Nurius'(1986) idea of possible selves as a core component of identity development, Greenberg and colleagues concluded that the imagined coping choices and consequences were viewed as more controllable, thus providing more opportunity for mastery and fostering conceptions of competent, successful future selves.

Improved emotional regulation also results from habituation to strong emotions and extinction of negative emotional responses (Sloane and Marx 2004). Changes in cognitive processing have been found; as people write about emotionally laden experiences, they label, structure and organize the experience, resulting in a more integrated and coherent narrative that they're more willing to talk about with others (Pennebaker, 2004; Pennebaker & Graybeal, 2001). Successful outcomes in expressive writing are believed to result from the revealing of subconscious thought processes, being able to discuss the writing with another significant person, and expression of both emotions and facts (Balkie and Wilhelm 2005). The reworking of difficult life experiences through fanfiction may allow for a similar replaying of the contents of that experience within a supportive group while remaining in control of the outcome.

Narrative Approaches, Identity and Change

Our exploration of the mechanisms of change that may underlie some fans' experience of fandom and fanfiction as therapeutic is also enriched by an understanding of narrative therapy. A narrative view of change assumes that meaning is socially constructed, as people construct personal stories that organize and give meaning to experience. As the narrators of our own life stories, we use the stories to consolidate who we are, script the way we go through life and how we relate to other people, and create our identities as human beings (Stewart, Alan and Neimeyer 2001). The approach is based on a conception of the post-modern experience of a self which is changeable, engaged in the process of "becoming"(Rogers 1961, 122). Assuming a sense of self as fluid makes the process of narrating our own life stories far from static, which opens up the possibility for therapeutic change. Since the stories we develop about ourselves are sometimes limiting, influenced by the dominant narratives of our culture (especially ideas related to power and gender) and the paralyzing experiences of trauma, they can result in emotional and psychological problems (Meekums 2005).

Traumatic events are not always processed and stored in the same way as "normal" events, existing outside the flow of time and isolated from the rest of autobiographical memory. In fact, such memories may be encoded in a pre-verbal, non-linear form which makes them difficult to access or to assimilate into the rest of the ongoing life story. They instead remain frozen and unprocessed, and thus unable to be revised and unavailable for the making of meaning, undermining our sense of self and continuity. Expressive writing and narrative therapy help us make meaning of trauma. (Stewart, Alan and Neimeyer 2001)   Recovery, according to Judith Herman in her seminal book *Trauma and Recovery*, is "the process of weaving the raw fragments of traumatic memory into a narrative that can then find a place in the lore—that is, the larger fabric of narratives—that constitutes the person's life experience and sense of identity."(Herman 1992, 177).

Traditional narrative therapy utilizes autobiographical stories co-constructed with the therapist to create change, with the process of being heard a crucial component of recovery. Psychological distress is seen as a breakdown in the coherence of the life story and the human need to make meaning, and therapy as an exercise in story repair that allows the reconstruction of a meaningful narrative. Clients are helped to uncover the life story that's defining and circumscribing their lives, to try out alternative narratives, and then to rewrite their own story in an empowered, genuine, way. Identity is viewed as constructed, and thus as open to reconstruction (Meekums 2005).

In individual therapy, a level of displacement is often effective in helping clients engage in the process with less denial and defensiveness. One of the most powerful methods of helping people rework their own narrative is the technique of putting the client "in the director's chair", encouraging them to step outside their own experience and view their life story (including the traumatic scenes) from a position of displacement. In imaginal exposure and rescripting therapy, for example, clients imagine their adult selves entering the scene of childhood trauma to rescue or comfort their child self. The clients "film" their own story, narrating as they go, changing settings and characters and events as they see fit—at times to express the repressed emotions actually associated with an event, at other times to rewrite a scene with a more optimistic ending. The client's perception of self as a powerless, helpless victim is thus unfrozen and replaced with a sense of empowerment. (Smucker, M.R. and Niederee 1995).   In traditional narrative therapy, the therapist plays a challenging as well as a supportive role. Much of the work, however, is done by the client, using his or her own accumulated wisdom and resilience to find meaning in the created "movie"; the most effective and internalized insights are those the client comes to independently once they are in touch with their own stories and emotions. We suggest here that the writing and sharing of fanfiction can serve a similar function of narrative repair, although fandom norms for feedback tend toward the supportive and away from the critical. Nevertheless, many of the themes and functions are similar, including the displacement offered by the writing and sharing of fictional stories. The motivations may also be the same; humans have a strong need to make meaning from their experience, and a healthy drive to process the more painful aspects. As we have seen in this chapter, fans who write fanfiction often express a need to tell their stories, especially the most difficult and defended chapters.

A sense of otherness is closely connected to the experience of trauma—not just the stereotypical instances of natural disaster, car crash, sexual abuse or physical injury, but trauma with a small 't'—those events that outpace our ability to emplot these events from the perspective of our dominant life narrative and thus make meaning of them, encompassing everything from a sprained ankle to a leaked email to divorce, addiction, and poverty. We experience a sense of powerlessness, having been through an intrusive event we didn't anticipate and couldn't control. Healing depends on the opportunity to express emotions, engage in the grieving process that accompanies trauma, and reclaim a congruent sense of self and agency (Herman 1992, 70). Unfortunately, that opportunity to feel the pain of loss and share it with another is complicated by our typical reactions to trauma. The sense of otherness brings an internalized shame that encourages silence, which unfortunately intensifies the isolation and makes psychological difficulties more likely.

Fans often describe a similar sense of otherness which draws them to fandom.

> Anon: Let's be honest here and say that a lot of fangirls (and boys) do not fit the social norm in some way, shape, or form; if we did, we might not be spending quite so much time online. We're the 'others,' and it's natural for us to identify with other 'others.' It affirms us, makes us less alone. Part of the appeal of the community of fandom is that it's a community of 'others'—and not just that, but a community of people who embrace their otherness and bond together and take power from that status. I can't speak for anyone else, but I know that there are days when I really need to know that space is out there, that I am part of this place where being 'other' is something to be proud of, not just a danger and a difficulty to endure (anonymous *metafandom* post).

Fanfiction and Narrative Change

As discussed in the research on expressive writing, the created story of *fiction* may facilitate emotional expression and healing, as the metaphors inherent within the story allow for increased emotional distance from painful experience. In writing the fictional story, the author also creates and positions the characters, taking a stance through each. This ability to reposition one's characters may be particularly powerful for someone who has endured forced self-positioning as a result of abuse or in the patient or "victim" role. The narrator can speak through each character, perhaps feeling heard for the first time. The anonymity afforded by the internet makes the process even less threatening. The writing of fanfiction can be seen as a relatively pure form of re-authoring one's own narrative, a freedom emphasized in the research as crucial to therapeutic outcomes. As several fans quoted in this chapter have recognized, with fanfiction there is also no additional goal for the writing—no publisher to court, no audience to woo, no financial incentives to censor oneself. The writer can write without having to please anyone—except herself. In fact, fanfiction writers describe a "need" to write fanfic, and an ease of writing which suggests uncensored tapping into unconscious processes. Says a fanfic writer interviewed in a research study by Angela Thomas, "We rarely think about what we're doing, we just write like heck" (Thomas 2004, 140).

The opportunity for displacement and the provision of a safe place to rework identity have been theorized by several researchers as part of the appeal of slash fanfiction. In slash writing, the identity of the writer may be displaced onto male characters, freeing her from both the constraints of female gender roles and circumscribed behavior. Researcher and fanfiction writer Suzanne Jung considers the appeal of "using" male characters:

> One of the appeals of slash writing for women may be that this genre allows for exploring scenes of male dominance and submission in a safe environment—over equal, preferably male bodies, as these have never been constructed as sites of subordination the way females bodies have. Without invoking institutions of gender inequality, the (female) reader—[and, we would argue, the writer] is free to choose to identify with either the dominant or the submissive male, switch identifications during the exchange, or simply remain voyeur to the scene (Jung 2004, 17).

Either way, the writer is empowered, and can choose to retain or relinquish control as she switches identifications, putting herself in the shoes of multiple characters and gaining a less restricted view of her own (displaced) experience. For women who have lost voice and power as a result of trauma (or simply from being female), mapping of identity onto a male character can be seen as a means of empowerment as well. Henry Jenkins has argued that slash is "not so much a genre about sex as it is a genre about the limitations of traditional masculinity and about reconfiguring male identity"(1992, 190–91). We agree that slash allows writers to free males from macho restrictions and discover their vulnerability, something that both females and males may welcome in real life as well. We would add, however, that sometimes slash is not about reconfiguring male identity at all—It's about reconfiguring *female* identity.

In her essay, Jung overtly sets out to "subvert mainstream culture" by creating an alternate universe in her fanfiction that excludes cultural mandates about femininity and masculinity. She creates a character with whom she identifies, then contrasts his identity in the dominant culture in which she herself has been raised with an alternate version in the utopian universe she's created. The character Ben in the dominant culture is a "shy, wary child, aware of the necessity of hiding from his homophobic father certain parts of his life," particularly his relationship with another boy. The alternate Ben, freed from the constraints of such a culture, is a playful, happy, open ten year old. The author thus explores her own identity and personality development as constructed by environment, externalizing those aspects of identity with which she struggles and trying on newer, more ego syntonic versions of self. At a few points in her essay, Jung seems to realize the transforming power of writing this piece of fanfiction. She expresses a desire to hang onto some of that feeling of being in a land "somewhere over the rainbow" and wanting to share it with others—analogous to the process of validating and solidifying the alternative narrative and being heard.

Angela Thomas, in her analysis of teenage fanfiction writers Tiana and Audriedi, also recognizes the transformative power of their evolving fanfic narratives, which at first reflect and later begin to allow evolution of the girls' identities. As in narrative therapy, there's a gradual reworking of the dominant narrative into a life story more congruent and cohesive. Tiana describes the process of writing fanfiction with an awareness of the subject/object duality. "I sort of become two people, Tiana and the narrator. I make myself see things from a third person point of view" (2004, 144). It is this displacement and ability to step outside oneself to view one's own experience that allows reconstruction of the narrative. Thomas notes that her subjects also have some awareness that writing a character, even one based on the self, allows them to take down their customary emotional defenses and reveal—and *feel*—more than they ordinarily would without such displacement. Pieces of their own pasts, especially painful memories, are recalled and embodied in an emotional way. Tiana talks about writing a recent emotional scene, reconstructed from her own painful past: "The scene(was) nerve wracking to my real self, who was crying through some of it" (2004, 143). As Thomas' subjects analyze the evolution of their own fanfiction writing, they begin to see their writing as not so much an infusion of themselves into their characters, but more an infusion of the created characters into their real-life selves. This, in essence, is the therapeutic potential of the process—the characters, who express their creator's pain and then find a safe place in which to rewrite their creator's life story, influence the writer's own identity. Thomas quotes Audriedi: "I've found that since I've been using her as one of my main characters, I have been…well… rubbing off on myself, in a way. I'm more outgoing than I used to be." Audriedi and Tiana have written themselves into new identities, empowering their realities through their fanfiction (2004, 161).

The potential for change through fanfiction writing is also seen in Jeanne Rudmann Grunert's essay "Why I Write Fan Fiction." Grunert describes her reasons as inexorably entwined with who she is as both a woman and a writer, and understands her chosen fandom as a place of solace and a refuge from her mother's terminal illness, her father's temper and her classmates' bullying in adolescence. She begins writing fanfiction by inserting herself as a character helpless and in need of rescue. Her early works of fanfiction are, she says, gramatically correct but lacking true emotion. Driven to keep writing fanfic, however, over the space of two years Grunert realizes her stories have changed, the main character increasingly strong and competent and the writing increasingly emotional. As the years of repressing her feelings of grief and rage give way to strong emotions displaced onto her characters, Grunert notes that something inside her psyche changed. She recognizes this as the emergence of her authentic self, and the shedding of the false self she had acquired to please her father and keep the peace in a chaotic home, specifically acknowledging that the end to the process of metamorphosis came with fanfiction (Grunert 2008).

Emo!Porn and the Value of Emotional Expression

Fans also realize that fanfiction may be particularly suited to the expression of emotions. In a recent metafandom post on what constitutes the best fanfiction, goldjadeocean cites the ability of fanfiction to hit readers' emotional buttons efficiently, effectively and powerfully:

Goldjadeocean: (Fanfic) is judged by how well or profoundly it impacts the reader. (Fanfic) is built on existing characters, tropes and situations. In the fannish context, what matters is how well you can use the existing tools to produce a certain effect, partly because the established tools can hit certain buttons on the readers far more quickly and effectively.

Stultiloquentia: That's it in a nutshell. For some of us who answered the best of poll, the question "Did it get me in my feelings?" spectacularly outranked "Does it have gorgeously deft prose and profound, original insights?" Screw the prose. Gimme emoporn. That's the fanfic that is doing its job right. (metafandom, 2010).

Perhaps not coincidentally, the progression from repressed emotions and a fragmented identity toward open expression is reflected in Jenkins' description of the prototypical plot for a slash story as "a series of movements from an initial (intense, close) partnership, through a crisis in communication that threatens to disrupt that union, toward its reconfirmation through sexual intimacy" (Jenkins, 1992: 206). This prototypical plot also describes the progression from an initially cohesive sense of self to one fragmented by trauma into a dominant narrative which divides the self and circumscribes life options, and finally to the re-authoring of a narrative which reconfirms a unified, reconstructed identity and allows the development of relational intimacy. Science fiction texts often provide a fertile playing field on which to base the prototypical slash or hurt/comfort plot, and on which to displace and reconstruct the writer's narrative. *Supernatural*'s Dean Winchester is the near-perfect embodiment of a self fragmented by trauma, emotionally repressed and isolated, expecting rejection and abandonment. The character of his brother Sam as the only one he can trust or allow himself to love often represents in fanfiction the longed-for supportive figure, and the author's own emerging resilient self, with the narrative gradually moving the two toward reconnection and restored intimacy. In more recent seasons of the Show, the character of Sam is literally fragmented, first by the loss of his soul with complete repression of all emotions, and then by the abrupt reintegration of his emotional and physical selves, which is experienced as intensely painful. Dean becomes the one who holds Sam together and facilitates his healing, as the brothers switch roles once more.

In Meekums' (2005) research on the use of fiction in narrative therapy, her client's fictional stories early in the course of therapy are of failure and inadequacy, featuring characters who are deadened and unemotional. The characters eventually begin to grapple with their feelings and experience great pain or even threat of death. The second phase of fanfiction as articulated by Jenkins—separating the characters, cutting off communication, creating or recreating trauma, inflicting pain and loss (angst angst and more angst)—serves as a way of finally expressing the writer's own emotional experience. The frequent use of hurt/comfort scenarios can be the beginning of the writer's acknowledgement of her own needs. Here the characters occupy both sides of the writer's longing—the need to express pain and the capacity to receive comfort and consolation that may never have been offered, or which came at too high a psychological price. In some fanfiction, the hurt/comfort is sexualized, the physical contact allowing a breaking down of the boundaries keeping them physically and emotionally apart. In other stories, the hurt/comfort is the goal in itself, and the reconnection and reassurance of love the demonstration of intimacy. In both instances, it is the restored intimacy, the sense of connection and completion, which conveys the rewritten narrative. It's no coincidence that there are vibrant and popular online *Supernatural* communities devoted to Hurt!Dean or Limp!Sam.

Later in Meekums' description of her client's narrative therapy, the client's fictional stories begin to express rage and a previously buried desire for revenge. With the expression of this range of emotions and subsequent narrative revision, Meekums recognizes in her clients an emerging theme: the struggle between death/deadening and life/embodiment (2005). A similar progression can be seen in some fanfiction. A multi-chapter Wincest story (Live Journal post, November, 2008) illustrates the gradual process of self-disclosure, risk taking, and feedback in the reworking of narrative. The author's summary describes the story as dealing with Sam's sexual abuse by his father, and his subsequent guilt and desire for punishment over his own sexual impulses, here represented by his attraction to his brother Dean. Sam at first represses, then haltingly begins to express the powerlessness, fear, confusion and self-blame which can normatively result from such trauma:

> "At first I tried to fight him off, you know? But I was little, and he was…scary, and big…after years upon years of it, as I learned to like it, to fucking *enjoy* it…*that*, that's what really made him mad. Probably made him realize how sick it was. How sick I was, because of him."

The character of Dean embodies and articulates the longing for support and acceptance, and the reassurance needed to begin the revision of the self-blaming narrative, saying:

> "He did this to you, Sam. If he'd never touched you, you never would have had to learn to tolerate it. It was how you survived. You're not sick, you're broken. Dad broke you, Sam. It's his fault. You're not alone anymore, okay?"

Readers responded to the expression of feelings and the risk taken in disclosing them, validating the realism of the story and expressing the desire for a sequel which would give the battered boys some closure. The readers' encouragement allows the writer to continue the story, reducing the displacement explicitly by writing the next chapter in first person. As she does so, the author comments that writing from Sam's pov "makes me cry every fucking time I look at my screen" but she also thanks readers for encouraging her exploration of her "darker side" and says she's slowly getting more confident about letting it out. The next chapter is painful to read, as Sam vividly describes the dissociation in response to trauma in terms most therapists have heard many times, and the self-blame and guilt left behind by sexual abuse. The story concludes with the happy ending of Dean and Sam together, but both readers and writer seem to realize that the sex is representative of a newfound capacity for intimacy and acceptance of self far beyond the physical. As the writer says:

> …For me it is definitely more about them finally being able to express themselves to each other and heal each other and love each other (in admittedly unconventional ways) than specifically about the sex (there was some major sex in there though. it kind of makes me blush)…Sam's whole journey from fear and shame to just feeling so taken care of and loved by Dean kind of heals me a little. I feel good about the place he's gotten to in the story arc. I do think they'll be okay. They're both survivors, and it's important to me to show how you can come back from trauma like that and be able to heal and find love. I'm all about the hope and the striving for the happy ending.

In a 2005 article in *The Chicago Reader*, Anne Ford interviewed Sarz Maxwell, a physician who had recently been appointed president of a local medical society. Maxwell described her own therapeutic journey through fanfiction in an article subtitled "Drugs and alcohol nearly ruined Sarz Maxwell's life. Writing dirty stories about hobbits made it worth living again." Estranged from her family, divorced, depressed and struggling to stay sober, one night Maxwell, a longtime Tolkien fan, went to see *The Fellowship of the Ring*. The film, and Frodo's pain and anguish in particular, tore long-repressed emotions loose in Maxwell, and she found online fandom as a place to share her new obsession, discovering slash and hurt/comfort fanfiction. Soon Maxwell was writing slash herself, and forming friendships with fellow fans and fanfiction writers. Sexually abused as a child, Maxwell's experience of trauma shaped her response to LOTR and fanfiction. Just as *Supernatural* fans respond strongly to Dean or Sam's suffering, self-sacrifice, and intense emotional bond, Maxwell reacted powerfully to Frodo's. When she reacted to Frodo's anguish,

Maxwell was also expressing the emotions she had repressed for almost thirty years. "All the things that Frodo felt, it really was just like a veil ripping," she described. Writing hurt/comfort slash with Frodo as an abuse survivor gave Maxwell a way to construct a backstory for Frodo that would bring his experience even closer to her own. Portraying Sam as the loving companion who nurses him back to physical and mental health mirrored Maxwell's own healing. Maxwell uses the commonly maligned fanfic trope of "healing cock" to work through her own need to redefine sex as an act of love instead of one of violence and invasion.

> "'Please,' Sam whispered. 'I need you in me. Please.'
> "Frodo looked down into the eyes of the person he loved most in the world and saw there only tenderness and longing. His body was shaking at the thought of performing the act that had been done to him so brutally, but the memory of the brutality was washing away in the sweetness flowing from Sam's eyes."

Maxwell said in her author's notes: "Frodo is helping me so much. In telling his story, I can speak the truth." She not only expressed her own pain through Frodo's suffering, but created a relationship that was both sexual and loving, instead of abusive. "That's why the whole slash thing was so incredibly liberating," she says. "I guess if there's safe sex, there's safe voyeurism. I was borrowing other people's bodies to explore my own head" (Ford 2005).

The Fan Community as Support Group: Disqualification of Uniqueness

Both Maxwell and the fan who wrote the story of Sam's abuse moved towards healing through both emotional expression and the support of the fandom community. Fans who have experienced trauma with a small 't' – bullying, divorce, breakups, shyness, injury, illness, discrimination, stigma, and anything else that brings significant pain, which includes just about everyone – also benefit from the acceptance of the group.

Sandvoss (2005) and others have established that fans perceive themselves as members of groups, even when they are not part of an organization or interacting with other fans face to face. Online communities have been compared to tribal cultures, with patterns of interaction that often seem closer to oral communication than written, and in which identity is wrapped up in the question of how many people know you. The intensity that goes into forming and defending the boundaries of social groups has an evolutionary basis. Belonging to a group was literally a necessity for survival, and being excluded from the group resulted in death. Indeed, in many early civilizations, exile and death were equivalent punishments, and we still retain our intense fear of being rejected. Social inclusion is critical to our ability to experience happiness. We all have a powerful and pervasive need to belong, and it is within the group that we define ourselves (Baumeister and Leary 1995).

A variety of psychological approaches recognize the risks inherent in remaining isolated and relying on denial and avoidance instead of sharing experience and emotions. Psychoanalyst Estrella Weldon describes the power of a community to replace secrecy and isolation with disclosure, cohesiveness, connectedness and mutuality. In the group, people feel supported enough to confront past pain and come to terms with their need for revenge. Otherwise, by staying in denial and keeping trauma split off from conscious awareness, the tendency toward the repetition compulsion can result in re-enacting the trauma, taking it out on one's own body through cutting, eating disorders, drug abuse, and other forms of self-harm. Coping strategies such as sadomasochism are also believed to be an attempt to master early trauma by reliving the experience under controlled and safe circumstances, an unconscious participation in a familiar scenario (Weldon 2002).

The default belief for most of us who have confronted some type of trauma is the disquieting thought that we alone have certain unacceptable reactions, problems, impulses or fantasies, as discussed in the previous chapter. When individuals remain isolated and without an opportunity to share these fears, no corrective experience can take place and intimacy is precluded. The disconfirmation of an individual's uniqueness, in contrast, provides a tremendous sense of relief. As Irving Yalom describes:

> The phenomenon finds expression in the cliché "We're all in the same boat", or perhaps more cynically, "Misery loves company." There is no human deed or thought that is fully outside the experience of other people. I have heard group members reveal such acts as incest, burglary, embezzlement, murder, attempted suicide, and fantasies of an even more desperate nature. Invariably, I have observed other group members reach out and embrace these very acts as within the realm of their own possibilities. Long ago Freud noted that the staunchest taboos (against incest and patricide) were constructed precisely because these very impulses are part of the human being's deepest nature (1998, 11).

If we consider the fandom community as a source of this same disconfirmation of uniqueness, the appeal of certain media texts as a forum for exploration of these "secrets" is clear. Yalom goes on to note that the most common secret is a deeply held conviction of inadequacy, followed by a sense of being unable to love another person. The third most common secret, according to Yalom, is something sexual. That such themes are repeatedly confronted in fanfiction is no coincidence.

The therapeutic factors of groups are interdependent; neither catharsis nor universality is itself sufficient for change. Rather, it is the expression of feelings and the discovery that others share them that are important. The community's acceptance challenges the individual's fear that they are basically unlovable and unacceptable. Cathartic expression of emotions within any group, whether an organized counseling group or a fan community, results in a sense of cohesion and greater self-understanding. Group members sense that they are not alone in their struggles, identify with one another, and begin to view their life challenges as universal instead of idiosyncratic.   The processes of catharsis, risk taking, and gradually exploring previously avoided or denied parts of oneself—recognizing that one can still belong—are the ingredients of therapeutic change (Corey, G. and Corey 2006).   In order to open up a space for processing experiences of trauma, the events must not only be recalled and externalized, but must be heard in the telling.   Charles Anderson and Marian MacCurdy, in their book, *Writing and Healing*, assert that in the process of rewriting our narrative, "we become agents for our own healing, and if those to whom we write receive what we have to say and respond to it, we create a community that can accept, contest, gloss, inform, invent and help us discover, deepen and change who we have become as a consequence of the trauma we have experienced. This …process integrates the personal and the social and depends upon the community's capacity to be both supportive and critical" (2006, 7). Anderson and MacCurdy are talking about a university writing class, but they have just vividly described the supportive (and occasionally challenging) role of online fandom communities as well.

In traditional therapy, the therapist is the one who's witness to the expression of long-buried pain and reinforces the rewritten life story. Similarly, the support and feedback of the fandom community appears to play a role in facilitating change for fanfiction writers reworking their narratives. As we read in fans' own words in the beginning of this chapter, the writing and posting of fanfiction is far from a solitary process; it is a communal one. Writers are also readers, and readers are also writers, all of them "playing in the same sandbox."   Readers empathize with the writer's experience, sharing her pain and validating it as genuine. A 2008 WIP fic in the *Supernatural* fandom which at last count was well over 70 chapters garnered hundreds of readers along the way as it explored themes of major depression, self-harm, psychosis and suicidality.   Readers thanked the author for her courage in telling such a story, and for trusting the community enough to tell it in way that resonates, realistically and openly. And then they shared some of their stories of trauma, breaking their own silence and isolation. The writer feels heard; the reader feels understood. Both feel validated, and empowered to work toward change. Fan communities often band together against the perception of outside forces of disapproval or imposed control, increasing cohesiveness even more. Without this sense of safety, writers and readers would not be able to benefit from the re-creation of a holding environment similar in some ways to that of the therapy room.

But is the "safe space" really without risk? In the next chapter, we examine the dark underbelly of fan communities—trolling, bullying, backstabbing, shaming, and relational aggression, also known as fandom wank.

CHAPTER FIVE

ONLY LOVE CAN BREAK YOUR HEART:
FANDOM WANK AND POLICING
THE SAFE SPACE

Our first experience of fandom "wank" came shortly after our discovery of online fandom itself. We were happily devouring everything Supernatural we could find, both online and off, and reveling in the discovery of a like-minded community of fellow fans. It seemed like utopia, a world where everyone got along and fans from all over the world were united in their love of Show. Our expectations, in retrospect, were unrealistic—we were in our fandom honeymoon phase, after all. That we were naively expecting a lovefest made the wank which came out of the first Supernatural convention even more shocking.

Asylum, the first fan convention to include stars of Supernatural, took place in Birmingham, U.K. in 2007, with series star Jensen Ackles in attendance. Unhappily stuck on the wrong side of the pond, we followed the con as most fans do—online. There were photos and videos and squee-ful posts—and then there was a flurry of reports that Ackles had been "attacked". Fandom responded with horror. What had happened? A robbery attempt? A conspiracy of jealous husbands? According to fandom, the truth was even worse. The attacker was a fangirl. Apparently overcome by her emotional reaction to Ackles, she jumped onto him and refused to let go, prompting the meager security force to swing into action—and ensuring that security around the actor at cons would never be meager again. Fandom dubbed her "the Flying Fangirl", and proceeded to rip her apart.

As fans berated The Flying Fangirl online, we watched the story morph from that of overly eager fan to veritable evil superwoman, leaping from a staircase and tackling the hapless actor as he tried to escape into an elevator. Reports of her sobbing and begging to be readmitted outside the convention center did nothing to stop the vitriolic attacks, and The Flying Fangirl was unceremoniously kicked out of both the convention and the fandom community. Fans even made tee shirts calling for her ostracism—or worse—to wear to the next convention. From our vantage point as new fans, what this showed us was that fandom is a place of strictly defined boundaries as much as a space of freedom. There are lines fans are not allowed to step over, even if sometimes you don't know where they are until you've crossed one. But once you do, the fans themselves will let you know. And it will not be pretty.

We were still reeling from the swift and lethal way that fandom turned on one of its own when another incident at Asylum brought to light one of the nastiest rifts within what until now had seemed like an idyllic fan community. A fan dared to ask Ackles his opinion of fanfiction, and the audience literally gasped in horror. Loudly. The actor responded, to the even greater shock of the convention and the fans following along online, by saying, tongue firmly in cheek, "My favorite is Wincest." Ackles' decision to explicitly acknowledge one of the fan practices that fans would prefer to keep hidden took the question in an even more taboo direction, even as the actor eased his way out of further discussion by adding with a smirk, "I just hope my grandmother doesn't stumble over it." Unfortunately, the fandom's strong sense of self protectiveness and internalized fan shame didn't allow recognition—let alone appreciation— of Ackles' sense of humor. Although the fan's question had actually been about fanfiction in general, within hours, the fan's question was posted as the First Rule of Fandom rule-breaking "She asked him about Wincest, omg". This fan, and the Flying Fangirl, were tarred and feathered online for months—even years—to come.

As we've discussed, there has been a welcome trend in the past several decades shifting the focus of study away from pathologizing fandom and instead to examining its benefits—finding a community of like-minded others, a safe space to explore identity, and just plain having fun. At the same time, whenever a group of people comes together, there are issues of social standing, popularity, norms and identity on which they will inevitably not agree. Fandom is no exception.

Fandom interaction itself has shifted in the last several decades to occur primarily online, changing the ways in which fan communities form and function. There is a growing body of research on online interaction and social media in general, which can provide a lens through which to examine online fandom. In 2011, the American Academy of Pediatrics published their Clinical Report on the Impact of Social Media on Children, Adolescents and Families in the journal *Pediatrics* (Pediatrics 2011, 2011:800–804), emphasizing that a significant portion of social and emotional development is now occurring online and on ipads and smartphones. The report cited a wide range of developmental benefits, including enhanced communication, social connection and technical skills, and noted that nearly 25% of teenagers log onto their favorite social media site more than ten times a day, with over 50% logging on at least once daily. On a less positive note, the AAP noted the down sides of online interaction, including the risk of cyberbullying and social rejection. Both have serious negative effects, including academic and work difficulties, low self-esteem, relationship issues, increased susceptibility to depression, and higher rates of self-harm and suicidal ideation (Sharp, S., D. Thompson and Arora 2000). A large-scale survey of adolescents and young adults for a 2009 MTV and AAP special found that half had been the target of some type of digital abuse, including someone spreading lies, writing something embarrassing or hurtful, or forwarding online content without permission. (AP-MTV 2009) Anyone who participates in online fandom has seen the same.

The study also found that victims of online harassment or bullying were more likely to engage in high risk behaviors and to contemplate suicide, and were twice as likely to seek mental health services, making the issue a serious one. Every online platform dispenses advice on how to use—and how not to use—social media, including this rather specific advice to new Facebook users: "Don't use Facebook to bully, harass, spread rumors, challenge fights or otherwise incite violence. Facebook is a social utility, not an anti-social utility." If only it were that easy.

Why Can't We All Just Get Along: Reactive Aggression and the Problem of Anonymity

Bullying, conflict and aggression occur in all corners of the worldwide web, and fandom is no exception. As discussed in previous chapters, fandom is widely viewed as a safe space where we can express ourselves and connect with like-minded others, but there's also a popular saying: You can't stop fandom from wanking. "Wank" is used here in a metaphorical sense to refer to fans who've gotten carried away, usually with anger and accusations. There has been an online *Fandom Wank* LJ community, dedicated to making fun of drama caused by fans on the internet, since 2002. Their motto is "because we think 'Fandom is fucking funny' isn't taking it far enough." The site is so popular that it has spawned numerous spin-off sites, including I-Wank, for reporting wanks you instigated yourself; Wankitywank, where you mock the people who mocked, in a headsplittingly meta fashion; and Unfunny Business, where topics deemed too serious for FW are banished.

Fig. 5-1

The types of bullying, marginalizing, and jockeying for position that occur in fandom are mirrored in most other groups, online and face to face. Aggression is, of course, a normal component of human behavior, and not all aggression is problematic. Researchers distinguish between reactive aggression (an affective, defensive, impulsive response to an actual or perceived threat) and proactive or instrumental aggression (aimed at influencing or dominating others) (Poulin, F. and Boivin 2000). Reactive aggression, characterized by impulsive, irritable and emotionally dysregulated behavior, is strongly associated with both bullying and victimization. We've all encountered people in fandom who seem to constantly be lashing out at someone. While it may seem like a personality trait, researchers believe the tendency is at least partially explained by experiences within the social group. People who have been socially rejected in the past may develop what researchers call a "hostile attributional bias." (Bushman, B.J. and Anderson 2002; Dodge, K.A. and Coie 1987). They become overly defensive, constantly perceiving threats or provocations even when they don't actually exist. Expecting whoever you're interacting with to be rejecting or competitive causes a pattern of reactive aggression, and sets up an escalating cycle of conflict. Experiences of social exclusion foster a particularly strong hostile cognitive bias because of the evolutionary significance of group affiliation. Belonging to a group was literally a necessity for survival, so we still retain our intense fear of being excluded. Thus people react with what on the surface may appear to be an out of proportion response.

People are aggressive both online and face to face, but the perception of anonymity online may increase the severity of the problem. Anonymity contributes to the depersonalization of others, and can lead to a real disconnect between action and consequence. Those who criticize or bully others online are not personally confronted with the way the targeted person reacts, and the absence of social cues fosters uninhibited and impulsive behavior and lowers thresholds for aggression without the fear of negative consequences (Dehue, F., C. Bolman and Vollink 2008; Finn, J. and Banach 2000; Meerkerk, G., R. Van Den Eijnden and Garretsen 2006). Also contributing to the problem is ambivalence about how to deal with instances of people attacking others when we're only witnessing it online. More than half of the young adults in the AAP survey reported that if they witnessed someone being bullied physically, they'd report it. But when aggression happens online, less than a third felt it was okay to report the bullying (AP-MTV 2009).

Within *Supernatural* fandom, the *spn_permanon* community on LJ was created as a place of free expression, and has developed a community norm of encouraging criticism of other fans and fanworks. All posting is anonymous, so fans feel comfortable expressing overt ad hominem attacks on other fans. The consequences are sometimes devastating for the victims, some of whom withdraw from fandom completely rather than risk further bullying. Each year, much of *Supernatural* fandom participates in the *spn_j2_bigbang* challenge, where writers team up with artists to compose novel-length SPN-based fanfiction. For the past several years, the anon meme weighed in on each and every one, replacing the norms of the broader fanfic community about constructive feedback with sometimes brutal attacks on the writing, the art—and the fan writers themselves

> Anon: I fear the anonmeme. I fear being the target of the next shit-storm or an ongoing grudge because I said the wrong thing …. The internet is the only place I can think of where people can speak their mind in a public forum with no consequences and believe they are entitled to do so. This entitlement should be balanced by responsibility, but it isn't. And the anonmeme is a social entity with real power. Unfortunately too often that power is directed at intimidation and fear and the manipulating of real lives.
>
> Anon: I almost didn't (write a big bang fic). Things for fun that aren't hurting anyone shouldn't be subjected to that kind of crap. We only get paid in feedback, so the urge to search out your own name is hard to resist….And for some reason it seems like a single nasty comment

dramatically outweighs all of the genuinely positive ones. Not useful criticism, just pointlessly nasty viciousness... under the guise of 'honesty' and the protection of anon....is cowardice and a kind of bullying.

Anon: The amount of bullying that goes on in LJ is disheartening and concerning. Because that's what it is to me, bullying—making yourself feel better by putting someone else down. It's not okay when kids do it and it's even worse when those over the age of 12 do it because frankly, people should know better by then. Somehow, somewhere it started to be 'cool' to be mean and snarky. And really uncool to be sensitive and/or respectful. And it's not right.

On the other hand, some fans who participate in the meme argue for its benefits, especially as a place to vent and a sort of group stress reliever, citing the ability to say what you really think without fear of consequences. The anonymity is also attractive because it erases the fandom hierarchy—nobody knows if you're a BNF or a newbie or a lurker or how many friends you have. Everyone starts fresh, without any reputation in fandom, and is judged solely on what they say within the community. Some fans argue that the anonymity also makes it easier for disagreements to actually be settled, since no one loses face by backing down. Nevertheless, disagreements, relational aggression and outright bullying are common on the meme.

Group Dynamics

Aggression is a specific type of social interaction, one which is influenced by both personal characteristics, as discussed in the previous section, and social pressures. Aggression serves instrumental functions within a group by helping to enforce norms, build cohesion, and defend against outsiders. According to a widely referenced online essay by Clay Shirky, there are three things that groups do, online or face-to-face, even if those three things are not part of the group's ostensible focus. First, in what is probably surprising to no one, group members will flirt and talk about sex. The second basic pattern is the identification and vilification of some external enemy, whether real or manufactured, which in either case creates a sense of group cohesion. Third is a pattern of religious veneration—nominating and worshipping some sort of religious icon or set of religious tenets which is then held up as beyond critique. Shirky uses a fandom example here, advising anyone who doubts the truth of that pattern to go into a Tolkien discussion forum and try saying, "you know, The Two Towers is a little dull." He could just as easily have advised going into a *Supernatural* community and suggesting that '67 Chevy Impalas are lame) (Shirky 2003).

Sex, defense, and something to worship—No wonder there's so much wank in fandom!   At times, number one seems to take precedence over just about everything else in fandom, as we've seen in the previous two chapters, but 2) and 3) are equally influential.   There are plenty of fans who joke that their religion is *Supernatural*, and fannish devotion is part of the stereotype, so the third function fits, as Shirky himself notes. As to number 2, if groups are in part defined by hating some enemy, then it makes sense that we spend a lot of time looking for one. In fact, Shirky claims that groups often gravitate towards members who are the most paranoid and make them leaders, because those are the people who are best at identifying external enemies.   In our experience of the past six years of *Supernatural* fandom, those who have emerged as leaders tend to be the moderators of influential online communities. Usually defined as BNFs (Big Name Fans), these individuals influence the dissemination of information within the fandom.   Some appear to be leaders because they have the time, motivation, creativity and technical skill to compile and organize the ever-increasing volume of *Supernatural*-related news, media coverage, tweets, posts, and fan creations which are strewn across a wide variety of online spaces. The Superwiki, an award-winning site maintained from its beginning in 2006 by missyjack, is the most comprehensive example.   The Superwiki has been remarkably free from wank through its six years of existence, perhaps due to the diplomatic talents of its maintainer and her ability to cross boundaries gracefully between diverse fannish spaces—or because the wiki archives information mostly without commentary, an example of affirmational fandom instead of the more wank-prone transformational fandom.

On the other hand, some of the group leaders who emerged from other sites, including the popular Television Without Pity (TWoP) *Supernatural* community, have remained controversial both within and outside fandom. *Supernatural* creator Eric Kripke, himself a frequent reader of the TWoP site, even wrote two of the most influential posters, Demian and Barnes, into an SPN episode, shattering the fourth wall and commenting on the fans' tendency to vilify the series creator as the identified villain, a dynamic we'll explore in depth in the next chapter. Various LJ communities have vied for most influential status over the past six years, with *Supernatural_tv, dean_sam,* and *all_spn* serially establishing themselves as go-to places for current information. The moderators of these comms provide a valuable service to fans, but occasionally someone also exhibits a bit of the paranoia that Shirky references, periodically accusing other fans of everything from lack of appreciation to theft to rumor-mongering, and threatening to close the comms in order to re-establish some control over the group. The mods, as BNFs, are also frequent targets of fandom wank. In fact, in the *Fandom Wank* community, a BNF is defined as someone not only well known in the fandom, but perceived as committing excessive wank. Once the BNF reaches a certain level of infamy, they are rewarded with their very own page on the FW wiki.

Sometimes wank is created as fans jockey for positions of power and influence within the group. One of the *Supernatural* fans we interviewed described her own history of being a BNF and its painful consequences. She ran a popular website devoted to an actor for years, becoming so successful that she was invited to the actor's house for charitable and social events. Other fans soon accused her of breaking boundaries, and came up with a particularly effective way of removing her from BNF status—outing her as a slashwriter to the actor himself, with a printout of her NC17 story (that featured him) in hand. The "outer" then took over the website, and with it the BNF status.

Identifying an enemy thus seems an integral part of the functioning of a group and the development of group cohesion. Sometimes the identified enemy is indeed external (TPTB, the network, showrunners Eric Kripke or Sera Gamble, the failings of society in general). Other times, however, the enemy is identified by creating an out-group within fandom itself—Phillies fans versus Dodgers fans, slash writers versus gen writers, Wincest fans versus Destiel fans, Sam!girls versus Dean!girls. Add to this the intense emotion created by Shirky's number 3, defending the object of worship, and wank is even more likely.

The intensity that goes into forming and defending the boundaries of social groups has an evolutionary basis, with social acceptance crucial to human survival and happiness (Baumeister and Leary 1995). Several lines of research have established that fans perceive themselves as members of groups, even when they are not part of an organization or interacting face to face (Sandvoss 2005), and explicitly categorize themselves and others as in-groups and out-groups (Voci 2006) The construction of in-groups and out-groups is part of the identification of enemies, as we've seen. It is also important to identity development, since it is within the group that we define ourselves.

According to social identity theory (Tajfel, H. and Turner 1986) a person's social identity is composed of the aspects of self-concept that are created out of the social groups to which the individual belongs. Group members are motivated to enhance their self-concept by positively differentiating their group (the in group) from other comparison groups (out groups), particularly when the comparison group is similar. This may seem counter-intuitive at first, but when an out-group is similar, it may be perceived as a threat to the distinctiveness of the in-group (Jetten, J., R. Spears and Manstead 1996). The purpose of aggression is often to enhance the status of the in-group, especially when another group poses a threat to that status. Several studies have found that fans strive for a positive social identity and attempt to avoid a negative one, sometimes by derogating out-groups to protect their self esteem and the positive perception of their in-group (Boen, F., N. Vanbeselaere and Feys 2002; Bizman and Yinon 2002; End 2001). Groups tend to show elevated in-group favoritism, attributing more favorable characteristics to the in-group, and are more likely to criticize or attack an out-group member (End 2001).

This dynamic can serve to unite fans and create a strong sense of community within fandom, vilifying the "outside world" who "doesn't get it". However, the dynamic is different when the out-group is not composed of outsiders. We also police our fellow fans, ostensibly members of the in-group, a practice which is implicated in a great deal of fandom wank. According to social identity theory, if an in-group individual does not behave in accordance with group norms, they are likely to be the target of aggression (Ojala, K. and Nesdale 2004). In fact, the "black sheep effect" describes the tendency to derogate an unlikeable or deviant in-group member even more than an equally unlikeable and deviant out-group member. This type of bullying serves to protect the positive perception and status of the in-group and enforce its norms, by excluding from the in-group definition anyone who breaks those norms (Abrams, D., A. Rutland and Cameron 2003; Eidelman, S. and Biernat 2002). According to Goffman's (1963) work on social interaction and human behavior, individuals become vulnerable when they are "out of role", and are then fair game to be attacked by other group members policing the group norms. Out of role could conceivably apply to everything from asking an actor his views on fanfiction at a *Supernatural* convention, to being a Sam!girl instead of a Dean!girl, to thinking that Castiel ruined the show instead of saved it, to writing RPF or slash. There is an increased need to view each other as similar and an intensification of group norms whenever the in-group feels threatened, known as the "in-group homogeneity effect" (Marques, J., D. Adams and Serodio 2001) (which, it could be argued, is always the perception in online fandom).

The sanctioning of deviant in-group members is particularly harsh when there is an external audience with some powers of sanction (which it can be argued is always the case on the internet, as opposed to a deserted high school hallway). In fact, one of the most frequently recorded forms of textual criticism found in Dunlap and Wolf's (2010) analysis of the *Fandom Wank* community was a variation of "Get out of my fandom, you make my fandom look stupid,", in which the community members feared that an outsider's perception of the wanker's behavior might reflect poorly on fandom itself. The rancor with which fans attack other fans who they believe are "doing it wrong" is testament to the strength of this drive. Within *Supernatural* fandom, as we will discuss in depth later in this chapter, contempt for fans who read or write RPS is an example, with such fans accused of everything from lack of respect to fundamental moral and ethical failings.

Fandom: You're Doing It Wrong

Creating an out-group within the fan community is often accomplished with the accusation of "you're doing it wrong" hurled at other fans. An example of the vehemence of fandom in policing fans perceived as stepping out of role is the almost universal derision for Mary Sues, loosely defined as blatant self-insertion narratives in fanfiction. Sometimes the Mary Sue character is disrupting the "ship" of the reader, the preferred romantic relationship. Sometimes she's a romantic rival for the reader herself, thus the target of jealousy and derision. Sometimes the Mary Sue may just be too obvious, too invested, too much. The fan who writes a Mary Sue is "doing it wrong", and therefore threatening the integrity and status of the fandom as a whole. The vehemence of the resulting attacks suggest a significant threat to personal identity and social status, as evidenced by a fan addressing a newbie who had inadvertently committed this fandom sin:

> Mystifyingbliss: STOP putting yourself into the stories you write. That's the biggest and most terrifyingly awful kind of Mary Sue. Fyi, a Mary Sue is not a good phenomenon. A Mary Sue is a phenomenon that should first be stepped on by a giant, then cut into little pieces with a kitchen knife, then sowed (sic) together, then drowned, then hung, then shot, then disemboweled, then sliced into tiny little pieces with a bloody kitchen knife, then crushed with a sofa, then chewed on by a llama, then digested, then spit out (from either side) by another llama, then dropped from a space station, then buried 25 miles underneath the surface of the earth, then finally devoured by the lava in the earth's core (mystifyingbliss 2007).

"Doing it wrong" can also extend to the more basic taunt of "my fandom's better than your fandom"—sometimes with so much rigor that certain fans are accused of not qualifying as fans at all. In 2009, for example, there was a great deal of wank about the increased female presence at Comic Con, especially the vocal and demonstrative *Twilight* fans. The Laweekly.com blog ran a photo of a young man holding a handmade sign that read "Twilight ruined Comic Con. Scream if you agree!" The response was apparently quite loud at times. Some of the ensuing online wank took on a gendered nature, with female fans challenging a perceived underlying assumption that girls and women don't know how to be "proper fans"—that their fannishness is superficial in some way, that they're just there for the hot guys. Other fans responded by reminding everyone that there's a prurient interest in most fandoms, regardless of gender (Ohanesian 2009).

A few commented on what they saw as a more pervasive issue.

> J.M. Rossi: Lots of fans want to believe that there is an objective goodness or suckiness to entertainment. They want to believe that their favorite things are inherently, undeniably, empirically better that other folks' favorite things....they tear down other people's faves in order to build up their own. So here's Twilight, outshining the complainers' faves. That apparently threatens their idea that whatever they like is the Best. So they start to deride, to gripe, to try to "prove" that Twilight isn't deserving of the spotlight. One way to do that is to attack Twilight's fans....It happens in music fandom. "Only dumb people listen to Frog Rock. People who understand music, like me, listen to Turtle Rock." It's Us vs. Them thinking....we love to ghetto-ize ourselves. Tabletop RPGers think that LARPers are so weird. Boardgamers disdain Magic The Gathering players. Star Wars vs. Star Trek. Manga vs. American Comics. It's not enough to get shoddy treatment from the larger culture, we have to treat each other like crap, too?
>
> Robin Brenner: I find it especially distressing that the SDCC (Comic Con) crowd, made up of fans who have been typically dismissed and marginalized by the larger culture...., seem to think it's perfectly warranted to dump on fans who you would think they have a lot more in common with than traits to divide them.

In other words, in-group versus out-group. It's just that the out-group here is also fandom.

In her popular blog "FanStuff Guide to Fan Etiquette," Tracy Wilson tries to tell fans to "just get along" while acknowledging the emotional investment in fandom which makes that challenging.

> Being a geek is about loving something so much that you open yourself up to ridicule. Fans tend to be opinionated people who are quick to defend whatever they're passionate about. ...But it also has a dark side. One of the

things I really don't love about fandom is the underlying "you're doing it wrong" attitude that so often runs through it....If you like something I don't like, you're wrong. If you don't like something I like, you're wrong. If you disagree with me about some point of whatever we both like, you're *really* wrong. That heated debate can be fun for a while, but eventually you get tired of talking about whether a Balrog has wings (Wilson 2011).

Within SPN fandom, we've encountered numerous posts about fan etiquette, including one that advised us to "dress up" for the community theater production of *A Few Good Men*, and another posted on the bathroom doors at a Creation SPN convention listing do's and don'ts and basically admonishing fans to "behave". There is often a sense of self-righteousness on the part of those attempting to police other fans' behavior, a sense that this is a necessary step to protect the community and maintain standards. The very act of declaring that someone who has not followed the rules is not "one of us" ensures that this person or "those people" are excluded from the usual protections we offer one another.

Some of the wank that occurs in fandom includes accusations of "!fail". Survey!fail , as we've seen, targeted an external enemy who had invaded fandom, but often the target is another fan. Race!fail revolved around accusations not that SPN itself was racist (although that was argued separately), but that certain SPN fanworks were. The contention here is that someone on the inside has failed to maintain the norms of the fan community. A high profile example of this version of fandom policing occurred after WisCon in 2008, when an attendee took photos of fellow con attendees and then posted them publicly with the specific intent to mock them in glaringly misogynistic, homophobic, racist, ableist ways. Fans retaliated, outing the poster with her real name because she had established herself as "not one of us" and was felt to represent a threat to safety in a space where women are expected to have the backs of other women. In this case, the group determined that the customary protections held sacred within the community (specifically, the prohibition against outing) no longer held for this particular fan.

The fan at Wiscon clearly diverged from established norms of the fannish community, but often fan-on-fan policing is carried out for much more subtle infractions. Fans respond to perceived external criticism with a tendency to reactive aggression whenever a fellow fan appears to be supplying evidence for outside conceptualization of fans as "crazy, fanatic, obsessed, perverse, or stalkers". When outside criticism does occur, fans react in markedly different ways. When the 2010 TV.com poll declared that *Supernatural* had the craziest fans, perverse enough to make someone want to "claw their eyes out", some fans proceeded to demonize other segments of the fandom for doing it wrong. Not all fans indulged in intrafandom wank, however. Some placed the blame on the (male) writer of the article instead of the fandom, taking him to task for his shaming and refusing to project their anxiety onto fellow fans.

Loving Too Much

The above article's discomfort with fandom seems connected to the level of emotional and psychological investment *Supernatural* fans display. One of the accusations most often thrown at fandom revolves around our obvious enthusiasm. Thus, another common fandom wank is policing fans who not only are doing it wrong, but are doing it too damn much!

From an evolutionary standpoint, we're built to become deeply connected to outside entities. The brain's mesolimbic system functions as a reinforcement circuit between the opiodergic system (which influences what we like) and the dopaminergic system (which influences what we want)—so when we like watching *Supernatural,* we want it again, and again, just as soon as it's available—if not sooner. The system developed to help us find our next meal, not our next fix of Sam and Dean, but obviously things other than food can trip the same circuits. Jeff Rudski, a psychologist who studies Harry Potter addiction, puts it like this: "For fanatics, liking may trigger an unusually high degree of wanting" (S. Booth 2011).

A similar idea in Goffman's (1963) social identity theory is that of "involvement"—defined as the degree to which individuals are cognitively and affectively engrossed in a situation or activity. We are all uncomfortable with displays of over-involvement. For example, rules of etiquette demand that we "eat relatively slowly" no matter how hungry we are, resisting the temptation to take food from our neighbor's plate and in general behave as if eating wasn't at that moment the most important thing in the world. We're expected to project detachment, even when we don't feel it (Gimlin 2010). Those who violate this expectation can expect censure, whether they're *Twilight* fans waiting in line for two days at Comic Con, or *Star Wars* fans who know all the specifications of a certain spacecraft, or *Supernatural* fans who watch twenty-two back-to-back episodes in DVD viewing marathons.

Reysen and Branscombe (2009) developed a measure of what they called "fanship" in an attempt to explore fans' investment in terms of emotion, time, energy and money. They found positive correlations between fanship and entitivaty (the perception that the in-group is a distinct entity), group identification, a positive social identity and collective happiness. In other words, merely thinking of yourself as part of an entitative fan group is associated with a positive emotional state that the researchers called "collective happiness". On the other hand, there also seems to be a connection between fans' emotional investment and aggression; sports fandom research has identified the level of team identification as an antecedent to fan aggression (End and Foster 2010; Wann, Daniel, M. Melnick, G.Russell, G and D. Pease 2001). More highly identified fans have been found to exhibit higher levels of both hostile and instrumental verbal aggression (Wann, Daniel, M. Melnick, G.Russell, G and D. Pease 2001), and to feel that aggression was more appropriate in a given situation. This may be because highly identified fans experience greater arousal and anxiety during a sporting event, and thus are more likely to impulsively act out. They also have more vested in the outcome, because of the connection to their self-esteem. In July 2011, the consequences of such emotional arousal and impulsivity proved lethal when a baseball fan plunged twenty feet headfirst to his death at a Texas Rangers game. The fan, there with his six-year-old son, had been attempting to catch a foul ball tossed into the stands. A few days later, another baseball fan escaped a similar fate when fellow fans grabbed his ankles and prevented his fall to the concrete stadium floor thirty feet below. Media fans exhibit similar lapses of good judgment and succumb to impulsive behavior when there is an opportunity to shore up self esteem and distinguish oneself in the fannish hierarchy.

We are admittedly not immune. On our first trip to Comic Con, we got up at 4 am to camp out on the sidewalk outside San Diego's convention center to secure front row seats at the *Supernatural* panel. We also ran— literally—the route we'd rehearsed the day before to be first to arrive at the panel's ballroom, deliberately ignoring the admonitions of dozens of Comic Con volunteers to "slow down!". When you want that baseball—or that front row seat at the feet of Eric Kripke, Jared Padalecki and Jensen Ackles—you just go for it. Consequences be damned.

In 2011, Comic Con recognized *Supernatural* as one of the most popular television shows, moving their panel from the smaller ballroom where it has been housed since 2005 into the cavernous Hall H, vindicating the Show's long-time fans. *Supernatural*'s success brings with it an even more intense identification, and an increased desire to ensure the continuation of that success, sometimes by policing other fans, and sometimes by attempting to influence the direction of the show itself. According to social identity theory (Tajfel, H. and Turner 1986), the ability to claim a positive social identity and bolster self-esteem is facilitated when your team (or show, or group, or film) is successful. The inability to distance oneself from failures of the fannish object makes the highly identified fan even more emotional about perceived outcomes. There are very real personal consequences for these fans, and they are therefore more than willing to fight for the outcome they desire (End and Foster 2010).   Sometimes that's the Eagles winning the Superbowl; sometimes that's Mulder and Scully finally kissing. Sometimes that's Misha Collins staying on *Supernatural*, or *Supernatural* just staying on the air.

Similar to the concept of reactive aggression, Wakefield and Wann (2006) suggest that it is not only identification which is related to verbal aggression, but also the level of what they call "fan dysfunction," the extent to which fans complain about various components of the fan experience and the degree to which they're confrontational. They developed the "Dysfunctional Fandom Scale" to measure this rather frightening sounding construct, and found that sports fans high on the scale were more likely to call in to radio talk shows to vent and to attend away games where they could confront other fans. This may be analogous to joining the *Fandom Wank* community, posting on the *spn_permanon* LJ community or frequenting the Stern Fan Network online. Wann interprets these results as the difference between trait aggression (dysfunctional fans) and state aggression (highly identified fans, caught up in the moment—perhaps, for example, cutting in front of other fans to race to a *Supernatural* panel at Comic Con.)

Fans' emotional investment in fandom is also high because, as we've discussed, fandom can be an important coping strategy, offering escape from stress and a sense of belonging and validation. The emotional significance can be seen in all types of fandom. Stephanie Booth describes the draw for a film fan "who's seen *Avatar* 23 times and still found time to post fanfiction online" as the desire to remain cocooned in the celluloid world, a welcome escape from a stressful real life. She also sees participating in online fan communities or dressing up as a favorite character and attending conventions as a way to sustain involvement in the movie and the emotional relief it provides. Similarly, Booth describes a music fan who has seen a pop group forty four times, noting that the intensity of emotion that the music evokes stokes the brain's pleasure center, like a temporary roller coaster with no severe consequences. The intensity of the feelings is highly reinforcing. In fact, concert-going fans in Booth's interviews described it as an almost religious experience—pounding heart, tears, no adequate words to explain their emotions.   So might a *Supernatural* convention first-time attendee, after finally getting up close and personal with Jared Padalecki in a photo op. We've observed fans burst into spontaneous tears after such an encounter, and many are rendered speechless by a celebrity's simple hello. Similarly, sports fans have been found to experience a vicarious sense of success as intense as the actual players when their team wins or plays well, with the same hormonal surges as the athletes and the same sense of optimism about life in general. (S. Booth 2011). Whether you're a fan of the Phillies, the Grateful Dead, or *Supernatural*, fandom is deeply, emotionally important.

The Ship Wars

One of the most emotionally intense disputes about "how to do fandom right" revolves around "ships". Originally called "relationshippers", shippers are fans who are invested in character A being in a relationship with character B. Sometimes the wank is about which pairing is the OTP (one true pairing). Is Dean destined to be with Sam, or with Castiel? How about Gabriel? Or should he have stayed with Lisa? In *Supernatural* fandom, wank about the right ships and the "one true pairing" brings up impassioned arguments. The most popular character pairing of Sam/Dean (*Supernatural*wiki, 2009) is not only a slash pairing, which kicks up wank even in 2011, but an incest pairing as well. Fans' discomfort with Wincest prompted a greater than usual amount of RPS (real person slash) in the fandom, pairing the two lead actors, Jared and Jensen, a coupling referred to as 'J2' or 'J-Squared.'

RPF made up half of the fanfiction in the annual bigbang fic challenge in 2011, according to the *Supernatural*wiki. This prompted the creation of icons wryly noting "*Supernatural*—where RPS is the moral high ground."

The addition of Misha Collins' character Castiel in Season 4 provided alternative slash pairings, both character (Destiel for Dean/Castiel and Sassy for Sam/Castiel) and RPS for Collins paired with just about anyone, attracting a whole new group of slashwriting fans to the Show. There is also a substantial amount of gen fanfiction and fanworks in SPN fandom which does not include any romantic pairings. Throughout fandom, fans have disagreed about whether writing any kind of fanfiction about real people is okay or yet another version of doing fandom wrong. Some of the most violent wank over RPF occurs between "tinhats" (fans who like to imagine a romantic relationship between two real-life and supposedly straight individuals, in which the term can mean either an insult or a tongue in cheek in-group reference) and "hets" (fans who like to imagine a romantic relationship between a male and female real person). Fans disagree about the appropriateness of all kinds of fanworks, with the threat of external judgment increasing the reactive aggression of fans who feel such fanworks may be contributing to negative views of fandom.

Shipping brings with it a strong emotional investment in seeing one's chosen OTP portrayed in the fandom universe, if not in canon or reality, so shipping-related wank tends to be highly emotional. One fan we interviewed wrote eloquently about her investment in her fannish OTP while maintaining a healthy grasp of the difference between reality and fiction. For a "tinhatter", whose fanfiction hypothesizes a romantic relationship between two real people, the distinction is critical. A fanfic writer in both the *Supernatural* and Adam Lambert fandoms, she explained it this way, after a virulent wank broke out pitting Adam Lambert/Tommy Ratliffe shippers against "Kradam" (Kris Allen/Adam Lambert) shippers.

Fig. 5-2

Rivers_bend: If I could ship in a less invested way, I would do it. As a writer... I inhabit the characters I'm writing about, whether they are the original characters from my novel, or Sam and Dean, or Adam and Tommy... I absolutely can tell the difference between my fantasy and actual Adam's reality....I do not, and can never, live Adam's actual reality. That is for him and his friends and family to live, and I have no place there. The ONLY reality related to him that I have access to is the one I can see. His persona. And that persona strongly informs the character I am writing. So when I (who takes the ONE and the TRUE parts of OTP very seriously) see or hear about that persona being with someone who isn't the other half of my pairing, it's genuinely painful to me….(so) It's up to me to filter and avoid places that are going to upset me. I am willing to take that responsibility and do that to the best of my ability. People should feel free to write about whatever they want to write about, however they want to write it, but they should not write with an expectation that everyone is going to want to read what they've written. We all have our own ways of interacting with fandom. (rivers_bend 2011).

Fig. 5-3

Fig. 5-4

Other fans stress the difference between real people and their public personas.

Poorchoices: I think it comes down to an issue of boundaries much more than an issue of investment? That is…it's entirely possible to ship, say, Sam/Dean *really hard*, and to be very invested in the relationship, and to not want them to be in other relationships. But once you start going out and telling people they're wrong if they like Dean/Castiel or Sam/Jessica, then you've crossed a line that, imo, should not be crossed. And I think with RPS it's a much--nastier problem? Because the bashing is of real people, and it escalates often in very gross ways.

Sulwen: I have always believed that writing about real people is no different than writing about fictional characters, and I'll tell you why. My characterization is based on public persona—what these people choose to show the world. I learned about Adam by reading his Twitter and watching interviews. That is all information freely given, and more than that, it's a role he plays, as we all do (and celebrities doubly so). That character is who I'm writing about. How could I possibly be writing about the "real" Adam? I don't know him. It would be more accurate to call him "an original character based on Adam." This is why it doesn't bother me a bit to read or write fanfiction about real life couples. I have no idea what they do with each other in private. If I want to take inspiration from what I do know about them, fine. I honestly don't believe it's any different from shipping two people who are not a couple or two fictional characters. However, I don't judge those who do find it unappealing. To each their own!

There is ongoing wank about whether or not writing fanfiction about real people, in any combination, is just plain wrong, with accusations ranging from disrespect to libel. The LiveJournal community *writingthewall* is devoted to meta discussion of the subject. Some fans question whether there's harm being done, and locate some of the discomfort in the internalized shame we explored in Chapter Three.

But what I find striking about this current set of events is to see how different, and indeed limited, the discussion of RP fic is in media fandom circles around LJ/DW compared to what it's like outside these boundaries. …As far as the general public is concerned, neither the media format, nor the distinction between fictional and real, nor even the idea of commercial vs. non-commercial seems to matter much. For that matter, real people make appearances in fiction all the time, whether they're celebrities or not. ….Media fandom writers seem to be surprisingly inhibited on this issue for reasons which don't seem to connect to what's being done outside its boundaries….. we tell stories about real people all the time, it is an equally longstanding human impulse. Sometimes it's called gossip, sometimes it's called fanfic, sometimes it's called published fiction (or art), and sometimes it's called a fictional biography. (With RPF) where is the actual harm being caused? Certainly the average celebrity gets much more hurtful, damaging things said about them, sometimes directly to their face, than ever appears in fanfic which, on the whole, tends to depict them as much more likable, and possibly interesting, people than they actually are (and certainly far better endowed)....I think the fans' perception of a celebrity needing protection from his/her fans' imagination seems a projection of fans' own deep discomfort in seeing their desires out in the open for public consumption (yourlibrarian: 2011).

Drawing the Line

When it comes to shipping and wank about who it is acceptable to include in fanworks and who is out of bounds, especially when fanworks are not G-rated, research on online sexual activity (OSA) may provide some insight into why the investment is so strong. OSA is broadly defined as the use of the internet for any activity (text, audio, or graphics) that involves sexuality, which would seem to include a significant proportion of fanworks that feature someone's OTP. OSA research has tended towards the overly pathologizing, but nevertheless may provide a useful lens through which to understand fans' emotional investment in their OTPs and in writing or depicting certain situations in fanworks. As discussed in the previous chapter, one of the reasons fans are deeply invested in reading and writing about certain specific experiences is to work through their own problematic self-narratives. The investment in doing so is at least partially tied to the need for emotional expression and reworking of past trauma. However, as we've noted, there are numerous reasons why fans produce and consume fanfiction and fanworks, some of which have more to do with finding pleasure than reducing pain, though both motivations are shaped by past experience.

In a widely referenced examination of OSA (Cooper, A., D. Delmonico, E. Griffin-Shelley, E. and Mathy 2004), the authors identify a common "obsessive" pattern as the desire to find the perfect image, story or erotic material that fulfills a favorite fantasy. Called "lovemaps", these internal maps guide our sexual interest, arousal and behavior. We're motivated to seek out depictions of our individual lovemaps, and finding them allows a pleasurable escape from stress that is both helpful and healthy in moderation. However, the desire to find our relevant texts suggests a reason for the intense frustration fans feel when they can't find whatever constitutes their particular lovemap. Hence the propensity of both ship wars and kink memes.

But what about the other side of the wank? If some fans are invested in seeing their lovemaps depicted or finding and creating fanworks to rework their narratives, why are other fans equally invested in stopping them? We've already noted the defensive need to police the group, censuring members who step out of role or are perceived as making the group look bad. Sometimes this is the motivation for wank, as one group of fans defines another as out of role and attempts to force them out of fandom. The created out-group could be Sam!Girls instead of Dean!Girls, or anti-fans instead of affirmational fans, or any other perceived division. When the cultural prohibitions around sex are added to the mix, the wank can become even more intense, and research offers some suggestions about why. Discovering lovemaps that are not congruent with one's own can increase feelings of anxiety and discomfort, especially if what one researcher calls "self-defined lovemap inappropriate sexual arousal" occurs (Noonan 1998). We all have more aggressive, violent and socially unconventional impulses which we're socially constrained to split off or disown, but which continue to exist, and exert an unconscious influence. If, for example, a fan inadvertently reads fanfiction that is both disturbing and arousing, the level of anxiety created can lead to reactive aggression when the individual feels threatened by the content—homosexual, heterosexual, sadomasochistic, pedophilic, or any imagery or idea that is in conflict with the person's perception of their sexual persona (Leiblum 2001). Thus, policing the boundaries of fandom can also mean constraining the topics that can be discussed, vidded, written or otherwise artistically rendered. Anyone straying outside the normative topics (according to the particular fan policing them) is fair game for wank. The reaction at times appears as a sort of "moral panic" that can lead to popular calls for greater outside control over online activity and a more repressive sexual climate online.

In 2011 alone, there were multiple outbreaks of wank in *Supernatural* fandom over where the boundaries should be set as far as what fans can write, draw, vid or request. The LJ community *blindfold_spn* hosted its fifth annual anonymous kink meme, where fans leave anonymous prompts for fic they want written, and other fans anonymously fill them. The comm's rules include "no judging of anyone's kinks" and "no kinks are prohibited." Nevertheless, several prompts were objectionable enough to inspire a wave of protest throughout the *Supernatural* fandom. Perhaps that was the anonymous poster's intention—"trolling" to create wank and then enjoy the resulting kerfluffle. Or the poster may have been an outsider attempting to incite a moral panic and inspire a call for censorship; fans did indeed respond to the more out-there posts with demands of the mods to delete them. At the same time, the wank contributed to an increase in fan shame and fan defensiveness, as fans argued among themselves about what should and should not be allowed within the wider fan community. As we've discussed, the post may also have been an attempt to work through past trauma by having someone write out a fictionalized version of a similar instance of abuse. Without context or explanation, however, there can be a disconnect between the motivation (conscious and unconscious) of a fan requesting or producing such a fanwork, and the perception of others as to its meaning and its delineation of fantasy and reality (Bivona and Critelli 2009). There was no way to know whether the post was intended to cause drama, invite censorship, exact revenge, or work through the individual's own past abuse.

A similar outbreak of wank happened at the *spnkink-meme* community a month later, again lining up fan practices as a source of shame on one side and a source of healing on the other. Once again, motivations were up for interpretation. Not surprisingly, much of this wank occurs around online communities specifically designed as fan spaces which welcome sexually explicit, kinky or dark fic. In late 2011, a fan posted that a prompt that included references to abuse and an underage real life person was "sickening and exploitative," going so far as to argue that anyone who thought otherwise was likely a real-life pedophile. The argument was passionate on both sides. Some members agreed that the prompt should be deleted; other fans protested, citing the therapeutic value of fanfiction for them as survivors of abuse, as discussed in the previous chapter. (All references here are anonymous, as the community is now locked.)

> Anon: You are making the ugly accusation that everyone who reads or writes underage fic is a paedophile, and that everyone who reads or writes the kink identifies with the abuser not the abused. There are two people on this post alone who talk about their own past and how these fics are therapeutic for them. And there's another with the exact opposite experience. They all have the same right to deal with their experiences in the way that works best for them, and demonizing people for their kinks and coping mechanisms is not the way to go. You keep trying to make this an issue where anyone who doesn't agree with you is somehow morally bankrupt and that they don't care about real life abuses. That's blatant emotional manipulation.

> Anon: Nobody in this post has ever said anything about condoning real life abuse, and for you to imply that survivors writing to cope with their abuse is some sort of slippery slope that will lead them to start IRL abuse is beyond the pale.

> Anon: So you sympathise with survivors but think it's perfectly okay to call them paedophiles and villify then for their chosen method of coping. They aren't victimising anybody by writing fictional stories on the internet.

Anon: You don't have the right to tell survivors that they shouldn't use fic (which causes harm to nobody) to explore their own issues. You seem to think you have the right to tell them to stop. For you to bring up actual physical abuse and imply that anyone, anywhere on this post suggests that child abuse should ever be condoned is completely wrong.

Anon: You do not get to police how survivors choose to deal with what happened to them. You can complain if it's posted unwarned or in an inappropriate place, you can hate that it exists and want nothing to do with it; but you don't get to impose your personal moral outrage on fandom as a whole.

Other fans, interpreting the purpose of the prompt as condoning abuse, were understandably shaken as survivors themselves.

Anon: It makes me sick to support people that actually condone what happened to me or any number of other kids out there. Shut them out, do not ever give them a place to indulge. It may be just a fanfic prompt now, just theory, but there is always the possibility for these people to make the step into reality. *No child ever wants to be touched! No child ever wants anything like what is asked for in some of these prompts! That is no Kink, that is sick!*

Still other fans, also survivors, interpreted the purpose of the prompt as motivated by the opposite of condoning abuse, and thus had wildly divergent—and equally impassioned—arguments for allowing such prompts and fills.

Anon: Also the opinion of a child abuse victim: You're not the only one who's lived through hell. And as someone who's been there, I'm not going to argue with your way to deal with it. Everyone deals with trauma differently, that's part of being human. But I want that section to stay. It is not the same as actual child abuse. Real life is uglier. And because of that, it's plain and clear it's just fiction. Fiction about something ugly, but still just (thankfully) fiction. And for me, I use that fiction to deal with what I lived through. To realise that what I grew up thinking wasn't accurate, wasn't what really happened. That no matter what they said, or what I believed, it was not ever even the slightest bit ok. I didn't understand as a child. (confusing, miserable, etc) But it helps me to come to grips with things as an adult. And to, very slowly, heal as I unravel the lies and the hurt and the sheer nightmare of it all.

Anon: It IS NOT the same as what either of us lived through. There are no real life children with futures and feelings being damaged by this. It's fiction. And for me, it's the only way I can face any of it, anything else is just too real. And when something triggers, I can close the window and go read fluff for hours until I calm down.

> Anon: Former abuse victim myself: I'm a real life incest survivor and I write in the underage section. It helps me. I don't know why but writing things like that is therapeutic.

Some fans viewed the created stories of fictional abuse, often written by someone who has actually experienced it as a survivor, as serving an additional purpose—remedying misconceptions that survivors encounter far too often from people who don't understand. The persistent sense of being "other" discussed in the previous chapter is in part created by this disconnect.

> Anon: Plus I know that fics like these make other people realise how much of a big deal it is to try and recover from. Which creates more support for the survivors. And that means there's less of those idiots who say "that was ____ years ago, why can't you just *get over it* already..." I don't know about you, but I hate it when people say shit like that because they just don't get it, they have no idea how much it is to try and deal with. So I see it as a force for good. You see it as something you can't deal with. But I don't think that means it should be deleted.

The original poster also expressed a concern that the real people being written about (especially those who were teenagers) could potentially discover disturbing fanfiction about themselves and be injured by it, to the point where their lives might be at risk, which seems to echo the research on the inadvertent discovery of incongruent lovemaps. Some fans agreed.

> Anon: Dean and Sam is one thing, RPS is another, I even feel the adult actors should be protected from underage prompts. Characters are one thing, real people is another.

Predictably, other fans didn't.

> Anon: Protected from what? From people imagining things that have never happened to them, in an alternate reality, writing things they've never said, to people they've never felt anything about, doing things they've never done? Not only can that concern be raised about everything fanfic. But more importantly, HOW does it "harm" them? It doesn't affect their real relationships. It doesn't mean they have to reenact anything. Everyone knows it's fiction, so they don't have to issue press statements saying "I have never been a spy. I have never blown up a bagel shop. And when I was fifteen, I did not sleep with my co-star (whom I didn't meet in reality until I was twenty-something) in my basketball cross-country tournament and also I never played basketball and I didn't grow up in Chicago and I've never had erectile dysfunction, polio, autism, or taken weed or cooked naked or gone to half the colleges in the USA. I do not have a twin, I was

not adopted, I have never been in foster care. I am not gay, bi, trans, asexual, or intersexed. I only ride horses from the top. I am not a secret billionaire. I do not own a jet, a villa in Italy or a..." I think you get the point. **If we thought it was real, we'd be labeling it "news."**

One fan seemed to intuit the research on incongruent lovemaps.

Anon: I find the arguments for "protecting them" to be full of bs. It's more like users who want to be "protected" from having to see something they don't like. Use some self-control and avoid what you don't like.

Threats to report the entire comm to LJ Abuse followed, which threatened the existence of the community itself. Eventually the beleaguered mod changed the rules to disallow the use of fellow fandom people and real underage people (under 18) in prompts.

In 2011's *angstbigbang* multifandom challenge, the mods decided to disallow any fanfiction about real people, "out of respect for the actors"(angstbigbang 2011). This caused a great deal of wank, since the challenge had already been running for a month welcoming "all fandoms" and then changed the rules on the first day of signups. One fan complained.

This is not 1990 when RPF was still being written with penlights in closets and posted under lock and key due to shame. So much disrespecting to do, so little time. I tell you, we need more hours in a day to make these celebs miserable.

A similar outbreak of wank also occurred on the *spn-hardcore* LJ community in late 2011, after a troll (an outsider looking to cause wank) posted:

This is not a threat, just a notice. I'll be reporting anyone who posts an entry to your community. Then I'll follow the link to their personal journal and report them there. I guess we'll see how long it takes for LJ to take action.

Community members protested the censorship of fiction writing.

If there's one thing I hate when it comes to writing, it's people who try to put a cap on what someone should be able to/not to jot down. Fictional writing and/or pictures DOES NOT equal real life and I hate how folks try to put the two together. If that's the case, any violent book or movie should be considered illegal and outlawed because going by their logic, it encourages everyone to replicate it in real life.

The community also eventually disallowed any reference to underage sexual contact, and went "members only" soon after. (Above posts therefore included here with names withheld.)

The Good Side

Fandom's invitation to share our genuine experience, including exposing our sexuality and fantasies, can be validating, normalizing and healing—but can also leave us vulnerable. Wank, however, is not all bad. Stepping away from our focus on individual transformation for a moment to revisit the transformative potential of fandom on a broader societal level, it's clear that wank results in discussion which can focus attention on important real world problems. Not only do fanworks explore the experience of marginalized or stigmatized people, which can increase empathy and create more positive attitudes (Batson, C., M. Polycarpou, E. Harmon-Jones, H. Imhoff, E. Mitchener, L. Bednar, T. Klein and Highberger 1997), but fannish discussion about how these issues are explored contributes to the cultural dialogue by challenging norms related to racism, misogyny, ableism, homophobia, and other social problems. Fans may disagree (often loudly) about what these norms should be, but discussion has the potential to be more transformative than silence. Fandom wank focused inwards creates a constant interrogation of our own fannish practices and their broader implications. For example, a recent metafandom discussion questioned the potentially transformative and political power of queering tv via slash. Does the time honored practice of seeing shows like *Supernatural* through "slash goggles"and magnifying every instance of perceived slashy subtext let TPTB off the hook for not including overt representations of glbt characters in canon? Is it in fact itself a potentially harmful and homophobic practice?

We'll revisit *Supernatural*'s interaction with its fans, including the propensity for canon and real-life queer subtext, in the next two chapters, but this sort of discussion is part of what fans value, and part of the transformative nature of fandom. In an unpublished online survey by a Hunter College grad student in 2011, fans talked about what they've gotten from fandom. Several fans referred to Race!Fail 2009, a sweeping outbreak of fandom wank that began with a work of *Supernatural* fanfiction that some fans found racist. The online exchange grew into a deep examination of racism in fandom that involved thousands of responses--many quite angry--and led fans of color to define their expectations for respect as well as the boundaries of their responsibility for challenging racism. Respondents who self-identified as straight and white said that such fandom wank had helped them recognize their own privilege. As one fan wrote, "Fandom has taught me to be less of an idiot" (Stern 2011).

Kathryn Dunlap and Carissa Wolf analyzed the Fandom Wank community itself in their essay on "Fans Behaving Badly" (2010), identifying a positive function in what at first glance seems like people going out of their way to be mean to other people. They argue that the "wankas" engage in a level of critical textual analysis that is reminiscent of Hills' concept of the fan-as-intellectual (2002), and challenge the forced dualism of "good" and "bad" fan practices.

In the *metafandom* community, kalichan argued for the continued existence of open dialogue in fandom, including criticism—and wank.

> We talk a lot about 'safe' spaces here in internet fandom, on both sides of this argument. I don't believe there is, or can be any such thing, although maybe the beauty is in the effort to make them so.... What I want to suggest, however, is that safety is, perhaps, overrated. I don't mean that we shouldn't fight the wrong things in the world; I don't mean that folks like you and me, who've been marginalized in whatever ways, should silently consent to injustice, or that folks (also like you and me) who have privilege, shouldn't continually strive to be better. The opposite, in fact. What I think I am trying to say is that the world I want to live in is filled with both peril and enchantment. To discard one, is to discard the other. Because......the things you love will hurt you......and you can fight the evil in the things you love and still never stop loving them (kalichan 2010).

In the next chapter, we'll examine the source of some of that peril and enchantment, as fans juggle their desire for a safe space with the increasing openness that exists between fandom and the creative side—especially on *Supernatural.*

CHAPTER SIX

AND THE (FOURTH) WALLS
COME TUMBLING DOWN

At the turn of millennium, we were just discovering the joys of online fandom and writing fanfiction. At the time, our obsessions ran more toward bands than television shows, so much of our fiction writing featured members of our favorites, the relatively obscure bands Placebo and HIM. Our friend and fannish enabler Laura (who would later be responsible for luring us into Supernatural) called one day in a panic. She had just gotten an email out of the blue from the keyboard player in HIM, a talented young man named Juska. He was writing to say he'd just finished reading a piece of fanfiction she'd written and posted online about the band, and wanted to compliment her on her research skills and comprehensive knowledge of the band and its music. "You got everything right," he exclaimed, then added, "Well, except the sex part."

Laura didn't stop blushing for weeks—the NC17 story portrayed Juska and band frontman Ville Valo as lovers.

Discussions of reciprocal relationships between fans and producers tend to portray these interactions as one way, even when stressing the newly acknowledged power of fans to affect cultural production. Fans ask and either receive (in the Utopian construction) or are denied by TPTB. The power dynamic is almost always top down, one of the reasons for the now traditional view of fandom as subversive in order to empower the "othered" groups that are popularly figured as making up media fandom. As a result, much of the focus of fan studies has been on what happens when fans appropriate the role of the producer, taking media properties and using them to create fan fiction, fan art and videos. In "Cultural Outlaws" Costello and Moore, writing in the wake of Henry Jenkins' *Convergence Culture,* say that "Internet technologies have empowered . . . fans to more effectively organize en masse as resistors and shapers of commercial television narratives," (2007, 124) an assumption that is confirmed by more than one showrunner. J. J. Abrams, Russell T. Davies and Joss Whedon, among others, have made no secret of how plugged into their fandoms they are, often citing their own status as fanboys in order to legitimize their online presence.

As fans have become more public with their opinions, producers have become increasingly active online, going to the source to find out what fans think about particular episodes, story arcs, and characters.   The assumption is that everyone wins when creators and fans work together, and that fans welcome the give and take of this reciprocal relationship.

But do they?

Before looking at how *Supernatural* has nearly erased the fourth wall entirely in its seven seasons on the air, it's important to understand how salient—and real—this otherwise symbolic division between audience and actors/producers is to fans. In this chapter, we'll explore the construction and maintenance of the fourth wall from the fan side, and fannish reaction when the creative side doesn't hold up their end of the "don't ask don't tell" rule. In the next chapter, we'll hear directly from the other side, as *Supernatural*'s actors, writers and showrunners share their views of fans, fanworks, and the reciprocal relationship.

Breaking the First Rule of Fandom

However much fan practices are celebrated within fandom (and within academia), many fans do not want those practices noticed—not by producers, or actors, or the mainstream media. Fans who bring certain fan activities to the attention of actors, writers and showrunners are sanctioned within fandom.   Fan shame is intensified when anyone outside the perceived safe space of fandom is allowed a glimpse inside. Nevertheless, the topic of fanfiction was raised at many of the early conventions. At 2007's Fangoria, a fan prefaced her question to Jared Padalecki with the apologetic, "I have the doom question, the fanfic question." Padalecki gave a serious "okay" and a serious answer as well. He had been given some fanfiction to read (fandom lore holds that it was beloved director Kim Manners who introduced the boys to fanfic) and was impressed by the quality. At 2008's Eyecon, Padalecki was asked specifically about Wincest. He managed to give a diplomatic answer without endorsing writing about fictional incest: "With fanfiction and RPGs (role playing games), it's like… everyone's taking part in *Supernatural* and they're not just watching it.…It's a great learning tool, and exploring tool, to explore this world. So I'm supportive."

Fandom was not reassured. The boundary between fans and the creative side varies from ironclad to fluid, but fans tend to prefer impermeability and to police the boundary diligently. In an LJ discussion of "fandom to celebrity interaction," fans posted their thoughts in language that is notable for its passionate—and violent—wording (bomb, suicide, assaulted).

> Adellyna: I, in fact, believe that the wall between fandom and the objects of fandom should be not invisible but rather *solid*. I want my fandom experience to take place in a fucking *bomb shelter*. Like, I want two layers of cement block packed with concrete, bricked, over, and then maybe, like, drywalled and wallpapered on the inside.
> Sunshinepill: I would commit ritualistic suicide before actually bringing up to any of the objects of my fannish adoration any of the things I've written about them.
> Overloved: It kills my fandom boner to think about the celebrities being assaulted with fandom (adellyna 2008).

Amanda Straw (2009), in an ethnographic study of the 2009 Creation *Supernatural* convention in New Jersey, described an incident of fan boundary breaking, situating the event in the context of conventions as contemporary sites of carnival. In such a view, events like a convention Q&A are "prestaged encounters" at which fans can interact directly with celebrities but cannot do so at will, and their requests must fit within tightly orchestrated limits. Fans, however, are not always aware of what those limits are. We happened to be there that day too, as a girl with a "Sam/Dean – gay love can save the day" tee shirt and green hair asked actor Richard Speight Jr. "What do you think of the Wincest?" There was a split second pause, during which audience members stared in horror at seatmates or at the fan, and then the room as a whole booed her loudly. Richard responded diplomatically, "I'm gonna say I'm not for it. Call me square, but incest is not my bag. Sorry." Sheepishly, the fan thanked him and scurried back to her seat.

According to Straw, actions considered normal and acceptable within the confines of online fannish space, are nevertheless clearly not acceptable outside in the "real world." Indeed, she describes the lack of clarity in boundaries between carnival space and real life as "dangerous" and disrespectful to the actor. While Straw wants to excuse the fan for her "lapse in judgment," she seems to share the "mundane" view of "free, unfettered displays of sexual expression" as abnormal and shameful, and above all, as something which should be kept private—in other words, secret.

Our own perspective on the occurrence is colored by a discussion with Richard Speight shortly after his Q&A. While he did he have to think for a bit about how to negotiate a very public answer, Speight was far from feeling disrespected or in need of protection—the fandom's projection of what he surely "must" be feeling. The green haired fan, on the other hand, might have. We followed her into the bathroom after the Q&A, where she was visibly upset and near tears. She was also rather young and new to fandom and its confusing distinction between online and "real life" rules, and genuinely shocked at the fan reaction to her question. We reassured her that Speight, at least, was not upset with her. Fandom, however, was another matter.

Missyjack, mod of the Superwiki, relates fandom's emotional reaction to the fan shame we've previously discussed.

> Fans have always felt some anxiety around the idea of fannish works being noticed by the original creators. On the one hand, some fans see the works as tributes to the source material, and many creators feel the same way. The gift of a fan creation to an actor or showrunner is an indication of how much the source material is valued and appreciated, and also often embodies a wish for approval. Yet some fans have wished to keep these works hidden, for both legal and cultural reasons. Many fans still hold the opinion that we do what we do for our enjoyment and it is not something to be shared outside of fandom, and particularly not with TPTB. Many people who are active in fandom do not share their activities with friends or family because of the negative stereotypes that persist about fandom. Of course, a lot of the pearl clutching reaction is due to people's own internalized shame at what they do (missyjack 2010).

Fans' discomfort with the creative side knowing about fanworks is particularly strong when the fanfiction is RPF and RPS, which can result in exposure to the real people whose personas inhabit the stories. As discussed in the previous chapters, conflict about whether writing fanfiction about real people is acceptable or shameful is a common source of wank. In the LJ *writingthewall* meta community, created expressly for the purpose of discussing the ethics of writing RPF, the discussion is more academic but still invested with emotion. Instead of debating the acceptability of writing about real people as a question in itself, some fans place the boundary between okay/not okay as dependent on the integrity of the fourth wall.

> RPF, I believe, when the fourth wall is kept entirely intact, is harmless. That wall is what keeps it from being aggressive and hurtful, and it's why we keep the wall in such high regard (silver_spotted 2010).

Fig. 6-1: Breaking the "First Rule of Fandom"

The *femslash_awards* in 2010 on LiveJournal disallowed RPF completely, with the mods stating that "we believe it is one thing to bend fictional characters to our imaginations, but another matter entirely when we begin to incorporate the lives of real people. It is our feeling that this becomes an issue of invasion of privacy for the actresses portrayed, and borders on the category of stalking". Fans responded with some confusion.

> Lady_amorika: I absolutely respect the fourth wall and would never violate the space of another person. I'm confused as to how I am stalking or violating someone I have never met, nor have I attempted to, nor have I attempted to cause any problems in their lives. In the case of people I have met, I find that my fannish interaction hasn't impacted my ability to be a respectful fan AT ALL.
>
> Seedyapartment: I think talking in a blog or a newspaper about an in-the-closet celebrity being gay has far more potential for harm than writing RPF about them being gay. So that in itself fails as an argument for RPF specifically being an aggressive/harmful act.

Outside fandom, people seem to worry a lot less about the possibility of offending a celebrity who might stumble across a fan's attempts at homage. Christopher Schulz, who also puts out Pinups Magazine, recently published an art book titled *Seth*, full of drawings of a nude man who looks remarkably similar to actor Seth Rogen. In an interview with New York Press (in which the author repeatedly refers to the book as fanfiction, though there seem to be no words in it at all), Schulz took pains to avoid saying that the drawings were actually of the actor, noting that he never used a last name, but allowed that "maybe he'll find out, I imagine. I'm sure someone he knows will stumble upon it and share it with him." He then proceeded to throw an open-to-the-public book launch party. Clearly no shame here. On the contrary, Schulz seems to be looking forward to Rogen's reaction (Winans 2010).

Real people make appearances in mainstream published fiction all the time. Our original pre-teen crush, David Cassidy, figures prominently in Allison Pearson's new book, *I Think I Love You*. Most likely, Mr. Cassidy will get a chance to read about himself, and perhaps be glad for the publicity. And way back in 1942, two volumes of what can only be described as "Hollywood RPF" were published, *Ginger Rogers and the Riddle of the Scarlet Cloak* by Lela E. Rogers and *Betty Grable and the House with the Iron Shutters* by Kathryn Heisenfelt (my_daroga 2010).

When it comes to fans' appropriation of texts and characters, some professional authors have recently come out in support of fanworks, and recognized their potential. In an interview for *International Business Times*, children's book author MG Harris encourages both fans and authors to explore the creative transformation of original fiction stories, saying that "Authors might want to noodle around there too. And it doesn't have to detract from the creativity of fandom. Some fans enjoy defining a text by their own reading." Harris confides that she herself began her writing career as a "textual poacher" in the 90s, publishing the first online zine of fanfiction for the much-slashed television show *Blake's 7*. "Without the literary multi-gym of fan fiction, I would probably never have become a published author. So I'm in favor of the fan-created world. Long may it live!" (Colby 2011).

Some of the most successful creators and showrunners are fessing up to getting their start with writing fanfiction. On the other hand, in Lev Grossman's *Time Magazine* article about fanfiction—one of the first mainstream articles to actually speak to fans and present a balanced analysis—he notes that creators are sharply divided on the subject. JK Rowling and Stephanie Meyer have given fanfic their blessing, acknowledging its impact as viral marketing for their work. On the other hand, other writers see it as a violation of both copyright law and their emotional investment in their own characters (Grossman 2011). Whether the open acknowledgement in various public forums that fanfiction isn't universally derided will eventually result in decreased fan shame and increased fan openness remains to be seen.

The Powers That Were and the Powers That Be

The views of aca-fans about just how reciprocal the relationship between fans and the creative side should be are as divergent as fandom's. In Henry Jenkins' online blog *Confessions of an Aca-Fan*, Kristina Busse, Flourish Klink and Nancy Baym recently debated the risks and benefits of a closer relationship between fandom, the creative side and TPTB.

> Busse: For me fandom is something that isn't connected to production and industry. As a fan I don't want to engage directly with actors/writers/directors, and as an academic, I don't care about that side either. I know it's an important area, and I'm very happy that we have good and smart people explaining and representing fandom, but to me fandom is mostly about what we as fans do. I'm passionately and hopelessly in transformational fandom, and I am interested in tracking and analyzing what fans do on their own rather than how fans interact with the industry.
> Klink: Right around the time that I was getting involved with fandom, my friends began getting cease and desist letters about their *Harry Potter* fanfiction - this would be around 1999 or 2000. Partially, I think, because *Harry Potter* was a more or less "feral fandom," people resisted rather than going underground—and it worked. So, on a personal level, I've never experienced fandom as something separate from industry; it was always very clear that industry knew about us, cared about what we did, and often misunderstood us.
> Baym: As fans we are constantly being viewed as ATM machines— "let's connect so we can monetize you!"—and I believe that the sustainability and long term future of the entertainment industries relies on a new kind of engagement with fans that must be informed both by those within fandom and by academic research (Jenkins 2011).

Baym interviewed thirty one musical performers about the impact of social media. Most felt an increased pressure to engage in "direct, proactive and increasingly interpersonal modes of interaction with fans" and felt it was important to show fans that you care. The performers mentioned fans as a source of support and instant feedback on new music and performances. They spoke about the powerful experience of learning that their music had helped someone deal with tragedy, and how this validated their work. They also mentioned drawbacks to this immediacy, one of which is the challenge for both fans and celebrities of keeping up with which social media platforms to use (Myspace? What's that?) Some set Google alerts so they know how and when they're being discussed on the internet; others avoid seeing anything about themselves. Facebook's 5000 friend limit has already snagged many on the creative side, including SPN's Jim Beaver, leaving him with the uncomfortable task of trying to decide who to friend and who to defriend. Decisions about how to balance divulging information and maintaining mystique are also challenging. As one musician Baym interviewed said, "You want to create an exciting experience of being a fan for your audience. And that involves both presenting and concealing information in interesting and surprising ways that make it fun to follow you, fun to wonder what you're up to or whatever…" (2011). In the next chapter, some of the *Supernatural* actors share similar concerns about how to manage the amount of information they want to divulge.

Baym agrees with fans who want the fourth wall to remain ironclad when it comes to fanfiction, and takes issue with RPF. She goes so far as to say that fans have a responsibility to listen to the voices of the industry and remember that actors, musicians and writers are "real people with real feelings". Busse, on the other hand, locates at least part of that responsibility on the creative side—don't Google yourself if you don't want to find out what's out there. She also connects the problem to violations of the first rule of fandom, placing part of the blame on fannish fourth-wall breakers.

> Busse: I think that fans behaving inappropriately is the issue and, just maybe, celebrities connecting to fans in likewise too intimate ways…. I blame a celebrity culture and a fan/industry intersection that makes it seem OK to erode boundaries that I am perfectly happy and comfortable keeping up (Jenkins 2011).

But keeping up boundaries may not be as easy as it once was. Both so-called celebrity culture and new forms of technology have changed the way we all relate to one another, from the public sharing of personal information and redefining of the word "friend" on Facebook to the immediacy of texting to the pseudo-intimacy of Twitter. The internet itself has changed modes of interaction between creator and audience in multiple ways. The entertainment industry historically related to their audience in terms of economic (market) exchange, while fans have related in terms of social (gift) exchange. But the internet has enabled fans to interact directly with the creative side in sometimes unexpected ways.

Some of this change has been driven not just by a cultural shift, but by the profit motive—the realization by TPTB that the production of fan works is a sign of an engaged viewer, one who will consume your product (and that of your advertisers). As a result TPTB are rethinking how they work, increasingly moving toward models of audience engagement that integrate social and economic exchange.

One of the ways by which TPTB are attempting to engage their audience is by capitalizing on fans' fascination with slash, gay subtext, and so-called "bromance", both in corporate advertisements and in interviews. GarlandGrey wrote in *Bitch Magazine* that he'd noticed a trend in Tumblr posts about the last *Harry Potter* film that joked about the three male leads being secretly gay for one another. Grey commented that "The idea isn't original to them, of course. The male leads of any science fiction or fantasy epic will be paired off in the minds of their fandom." (*Supernatural*'s Sam and Dean and Jared and Jensen included.) What's changed is the willingness of TPTB and the celebrities involved to jump on board and use it to their advantage. TBS ran an advertisement for a *Lord of the Rings* film with the song "Secret Lovers" as the background for Frodo and Sam. The BBC's *Sherlock Holmes* came close to overtly suggesting that the Holmes/Watson pairing is canon. Misfits utilized the fandom AU trope to allow male characters Nathan and Simon to share a steamy onscreen kiss, but only because one of the men has been zapped with a love potion tattoo, thus throwing a bone to the show's slash fandom. Actor Rupert Grint alluded to being slashed with another actor by wearing an "I Heart Tom Felton" tee shirt to a film premiere. Felton, Grey notes, has been the most willing to joke about being in love with the other *Harry Potter* actors. He plays a relatively minor character in the films, but has a disproportionately large fan following, which Grey suggests is due to his interaction with fans and especially his teasing them that the slash narrative might be the real one.

These and other examples "highlight how much of the cultural bandwidth straight men playing gay takes up, and how lucatrive being ambiguously heteroflexible can be in securing more of the fandom's attention," Grey says. He also asks a question that fandom debates regularly—why can't we have legitimate queer couplings in canon, instead of manufacturing them for ourselves and hoping for crumbs from actors and producers?

Commenters to Grey's article agreed. Not surprisingly, they also mentioned SPN.

BruisePristine: I do definitely think that some creators/actors are perfectly happy to court slash audiences in a limited way, and they're able to because throwing the audience a bone often comes in the form of joking about the male leads being gay/acting like a couple, which mainstream audiences (the ones raised on the comedic "bromances" of Boy Meets World, Scrubs, and Friends) are happy to accept because it is a joke in a way that they wouldn't accept a legitimate queer coupling.... friendships between men are "problematized" by the possibility that they could be a gay couple as opposed to close but platonic friends, and "problems" often lead to comedy.

Sharilyn: If you really want to complicate matters, there's also "*Supernatural*," which has spawned tons of slashy fics featuring real person slash about the leads, Jared and Jensen, as well as the 'wincest' fics between the characters they play, Sam and Dean, who happen to be brothers; so a bit of incest gets thrown into that mix, as well. There is also the popular slash pairing on the show of the character Dean with an angel, Castiel, and if you add in all the other slashy pairings between various and sundry male-embodied angels and demons on the show, "*Supernatural*' has to be one of the 'slashiest' tv shows out there right now. Even Bobby, the brothers' grizzled hunter friend, gets into the game when he's forced to kiss Crowley, a male demon, on the mouth to seal a deal between them. That scene caused much merriment and uproar in the "*Supernatural*" community when the episode featuring it aired (GarlandGrey 2011).

In fact, SPN has provided so much gay subtext and so many canon nods, that it would take an entire chapter to cover them all. The intimate relationship between the brothers is what draws fans of all genres to the show. That slash sexualizes that intimacy is based in both the show's canon subtext and the desire of slash writers to create as much intimacy as possible between the brothers. Writer/producer (now showrunner) Sera Gamble has referred to the show as "The Epic Love Story of Sam and Dean" (Borsolino 2006), inviting fanfiction which can rely on that bond as both a happy ending and the personification of the writer's reworked narrative. Catherine Tosenberger, in her article "The epic love story of Sam and Dean: Supernatural, queer readings, and the romance of incestuous fan fiction", argues that "Wincest is best understood not as a perverse oppositional resistance to a heterosexual, nonincestuous show, but an expression of readings that are suggested and supported by the text itself" (2008). As Camille Bacon-Smith put it, "Many women perceive a deep and loving relationship between characters on the screen because series creators put it there" (1992, 234).

Fig. 6-2

The affectionate real-life friendship the two leads share has provided plenty of subtext as well, and the raw material for fanvids and tumblr gifs. Ackles and Padalecki have jokingly acknowledged fandom's construction of their relationship as romantic, accusing each other of having crushes in video interviews, slapping each other's butts for gag reels, and pretending to almost kiss several times when the cameras were rolling. They have also acknowledged the fans' desire for some queering of canon. In a late 2011 interview for MTV, the actors were asked, what can fans really get excited about on Season 7? Padalecki replied, "Man on man." Ackles quickly responded with a surprised grin and a "Woah woah, that's a different show apparently."

The actors' willingness to engage the fans directly is a relatively recent development. Nancy Baym, in her examination of the evolution of performer-audience relations in the age of social media, finds that for many entertainers, what used to be clearly delineated boundaries have loosened, at times leaving relationships with fans resembling ordinary friendships. Celebrities used to be inaccessible other than from the occasional paparazzi sighting or convention appearance; now they tweet what they had for breakfast (2011).

Once again *Supernatural* has been on the forefront. Misha Collins jumped on the Twitter bandwagon before most celebrities, recognizing the power to be wielded in periodic 140 character tweets. He quickly contributed to the coherence of his Twitter fan group by putting his stamp of approval on their chosen name (Misha's minions) and then used his powers for good by mobilizing the minions into social action by founding the Random Acts nonprofit. When some fans questioned whether Collins knew what he was doing, Collins stepped directly into fan space and responded on the fan's own blog, prompting her to assure him that she would be more circumspect about her comments in the future (laurenist 2010).

The economic opportunities of Twitter are not lost on TPTB. Jared Padalecki finally got a Twitter account in 2011, after years of insisting he never would. In true reciprocal fashion, he announced it directly to fans at a *Supernatural* convention in Nashville, tweeting a photo of costar Ackles as proof that it was really him. He had over 100,000 followers in less than a week. The CW soon cashed in on the free publicity, making it easy to follow any of their celebrity tweeters with a full page of one-click links to more than 75 of their stars' Twitters. On the day that Padalecki joined, "@jarpad" was a trending term on Twitter, ensuring that thousands who had no idea what *Supernatural* was clicked through to see what all the fuss was about. That's the kind of publicity that the CW can't afford to buy. Or pass up.

A documentary by Laurie Cowan, *Participate: The Revolution of Fan Culture,* explored the changes in fandom from the 1960s to the present, citing the increased voice fans have been afforded by the internet, and their ability to show producers what they like through media feedback as well as purchasing power. Likewise, the people who are making the media have instant access to that feedback, instead of having to sift through fan mail or wait for advertising statistics. The film's title comes from another way in which the boundary between fans and creators has changed: fans don't just consume, they participate. The creator/enthusiast is becoming the norm as fans become major players in the industry. As Joss Whedon says in the film, "The internet has made it possible for creators to get in touch with their fans. It's never an easy thing for Hollywood to adapt to an idea, but this is more than an idea. If Hollywood doesn't tap into that, they'll be in trouble."

Creator/producers like Whedon, and *Supernatural*'s Eric Kripke and Sera Gamble, have been listening to fandom from the beginning. But what happens when TPTB (producers) move into fan spaces and appropriate fan practices, effectively breaking down the fourth wall from the other side, has received relatively little academic attention to date. We consider here why producer incursion into fan spaces can be so deeply problematic, and how that incursion has played out on *Supernatural*—both in canon and in face to face shared spaces such as fan conventions.

Shots Across the Fourth Wall:
Invasions from the Other Side

Particularly in the carnival space of conventions, where fans are face-to-face with their fannish objects, the actors have been the ones to bring up the forbidden subject of what fans do as often as the fans themselves. In her ethnographic study, Straw describes an incident at the 2009 Creation *Supernatural* convention in Los Angeles:

> Another interesting moment came during Misha Collins' panel. Someone asked "what was it like to have Keifer Sutherland on top of you?" (on an episode of 24). Misha's immediate response was, "Is this going to be a resource for some slash fic?" This time, the audience erupted in laughter, applause and cheers. He went on to say that fandom is "pretty weird… this slash fic thing. I'm kind of fascinated by it. I've read a few of them…and yeah, it's definitely stuck with me. I'm fascinated by subcultures and communities that seem to evolve organically…I'd love to find out more about it, without getting, you know, molested." There have long been rumors that the producers and actors read fan fiction, but I was quite shocked to hear an actor confirm the fact. The concept of the 'fourth wall' in film and television applies to fandom as well: fans are fans, producers are producers, and separation is expected to be maintained. The creative boundaries parallel the social boundaries (2009).

Here, Straw, as a fan herself, reiterates her own need to see the fourth wall maintained by all concerned, her shock at realizing that an actor "knows", and her own discomfort with feeling outed.

Clearly Collins wasn't as interested in policing the fourth wall as the fans. In fact, he seems to delight in breaking the "don't talk about fandom" boundaries as often as possible. At a 2009 convention in Australia, he surreptitiously took the microphone to ask the last question of castmates Ackles and Padalecki onstage, playing the role of a tinhat J2 shipper to a tee. "How does it feel playing brothers when you're lovers in real life?" he asked, as the audience gasped. At the LA *Supernatural* convention that year, he told the audience that he was fascinated with fandom as a subculture and would like to read some slash. Later he admitted to doing so, and pronounced it "a bit like finding your parents' pornography." He also acknowledged the fans' discomfort with his open discussion of forbidden topics like slash, joking that of course that's why he does it.

Collins isn't the only actor who has been comfortable with breaking the fourth wall, or the only one who has brought up slash. As we've seen, the wank that broke out at the very first *Supernatural* fan convention (Asylum) in Coventry, UK in 2007 was partly inspired by Jensen Ackles' joke about Wincest. And actor Jim Beaver broke the first rule of fandom even more explicitly when he showed up at his first fan convention (Eyecon in 2008) wearing a shirt that overtly proclaimed his knowledge (and approval) of slash. Fans reacted loudly. Some with glee, some with horror.

Figure 6-3. Never dare Jim Beaver to do anything.

Fandom was all too eager to believe Jim's explanation that he got the tee shirt from a fan and didn't understand what it meant, thereby allowing the fourth wall to remain in place, albeit shakily. The actual explanation is quite different, illustrating our own inadvertent contribution to *Supernatural*'s propensity for fourth wall shattering. On the eve of Jim Beaver's first convention appearance, we were in LA to interview him for the first time. We discussed slash, specifically the stories written about his character, Bobby, and John, the father of the main characters on *Supernatural*. In the course of the conversation he jokingly observed that he should woo fan favor by wearing a shirt to the convention that says "I Read John/Bobby". We jokingly dared him to do it, never thinking he might take us up on it. He did.

The reaction to his shirt when he walked out on stage sent immediate ripples through the fan community, with two dominant explanations offered. Horror! He goes online and reads what we're writing!! Or, Horror!!! A fan gave him the teeshirt and he has no idea what it means (which was the explanation he himself offered). Fans quickly latched on to Jim's explanation as the less horrifying of the two options, finding it much easier to blame and cyber-flog a hapless fan than contemplate actor involvement.

Breaking the fourth wall also occurs in canon, as it has in television and films from *Moonlighting* to "The French Mistake." In canon, meta is defined as a show that refers to itself, either explicitly through breaking the fourth wall and addressing the audience, or implicitly through vague references to the fact that the characters are on a television show or film. *Supernatural* has extended the inside jokes and self-referential content to include the fandom as well as the actors, producers, writers and showrunners. In the process, SPN has become the poster child for meta episodes and fourth wall breaking, partly because creator Eric Kripke has been savvy enough to monitor his fandom fairly closely from the start. He even attended a fan convention, answering the questions of hundreds of gathered fans. The online *Eclipse Magazine* ran a piece on that convention, Creation's 2008 Salute to *Supernatural*, describing Kripke as "practically orgasmic at the opportunity" to talk directly to fans (Bekakos 2008).

Armed with a great deal of fandom knowledge, Kripke and company were in the ideal position to take the gaze of the fan and turn it back on itself, putting the fan in the spotlight. And they did. When Buddytv counted down their 20 favorite shows that feature meta content, *Supernatural*, not surprisingly, ranked number one. SPN beat out even the beloved episode "Buffy the Musical", *Northern Exposure*'s addressing its "sophisticated audience," *Lost*'s response to audience hatred of new characters Nikki and Paolo by burying them alive, *Moonlighting*'s groundbreaking references to its own script, and *Arrested Development*'s overt pleas to its viewers to keep it on the air (Kubicek 2011).

Supernatural also eventually blurred the distinction between acknowledging fan opinion and outing fan practices. Academics, reviewers and the fans themselves have been divided in their opinions of *Supernatural*'s meta episodes and the Show's incorporation into canon of fans and fan practices, especially the more controversial ones. In the 2010

issue of the *Journal of Transformative Works and Cultures*, which was
entirely devoted to *Supernatural*, Jules Wilkinson analyzed the impact of
the meta episodes from the fans' perspective.

Fig. 6-4: The creator speaks. Eric Kripke fronts his creations at a con.

It all used to be so simple. There were fans and there were TPTB, the
show's creators. TPTB created stories that we, the fans, adored, consumed,
criticized, and chopped into bits and made into shiny new things for our
amusement. There was a version of the fourth wall – more a one-way
mirror, really – between the source text and fandom, with both sides
generally happy to keep it that way. But with *Supernatural*, that fannish
fourth wall has been demolished…. What happens when the creators of the
original work take the fans and their creative works and incorporate them
into source material that the fans in turn will further transform? (Wilkinson
2010)

The Monster at the End of This Book: Kripke's Marty Stu

In Season 4's "The Monster at the End of this Book" (air date April 2009), *Supernatural* began a series of portrayals of fans that closely mirror the show's own fanbase, and a tradition of poking fun at both sides of the reciprocal relationship. Sam and Dean discover a book series that describes their lives (the *Supernatural* series, obviously), and then discover that they—the characters in the books—have fans. In fact, the books have what is described as "a kind of underground following", a nod to the Show's four seasons of flying under the radar and lack of network support. At first, the boys are mistaken for Sam and Dean fans who are LARPing (live action role playing). It's clear the series is about them, but the boys are nonetheless portrayed as newbies here, lacking any understanding of fan terminology and hopelessly clueless of fan practices. This trope was continued in subsequent episodes—both the clueless status of the brothers and the superior knowledge of the fans, knowledge that eventually becomes crucial to preventing the Apocalypse itself. They will be mistaken for fans again in a subsequent episode when they are tricked into turning up at a fan convention and will be similarly judged by other fans. Later in this episode they will be indebted to a fan for her encyclopedic knowledge of their lives.

Sam and Dean quickly move from being mistaken for fans to misrepresenting themselves as fans to gain information from the agent for the writer of the *Supernatural* book series, Carver Edlund (a mash up of the names of two SPN writes, Jeremy Carver and Ben Edlund). The wary agent, who is also a hardcore fan and a stereotypical female fan, at least as constructed by academics ("The best parts are when they cry … If only real men were that open and in touch with their feelings.") will not reveal the real person behind the pen name until she's convinced that Sam and Dean, now posing as journalists writing about the series, are also real fans. They pass her trivia test, but she is still not completely convinced until they reveal the matching protective tattoos on their chests. This not only assures her that they're really fans, it also prompts her—since she is now in the safe space of fandom—to reveal her own tattoo (in a rather private location). Even though the scene played out as an extended comment on the (obsessive) detailed knowledge that fans have of their fanned object and the actual practice within the SPN fandom of getting that particular tattoo, fans were generally thrilled at this portrayal of the boys as fans of themselves. Making the tattooed fan "Sera Siege" was also seen as a positive point of identification, solidifying writer and eventually showrunner Sera Gamble's status as a fangirl, along with writer Julie Siege.

The Winchester brothers are once more mistaken for fans by the author of the books, Chuck, when they show up at his house to confront him. When Chuck categorizes them as nerdily zealous fans, he is dismissive, saying "I have some posters in the house." When they show him their car, a 1967 Impala just like the one his characters drive, the supplies they carry in the trunk of that car (rock salt, holy water, guns – lots of guns) and display their encyclopedic knowledge of Sam and Dean's (their own) lives, Chuck becomes frightened, thinking they are dangerously obsessed. "Is this a *Misery* thing?" he asks. "It is. Isn't it? It's a *Misery* thing." Chuck thus articulates the negative ways in which fans are often characterized.

Sam and Dean only manage to convince Chuck they are the real people he's been writing about when they reveal knowledge never written in the books. The tongue in cheek portrayal of Chuck here is one of the things that saves the episode from slipping into mean-spirited parody of fans. Chuck, as creator, is far from a role model for showrunners and is clearly a parody of Kripke himself. Fans of the show have often referred to Kripke as a god in their own fanworks, and here Kripke plays with this portrayal.

When Chuck finds out that his characters are real people, he jumps to the conclusion that he, as their author, must indeed be a god, "a cruel, cruel capricious god." (And though it's seemingly his self-inflated ego talking here, it turns out Chuck really is divinely inspired). Thus Kripke gets to both mock himself and validate his own choices as "creator" with generally amused approval from the fans. The use of the fictional versions of the already fictional characters allowed the writers to talk about real life fan practices that had heretofore remained hidden, at least on network television. Some fans reacted with uncontrollable laughter; others were scandalized.

In addition to being seen as fans, the brothers occupy another space in this episode, that of the objects of fandom. They buy all the books (they are all in the remainder bin), read them and react to the fact that someone has been writing their lives—much as fans fear real actors might react to the knowledge that RPF (especially sexually explicit RPF) is being written about them. They are not happy. They are particularly uncomfortable about having the intimate details of their lives there for anyone to read. At one point Dean throws a book down in disgust exclaiming, "This is freakin' insane! How does this guy know all this stuff? Everything is in here, I mean everything. I'm full frontal in here, dude!" The objectification is doubled when the boys find out that the books have fans and that there are fansites devoted to "them" as characters. They again do what fans fear actors/producers will do—they check out the websites.

Fig. 6-5

"For fans they sure do complain a lot!" Dean observes and then quotes one fan—Simpatico (an actual poster on the Television Without Pity boards that Kripke favors), who comments about the storyline being "craptastic".   Dean angrily responds, perhaps voicing the annoyance of the Show's creative team to negative fan reactions, "Well screw you, Simpatico, we lived it!"   (Thus, in the course of the episode, the boys move from being mistaken for fans, to being the objects of real person fiction, to being put into the defensive position of creators.)   The final hammer blow to the fourth wall was delivered when Sam and Dean actually read some of that fanfiction. Sam has to explain to Dean.

> Dean: Check it out! There's actually fans. There's not many of them, but still…Although for fans, they sure do complain a lot. Listen to this – Simpatico says, "The demon story line is trite, cliched and overall craptastic". Yeah well, screw you, Simpatico. We lived it. There's Sam girls and Dean girls and….what's a slash fan?"
> Sam: As in "Sam slash Dean—together."
> Dean: Like, together together? They do know we're brothers, right?
> Sam: Doesn't seem to matter.
> Dean: Well, that's just sick!

With this scene, Kripke has made public several hallmarks of fan communities that fans have kept mostly hidden—the criticism of the text, the divisions among fans (the Sam girls and Dean girls), slash fiction, and particular to this show, Wincest. That Wincest was mentioned only to be criticized actually worked in favor of several subgroups of fans. Those who disapprove of Wincest had that disapproval validated by the creator and characters. At the same time, those who write it could rest assured that their subversive hunt for subtext was still being met with resistance, at least overtly, from TPTB.

Kripke did not stop at simply portraying fans and fan practices, however; he appropriated those fan practices and made them his own. With this episode, he began what amounts to his own extended piece of multi-genre fan fiction. He has written himself into the text, in the character of Chuck, creating a Mary Sue/Marty Stu self-insertion narrative with himself as the divinely inspired hero, and writer of both Wincest and RPF (since Sam and Dean, in the canon universe, are real people). He has also written another type of real person fic—this time about fans. When Dean reacts to the criticism of Simpatico, he is reacting to the real criticism of a real fan of the real television show *Supernatural* (rather than a fictive fan of the fictive book series). Kripke is thus turning the tables, writing a fan into his story much the way fans have written him into theirs.

Not only did the Show break the fourth wall and "out" its fans on screen, but the Show's first mainstream media magazine coverage coincided with the filming of the meta episode "The Monster at the End of this Book"—and therefore outed fandom even more. We were on the *Supernatural* set the same day that reporter Alynda Wheat from *Entertainment Weekly* visited, and spent part of the afternoon watching filming between interviews. While we were frankly giddy with excitement over the depiction of fandom and the canon nod to Wincest, Wheat was clearly not. When her cover story came out, it included a less than flattering reference to "the intense universe of fandom" and the comment, "There's also a unique and very creepy subset of romantic fanfiction dedicated to siblings Sam and Dean called "Wincest"—the less said about it the better" (Wheat 2009).

The EW coverage cast a negative spin on the episode itself, making fans even more likely to interpret the fourth wall breaking as criticism of fandom instead of an affectionate poke. Having talked to Kripke and Gamble and most of the actors about fandom and fanfiction, as we'll explore in the next chapter, we felt certain the episode was intended as the latter. The episode was one of the most highly rated of season four, but it generated a great deal of fandom controversy. Some fans were excited to be written into canon, and happy to be poked fun at along with everyone else.

Within the first five minutes I was pissing myself in laughter and disbelief. Taking the mickey out of the fans and themselves was pretty fun there for a while. Especially since an episode that was *fictionally* a crossover between fiction and reality was at the same time *in reality* a crossover between fiction and reality. Art and life imitated each other into a tangled ball of timey-wimey, wibbly-wobbly stuff (to quote The Doctor.)

I loved this episode so much I can't even say. My boyfriend was laughing at me throughout for the honest-to-god (blasphemy!) squeeing noises I was making. I believe at one point I even did victory arms.

Simpatico, the real fan on TWoP, took the reference to her in stride.

I wasn't hurt. Just shocked and bemused that they picked me of all people. And struck by the irony, as I no longer really watch or post about the show, and the episode I did see and post about I actually enjoyed and praised. Apparently posts I made years ago have left permanent scars on their psyches (TWOP 4-18 2009).

From the rest of what she writes, it's clear that her comment is largely tongue in cheek, but it is also indicative of the preferred dynamic—fans affecting producers via their public criticism, rather than their private fan practices. A significant portion of fandom had less positive reactions. They felt mocked, shamed and unappreciated.

Sympathy for the Devil: Fan Girls and Stereotypes

The controversy accelerated when *Supernatural* continued its meta episodes with the introduction of fangirl Becky Rosen in the first episode of season five, Sympathy for the Devil, written by Eric Kripke. Becky's bedroom is a shrine to the series (and the fact that she's shown in her bedroom suggests she's still living at home—not in her parents' basement, but close). Her identity seems closely tied to her fandom. Her online avatar is "samlicker81", she proclaims herself Chuck's number one fan, and is the webmistress of More Than Brothers.net (which was apparently a real site that quickly disappeared after being referenced on the show). Fangirl Becky is depicted as both overly emotional and overtly sexual. As the scene begins, she's writing Wincest fanfiction that's clearly heading in an NC17 direction.

The brothers huddled together in the dark as the sound of the rain drumming on the roof eased their fears of pursuit. Despite the cold outside

and the demons who, even now, must be approaching, the warmth of their embrace comforted them. And then Sam caressed Dean's clavicle.
"This is wrong," said Dean.
"Then I don't want to be right," replied Sam, in a husky voice.

Kripke got the Wincest right—the brothers are hurt, isolated, alone. There's a nod to hurt/comfort fic, a reference to Dean's "muscular frame", an external danger, an emotional connection. And then, having established Becky as a slashwriting fangirl, Kripke does something surprising. The writer of the *Supernatural* book series, Chuck, contacts Becky for help when he's prevented from getting in touch with the "real" Sam and Dean. She responds by mirroring the real-life wank over the previous meta episode, "Monster At The End of This Book," complete with fannish protest about being mocked. While the fans watching are assured that Becky does in fact know the difference between fantasy and reality, one of the accusations most often hurled at fans, Becky also appears to harbor a close-to-conscious wish that the Winchesters really are out there saving people and hunting things. But really, who can blame her?

> Becky: Yes, I'm a fan, but I really don't appreciate being mocked. I know that *Supernatural* is just a book, okay? I know the difference between fantasy and reality.
> Chuck: Becky, it's all real.
> Becky: I knew it!

In other words, TPTB need the fangirl. And so does the writer/creator. And if there wasn't already enough meta to make your head spin, the person who created the show that inspired Wincest has now written Wincest himself, right into canon. Chuck's interaction with Becky is initially dismissive, devaluing her fannish adoration with a quick "I got your marzipan—yummy" even as he is reaching out to ask for her help. He needs someone crazy enough to believe him and knows his number one fan is his only hope, much as *Supernatural* itself has depended on fans "crazy" enough to fight for its survival in order to stay on the air. When Becky shows up at Sam and Dean's motel room to deliver the message Chuck has charged her with, she is the model of the inappropriate fangirl—the one that other fans so diligently police for "doing it wrong." She tells them she's a fan, and almost admits she writes slash, stopping herself just in time. She criticizes the show, saying that "the demon mythology was getting old", and she breaks an ironclad fan rule by touching Sam. Becky personifies the stereotype of the out-of-control fangirl here, calling up cultural fears of overt out-of-control female sexuality and hysterical women.

> Sam: "Becky, do you think you could stop touching me?"
> Becky: "No"

At the same time, many fans could relate to the wish to check out Sam Winchester's impressive physique for themselves, whether they'd be comfortable admitting it or not. Turn the tables and genders, and the wish—if not the action—appears closer to normal and farther from shameful. She is, after all, only patting his chest. This episode, though only briefly about the fans (Becky disappears after she delivers the message and the main storyline takes over) drew harsher criticism. Many thought the fangirl depicted was "creepy". One poster complained:

> I thought Becky was grating and embarrassing. Such an idiot. She just found out that the *Supernatural* books are real and that the Apocalypse may be coming, and she doesn't even seem concerned. Not a flattering portrayal of fangirls (TWOP 5-1 2009).

Other fans responded to Becky's overt objectification of Sam and the depiction of her sexuality as reinforcing gendered stereotypes of fangirls as "only there for the hot guys". Part of the objection was that the portrayal buys into the dominant trope of fangirls as sexually needy and deviant and part was to the disclosure of the practices that are seen as coding them this way in the first place. Some fans felt exposed and some felt outed by Kripke. "It makes me fearful as a teacher of what it would do to my career/future to be 'outed' (as a *Supernatural* fan)", one anonymous fan posted in her reaction to the episode.

A cartoon by counteragent captured the fear running rampant through fandom after this episode—fear of being outed as a fan and the possible real life repercussions. In the comic, a young married woman is happily typing away on her laptop, coincidentally checking off a ticky box about the worst fannish sin being outing a fellow fan. She's smiling, engaged with the fandom community. Later, their baby asleep, she watches *Supernatural* with her husband, only to be confronted with its depiction of fans. Horrified, her husband angrily demands to know if *that* is what she does on the internet. Ashamed, the woman tearfully informs her fandom friends that she won't be coming back – and closes the laptop.

The episode's outing of some of the most hidden fan practices spread fear throughout all of fandom. Phoenix64 posted:

I've never watched *Supernatural*, but I still felt the shockwaves when it portrayed slash fen in the show. I thought it was cute at first, but eventually the implications sunk in. The thought that a creator could take a subversive bit of fan culture and present it on television is intimidating. Fandom, slash fandom in particular, is a safe haven for many women who want to express their sexuality.

Fig. 6-6

Many fans felt that the situation portrayed in the comic was quite plausible, and worried that their own investment of emotional energy and open expression of sexual desire in fandom would threaten their (especially male) partners.

> Rivkat: One of the things SPN's specific portrayal of *Supernatural* fandom did was contribute to the popular denigration of women's icky sexualized overinvestment in fiction. The episode foregrounded the extent to which female fans' investment is about sexual desire for the male leads *and portrayed that as laughable.* Unsurprisingly, this is messy! Because one thing that might happen when a man sees a portrayal of female fans' sexual desire, and connects that to his wife's fandom, is that he will conclude that *her* sexual desire is focused elsewhere: she doesn't want him, she wants *them.*
>
> Platypus: Considering how many men watch visual porn, though, I'd be surprised if many of them considered smutty fanfiction a breach of

fidelity. It's like reading trashy romance novels, only they're about TV characters.

In fact, men are openly depicted in television canon as unapologetically consuming pornography, starting with Dean Winchester himself. It's even an acceptable and fondly received Christmas gift between the brothers.

> Cesperanza: Except men's dislike of their wives reading trashy romance novels is totally the subject of Janice Radway's "Reading the Romance," in which her subjects talk about having to hide their books, and how many books they buy, from their husbands. Sad but true! (Also sad but true: since when is what's good for the goose good for the gander?)

Reading romances is considered suspect in part because it can direct a woman's emotional energy elsewhere. In fact, as another fan adds, for many of us, the sex and the Wincest are only the tip of an iceberg that has much more to do with emotional intimacy and time spent on one's own desires. The cartoon positions the woman as mother and wife first, and paints her interaction with fandom as stolen time, her desires always subject to the needs of others. In fact, she needs to coerce her husband into watching the show with her with the promise of a foot rub, no pleasure apparently allowed without payment. This reaction harks back to the early days of fan studies when fan behavior was cast as subversive, giving it both political and gendered readings. Ironically, as we've discussed in previous chapters, the very secrecy with which fans guard their safe space and bolster the fourth wall can be disempowering and perpetuates their shame. Some fans, however, took issue with the shame expressed in the comic:

> Lierdumoa: Okay ... what? I totally agree that outing fans is bad news, but. The consequence here should be "I lost my job" not "I lost my family." I spend hours almost every day doing fannish things. That's a really big secret to keep from a significant other. Frankly if you're keeping secrets that big from your husband, your marriage is already *fucked up*, and Kripke is not to blame for your judgmental husband and crying baby. A gay male fan friend of mine once compared his experience of coming out as a fan to his experience of coming out as a gay man, and I think the parallel drawn is accurate. Both fall under the umbrella of "sexual deviance"—that is to say, having views of sex and sexuality that do not align themselves with the views of conventional society. If your family rejects you for being a sexual deviant because you are not heterosexual, or because you are into BDSM, or because you have a personal inclination towards risque, essentially *harmless* internet fiction, then your family is dysfunctional. Kripke is not to blame for your family's dysfunction.

Missyjack responded with a comic of her own, and some amusingly biting sarcasm –

Fig. 6-7 (credit missyjack, used with permission)

Here the existence of the First Rule of Fandom and the policing of the fourth wall seems predicated on the very fan shame we've been exploring.

The Real Ghostbusters: Fanboys and Fangirls

In another fancentric episode, "The Real Ghostbusters" (November 2009, episode 5.09), Show took another leap across the wall by depicting a *Supernatural* fan convention—airing on the night before an actual *Supernatural* fan convention. Becky has organized a SPN fan convention and tricked Sam and Dean into coming. Her motive is not to out them as the real Sam and Dean, but rather to show them what the fans are doing (in other words, breaking the First Rule of Fandom -- and a major breech of boundaries that mirrors Krikpe's own chipping away at the fourth wall from the other side). Some fans objected to Kripke's depiction of the SPN fandom in this episode, charging that he did not know who his fans were (in the episode the fans are almost all male, the reverse demographic for actual SPN fan conventions) and that they came in costume, not a common practice of real fans of the real series.

Margaret O'Connell, staff writer for the online "*Supernatural* Talk"

> Somebody who knew nothing about the *Supernatural* fandom beyond the fact that it exists might well come away from this episode with the impression that the show's writers and producers, at least, think that their audience is composed of a few women who want to sleep with the Winchesters (or otherwise sexually fantasize about them) and a lot of guys who'd like to be them. Unless they all have PhDs in denial, it's unlikely that anyone on the *Supernatural* staff seriously believes this. But, based on this episode, it certainly seems as if some of them would prefer it if that were the case. The striking dichotomy between the gender breakdown of real life *Supernatural* fandom and the way it's portrayed here seems more apt to be the product of the creators' uneasiness at their theoretically decidedly male-centric show being subject to, and significantly dependent for its success on, the female gaze (Chan 2010).

If *Supernatural* is uncomfortable with the Show's success being dependent on the female gaze, somebody needs to inform the director of photography, directors and showrunners, who seem to enable that dynamic with every other frame.

Other fans were simply uncomfortable with the fact that Kripke knew too much, and even worse, revealed too much about the real-life fandom. In fact, the panels at the fictional convention could have been lifted directly from the most prevalent *Supernatural* meta and fanfiction: "Frightened Little Boy: The Secret Life of Dean" and "The Homoerotic Subtext of *Supernatural*." The episode makes other comments on fandom as well. Two attendees at the fictional fan convention are fanboys Demian and Barnes, who come dressed as Sam and Dean. They, along with fangirl Becky, wind up as the (somewhat reluctant) heroes of the episode, saving Sam and Dean as well as the rest of the convention attendees from malevolent ghost. The episode also made the faux Sam and Dean lovers instead of brothers, prompting AfterElton.com to describe the episode as a "love letter to all *Supernatural's* fans, including the gay male ones." Demian and Barnes are, in the real world, moderators of the TWoP SPN fan forums that Kripke frequents. So the doubly fictional Sam and Dean were named after two prominent real life fans. In other words, the Show slashed its own fans!

With this episode, Kripke has slashed his fans **and** made a reference to the ways in which real fans of the real television show slash the actors. Barnes' gesture of laying his head on Demian's shoulder is reminiscent of a fan favorite shot (part of the extras on season 1 DVD) of Ackles laying his head on co-star Padalecki's shoulder, a shot that has been used over and over in J2 slash-centric fan videos. The gesture is also seen as a more positive canon nod to Wincest. Demian and Barnes are Sam and Dean roleplayers who also happen to be lovers. This is probably as close as Sam/Dean can get to canon and still make it past the censors (and also not scare off the non-Sam/Dean fans). Later in Season 5, we learn that Sam and Dean are described as "soulmates" (5.16, Dark Side of the Moon) who are "psychotically, irrationally, erotically codependent" (5.18, Point of No Return), and periodic references to the pair as a married couple continue throughout Season 7.

Our own reading of this episode is that Kripke was writing a piece of AU fan fiction (about his own fans), and that he, like his fans, knows the difference between fantasy and reality. This does not necessarily exonerate him of co-opting fan practices in a turnabout of the accepted dynamic of fans co-opting media properties for their own use. Kripke's inclusion of fans challenges the accepted dynamic of powerless fan and all-powerful producer in ways that, ironically, still make the fans uncomfortable. Fans objected to Kripke's depiction of fans in his text in part because of fan shame, but also because he upset the balance of power that has traditionally been theirs to upset and engaged in activities that have always been their purview. He took their subtext and made it text.

The fact that Chuck (Kripke) winds up with Becky (fangirl) at the end of this episode can be read as variously creepy, amusing, appreciative, or as politically savvy. Catherine Tosenberger saw mostly the creepy, writing that "The message of "Ghostbusters" appears to be: fanboys, keep on keeping on—you are dorky but lovable. Female fans, you are creepy, but you might be willing to fuck us real writers, so you aren't *totally* unacceptable" (Tosenberger 2010).

Alternatively, that Chuck/Kripke is literally in bed with his fans can be seen as indicative of the fact that we—the creator, the actors and the fans—are all in this together. That fanboys Demian and Barnes, along with fangirl Becky, end up saving the day can be seen as a love letter to fandom and an expression of appreciation to the fans who, quite literally, have saved the Show season after season. Some viewed the nod to fandom positively, showing the writers and actors' own fanboy roots, and making a definitive statement about how Kripke sees the fan/creator relationship. As Jules Wilkinson puts it in her TWC article:

> The episode subverts the cliched trope of the socially awkward, emotionally immature fan by making the *Supernatural* fans Demian and Barnes gay lovers who save the day and provide Dean with an emotional insight. Kripke's most definitive statement, however, is made through the

relationship between Becky and Chuck: the creator falls in love with the fangirl.

Fans discussed Wilkinson's article with as much passion and disagreement as we can expect from fandom. The final comment, on missyjack's LJ post was from madame_d:

> So basically you're saying that Show, like a supportive counselor, is coaxing reluctant slashfans out of the closet, to be out and proud and not give in to internalized homophobia (crossed out)pervy shame? ;) I like that theory (missyjack 2010).

From our vantage point straddling the fan/researcher fence, it seemed unlikely that anyone on the creative side of SPN had their PhDs in denial. We'd interviewed Eric Kripke several times by then, and, he'd asked us as many questions about fandom as we'd asked him about Show. Kripke had also been to the LA *Supernatural* convention as a guest himself, so he was intimately familiar with the gender composition of cons and fandom and made a conscious decision to portray fandom as less than 100% reflective of reality. As we'll see in the next chapter, he was also genuinely appreciative of the fans he was lovingly mocking.

The French Mistake

In Season 6, *Supernatural* once again decided to break the fourth wall, this time into such tiny pieces it's doubtful that reconstruction is an option. The episode title, "The French Mistake", is a reference to the Mel Brooks film which ends with the fourth wall being shattered, but fandom immediately picked up on urbandictionary's other definition of the term as well, which is "When an otherwise straight male is persuaded to, or on a whim in the heat of the moment, engages in a homosexual act of which he later regrets and is ashamed." This prompted some in fandom to wonder if Show was playing "gay chicken" with fandom. At the Jus in Bello convention in Rome that year, Jared and Jensen confided that even they were "worried Kripke was going to make us kiss" in the episode, perhaps the ultimate in fan service (tweet by @FiercelyNormal).

Instead, the episode depicted the alternate universe Jared and Jensen as less friendly than their real-life epic bromance, but there was plenty of fan service in evidence nevertheless. TV Squad writer Laura Prudom posted a preview of the episode, "5 Reasons Why You Can't Miss Friday's Meta-Filled Episode"

Few shows are quite as willing to poke fun at themselves as the CW's *Supernatural* which has tackled everything from turning its characters into the heroes of a pulpy (and little-read) book series, to sending them to a spooky fan convention. But after six seasons of self-referential madness, writer Ben Edlund seems to have decided that he's sick of "scratching" at the fourth wall, and would rather take a sledgehammer to it instead. What results is 'The French Mistake,' one of the most surreal, unpredictable and undeniably hilarious episodes that the show has ever produced—and if you've seen 'Changing Channels' or 'Tall Tales,' you know that's quite a feat (Prudom 2011).

In what has become known as "the meta episode", Sam and Dean are transported to an alternate reality where they're mistaken for self-centered actors Jared Padalecki and Jensen Ackles, stars of a struggling little-watched television show called *Supernatural*. Their colleague Misha Collins (played, of course, by Misha Collins) is a twitter-obsessed jerk with a fanbase who call themselves "Mishamigos", and Jared is married to Ruby (real life wife Geneveieve Padalecki, who played the demon Ruby on SPN). It's enough to give a fan a headache. Once again, the Show poked fun at everyone on it, including director Bob Singer and cinematographer Serge Ladouceur and stunt coordinator Lou Bollo, who played himself. New showrunner Sera Gamble complains that nobody listens to her, while executive producer/creator Eric Kripke shows up to save the day only to be gunned down by a pissed off demon in a hail of bullets and a pool of the blood Kripke is so fond of spilling all over his Show. Nods to the fandom were strewn throughout the episode, with the actual TV Guide fan favorite cover that the fans won for SPN, the People's Choice Award and the Constellation Award all strategically placed in the boys' trailers. Ackles even holds up an issue of *Supernatural Magazine* for the camera.

If the script itself wasn't enough to decimate the fourth wall, Collins actually tweeted the identical words that his character tweeted onscreen at the exact time of airing, so that fans watching the actor tweet on the show received the tweet on their iphones at the same moment! (One for the east coast US airing, one for the west coast). In-jokes that only fans and the creative team would understand were everywhere. The fake *Supernatural* was filmed at the KM Motion Picture Studios, named for the late and much beloved director and producer Kim Manners. The fake Bob Singer told the fake Sera Gamble about their stars' strange behavior, exclaiming "Now Jensen's living at Jared's house!" As every fan knows, Ackles really did move in with Padalecki in 2008. Singer also jokes that to cut some time from the episode, they'd "have to blow off the scene where they sit on the Impala and talk about their feelings," adding that there's no way he'd risk incurring the wrath of fandom for that one! As Sam and Dean watch their "fake selves" on an episode playing on a television screen behind them, both actors cast a knowing wink directly at the audience, literally sharing the joke. At the end of the episode, Sam walks right up to viewers' television screens to be sure the (fourth) wall is real, and solidly back in place.

In the online blog Sequential Tart, staff writers (who are also fans of the Show) commented on how well the so-called meta episode worked. Olywn Supeene recognized the meta tradition as well established already on *Supernatural*, saying, "After all the meta content we've had throughout the series, this show was ripe to break the fourth wall good and proper." The writers also noted that an episode that utilized such a complicated mix of real/unreal depends on an involved and informed fandom.

> Anita Olin: it seems an appropriate way to comment on the trials of Season 6 and to throw a nudge and a wink at the fans who've followed the show and the behind-the-scenes developments. The mixture of the true and the untrue "real-life" things that were used would not have worked on a show with a less enthusiastic fandom. It takes time to develop both a show and a fandom to the point that so many in-jokes can be layered into an episode.
>
> Olwyn: It's an interesting wink and nod to the viewers: dedicated fans will have noticed from the first look at Jensen's trailer that the versions of Jared and Jensen that we are given in this episode are nothing like the real thing—or at least, like the glimpses we've been given from interviews, DVD features and convention panels. They're sharing a joke with us, as though they're saying, *look, see how ridiculous we are? Watch us poke fun at ourselves!*
>
> Wolfie: I have to wonder, has there ever been a more Meta-tastic episode, in all the history of TV, than this one? ....All in all, I have more respect than ever for everyone involved in the show: in my opinion, self-deprecating humour is the very best kind!

Fandom was, as always, divided about the episode. In general, though, this meta episode was widely received as a thank you to fandom for six years of keeping Show on the air and countless online voting marathons that gained *Supernatural* the nickname "The little show that could" as fans voted it onto the cover of TV Guide and to the top of numerous lists and contests. As one fan posted in her episode reaction, "true love letters are never a mistake." She categorizes "The French Mistake" as just such a love letter, to both the Show and to the show's fans, interpreting this episode as clarification of the reciprocal relationship itself.

[F]illed with everything we love about SPN and J3+M (Jared, Jensen, Jim and Misha), and written to us in the same witty, snarktastic voice that made us fall head-over-heels in love with The Show in the first place. And perhaps more important than even the familiar and much-loved tone is the veracity of the sentiments expressed: every declaration of mutual admiration and respect, every expression of love in reciprocation for fidelity and unconditional support, every reminiscence of "remember that time?" or "wasn't it funny when?"'s are intimate conversations with *US*, the fans, that—while the rest of the world may understand the words used in the speaking—are designed to speak solely to *US*, the fans. And to speak to us on a totally different level than mere words can ever do. To speak *very intimately* to us about all the things we -- those who make the   show *and* the fans who love the show -- have in common and all the travails we've shared in this 6-year relationship that has been both blessed and cursed, both brilliant and so-not-even-passingly-acceptable that it aches. And most important of all, to us, the fans, to say, "We love you ... we really, *really* do. Even if we don't always listen to what you say. Even if we don't always say what you want us to say, or see things the way you want us to see things. We still *love* you, and we know that you love us, too. Even when we fight. Even when we disagree. Even when we insult one another or withhold good opinions in retaliation for bad scripts. Even then, we still love you. We really, really do..... And what *The French Mistake* tells us—the fans, the faithful, the hopelessly love-struck—in ways no words simply spoken could ever say, is that they love us, too. They *love* us, dammit. They really do. And they are willing to say as much—to shout it from the mountaintops, even—and to do so in a language specific to, and limited to, SF/TV fans in general and   SPN/J3+M   fans   in   specific.... finally, after all these years of wondering if it really *was* as reciprocal as so oft is claimed, the whole of you got together and didn't *say* you love us this time, you *showed* it (dodger_winslow 2011).

CHAPTER SEVEN

THE RECIPROCAL RELATIONSHIP:
HOW MUCH IS TOO MUCH?

The first time we blundered onto the Supernatural set, on location at a Vancouver hospital, was also our first trip to Canada. We were passionate about our brand new obsession with the Show and our brand new research line of investigating fandom, and feeling fortunate that the two came together in as beautiful a place as Vancouver. Accustomed to our roles as psychologist and English professor, and alarmingly naïve about TPTB, we handed over our business cards and asked if anyone on the production would like to be interviewed. We were sorry to hear some negative stories about fans in response, but other than that things seemed to be going fine—until the PA we were interviewing got a call on her headset. Suddenly instead of pleasant conversation we were being told in no uncertain terms to leave the premises. NOW. Somehow, we had been recategorized from researchers to stalkers. Confused and unexpectedly humiliated, we slunk off to our car, only to run smack into Supernatural's lead actors coming back from lunch. Now we really looked like stalkers! We came away from the set that day still stinging from the sense of shame the experience produced.

Fast forward twelve months and we'd learned to negotiate the boundaries between fans, acafans and the creative side a bit more smoothly. Our second set visit, to the Supernatural studios in Burnaby, was the opposite of our first disastrous outing. We interviewed everyone who happened to be at the studio that day -- the guys responsible for the Atmo smoke, the PAs, the production office staff, propmaster Chris Cooper, art director Jerry Wanek, director of photography Serge Ladouceur. Everyone was eager to tell us about their role in creating Supernatural, clearly proud of their contribution. Jared Padalecki spoke thoughtfully about fans and acting and the Show itself, his giant dogs Harley and Sadie asleep at our feet. We despaired of an interview with Jensen Ackles when he didn't finish filming until the wee hours of the morning; Ackles insisted on staying to do the interview anyway, even asking for more time when his driver came knocking. We ended up spending the entire day and half the night on the Supernatural set, asking and answering questions about fans, the Show and the reciprocal relationship that had developed between them. The contrast was striking.

The relationship between fans and the creative side is becoming increasingly reciprocal. The evolving technology-facilitated openness has left both sides struggling to negotiate boundaries, with fans alternately insisting "Let me tell you what I want!" and then exclaiming "Ohmygod, they know what I want!" and creators wondering "How much do we really want to know, and what do we do with what we've learned?" In the previous chapters, we explored fans' desire for boundaries, and the ways in which they police those boundaries with both TPTB and other fans. There is constant negotiation and re-negotiation, since individual fans and segments of fandom disagree on how much reciprocity and openness is optimal between fandom and the creative side. Fans simultaneously want to exert influence on a text in which they are highly invested, and yet remain hidden. A similar tension exists on the creative side, who must also negotiate their own boundaries with fandom. The creative side knows the value of maintaining fans' interest and is invested in pleasing fans, yet recognizes the risk of too much reciprocity in contaminating the source text or interfering with the need for mystery to sustain fantasy. As we've seen, *Supernatural*'s incursions into fan spaces, both in fourth-wall-breaking canon and in face to face interactions, have been welcomed by some fans and abhorred by others.

Nevertheless, both sides are enacting the convergence culture which Jenkins referred to several decades ago, with writers, directors, actors and fans all an integral part of the creative process (Jenkins, 1992). In this chapter, we examine the increased openness between *Supernatural* fans and the creative side—the risks, the benefits, and the continued need for boundaries in the reciprocal relationship. While many academic explorations of fandom have explored the fannish side of the reciprocal relationship, few have interrogated directly the experience of the creative side. We occupied an unusual middle ground as we did so, immersed in *Supernatural* fandom while also engaging in academic analysis. This put us in a position to answer questions about fandom instead of just asking them, and to poke holes in a few of the existing boundaries. We found that the creative side is sometimes as curious about fans as fans are about them. There are few opportunities for creators to discuss fandom with fans, and actors and producers are reticent to ask fans questions that might be interpreted as criticism or lack of understanding. Actor Matt Cohen (young John Winchester and the archangel Michael on SPN) told us, "It's crazy because I don't really get to have this conversation with people who sit out in the audience, so it's nice to hear how the fans are reacting. That's really unique actually." In our first meeting with *Supernatural* showrunner Eric Kripke, he wanted to know what websites he was missing. Actors and producers were also curious about fannish motivation – almost as curious as fandom itself. As Misha Collins asked in our first interview with him, "From a psychological vantage point, what needs is this fulfilling?"

Our dual role as fans and researchers provided us a position from which to answer Collins, but also inevitably biased both our questions and our responses. We did, after all, reside in a specific fan space, and that was the space we knew best. We were writers ourselves, researching the therapeutic aspects of fandom and challenging fan shame. Our discussions with *Supernatural*'s creative side reflected our agenda, although our interviewees often turned the conversation to their own as well. What the creative side learned about SPN fandom from our discussions may itself have had some impact on the reciprocal relationship. We've questioned that impact from an academic perspective, since it places us outside the detached stance that research usually entails, essentially breaking the prime directive of non-interference. On the other hand, we believe that the straddling of multiple identities facilitated a more comprehensive analysis of both sides.

Creative Control Versus Fan Service: Boundaries on the Fan Side

The question of fannish influence as a result of the reciprocal relationship is most relevant for those individuals who have the most creative control—for *Supernatural*, show creator and five-season showrunner Eric Kripke. Fans credit much of the good (and blame much of the bad) when it comes to *Supernatural* on Kripke. Like fellow sci fi showrunners Russell T. Davies (Torchwood) and Ronald D. Moore (Battlestar Galactica), Kripke has been a larger than life presence from the beginning. Fans have vacillated between anointing him as a deity and wanting to salt and burn him, depending on their feelings about the current season's trajectory. Kripke's breaking of the fourth wall from Season 4 on, a tradition continued by showrunner Sera Gamble in Season 6 and 7, removed any lingering doubts fandom may have had about whether or not he was wise to the ways of fandom, to some fans' glee and others' dismay. A common fannish concern is that the actors and producers are trolling the online communities, reading fanfiction and viewing fanvids and fanart. It

turns out SPN fandom is right about Kripke. He's a lurker, as fandom has
long suspected.

> Kripke: It's always there online, and often I wonder if it's an accurate
> representation. It's various websites, and I'm there quite a bit. I like
> *Supernatural*.tv, I pop around the various Live Journal stuff. The main
> question is, of the three million viewers, how many are online and how
> many are commenting? I'm on as many fan boards as everyone else, but
> never posted a comment.

The advent of an increasingly connected online and mobile culture has
made communication between the fan and creative side continuous,
something that is recognized by everyone who works on the show. In an
interview for Sky Living television (UK), Jensen Ackles recognized the
changing relationship between fans and creators, and the significant voice
individual fans now have.

> Ackles: Before all the social networking, and the tweeting and the
> facebook and the blogs and the posts, I'm not sure fanfavorite021 from
> Germany really had a voice about whether the storyline went a certain
> way, but it seems to me that now they do. They're getting paid attention to
> by the people creating the show, and that goes to show that there's an
> interesting relationship forming now with the technology we have between
> the fans and the creators of these shows (2011).

As Season 4 began filming, we asked Eric Kripke about his
relationship with *Supernatural* fandom and his thoughts on the so-called
convergence culture created by the increasingly reciprocal relationship
between fans and creators. One of the problems with the convergence is
that the communication streams are indirect, often filtered through third
parties, making it difficult for both sides to interpret the other. Kripke
described the challenge of interpreting the nuances of fannish reaction,
with the goal of deciding when to allow fans to exert an influence on the
show's direction.

> Kripke: We do pay attention to the fandom, with certain restrictions and
> conditions. One, we pay attention when general fan response is practically
> unanimous. But we actually welcome and encourage arguments. I think
> we're equally unhappy when everyone loves something. We're happiest
> when there's debate, when some people love it and some people hate it. So
> that's usually the stasis point we like to be at, because that means people
> are talking about it. When a character is sort of universally rejected, like
> Bella, we notice, and talk about it in the writers room. One of our first
> steps was to immediately devour as much information from the fans as
> possible. Our first thought is—do they hate her, or do they love to hate

her? It's very different. And part of the job is that you're supposed to drive the fans crazy, that's kind of the point. They'd be disappointed if they were satisfied every week with every character conflict.

In fact, that would leave fandom with very little to talk about! (Note: Bella was a Season 3 character reputedly shoe-horned into the show by the network to add some sex appeal for the male viewers who TPTB continued to mistakenly believe were the primary audience).

> Kripke: Exactly, that's the point, it's supposed to drive them nuts. After quite a few years of doing this, you know. If there's some ongoing piece of drama between Sam and Dean that's driving them crazy, you know they love to hate some things, so you have to separate that from if they just really hate something. It's a fine line. We think Bella was not loved to hate, because usually when people are just in suspense it's like, they're driving me crazy, how are they going to end this, which way is it going to go? But it was more along the lines of 'I turn off the episode when she comes on.'

Explicitly acknowledging the openness he's cultivated on *Supernatural*, Kripke views the ongoing story as, to a limited extent at least, co-constructed. While all media properties are inevitably influenced by viewer and fan response, in the case of Bella, fandom directly influenced the trajectory of the Show. Fans complained; Show listened. Kripke's discussion of the self reflection process that the writing team undertakes, and their lack of defensiveness, is an indication of such reciprocity.

> Kripke: We're really open to self reflection. We all started talking about it. I think the majority of shows have this attitude like, we know better, and we don't. We kind of examine it and see if it really works or doesn't. And with Bella, we had a hard time fitting the character into the mythology in a way that's seamless….every time she showed up, we had to write up some reason, and it started to feel sort of ridiculous and artificial and inorganic to the process.

Kripke was also well aware that there's no pleasing all of fandom, and that boundaries are necessary to maintain creative control while also sustaining popularity. The reciprocal relationship is, of necessity, limited. Drawing the fine line between creative vision and fan service, however, is not easy, in part because fans do not want too much of the control they clamor for.

> Kripke: As soon as you give them what they want, they're irritated that they're getting what they want, immediately after there's a burst of comments like 'fans are controlling the show.' The reality of this business

is this is serialized drama. I have the story I'm telling, what all the plotting and conspiracy is leading up to, and I've never deviated from that story, it's been right on since the pilot and that's what matters to me. That's the story I'm telling. Now over the seasons, subplots developed, and some of them work and some of them don't....and if there's a subplot that everybody hates, and even the writers themselves can pick out the flaws, I have no problem dropping it. I think it'd be foolish to hold onto it through vanity and pride. If it's not the main storyline, it's fair game. The fans don't have as much power as they think they do, but we will listen, and if it's unanimous and true hatred, not just suspense you love to hate, then if it's a subplot, it's completely negotiable. You pay attention to what people are saying, but you can't have any loud and vocal minority influencing any creative decisions on the show, you just have to pay attention to what's going on and who's saying what.

Kripke was eager to know if there was anything fans were really loving or hating, anything he seemed to be missing. Just as fans spend a great deal of time worrying that the actors/producers/creators wouldn't understand fandom and thus would harbor negative feelings about fans, the creative side worries that they're not understanding the fans, and thus at risk of alienating them. At the time, early in season four, fandom was debating accusations of misogyny, racism and homophobia on *Supernatural*. Eric told us that his awareness of fandom's discussion of homophobia had in fact already influenced the trajectory of SPN episodes.

Kripke: I think in my mind we had one line that went too far, and it was in "Bedtime Stories", and Sam is pointing out a reference to Cinderella, and Dean said, "could you be any more gay?" I think that went too far. And I disagree with it, but this is sometimes the way young men talk, there's that tone that gets taken on even if there isn't malice behind it. It's in the DNA of stupid men, and it's a reflection of our culture. But I think we made up for it in the "Ghostfacers" episode, the core of the story is how love supersedes anything, and I don't get it when people say because the gay character ends up dead that it's homophobic, because the hero is a gay man, and the other character is someone who comes to realize the power of love.

Kripke's frustration with fans' interpretation of his Show is less surprising than the fact that, as showrunner, he was listening fairly closely to fannish discussion and concerns. While they are clearly listening, the creative side of *Supernatural* is as invested in their creations as the fans are. Both feel a possessiveness about the characters, and a strong desire to maintain their continuity. We asked writer and Season 6 and 7 showrunner Sera Gamble, were there ever moments when Gamble felt that fans should not be listened to?

Gamble: I read something once, to the effect of "Eric Kripke doesn't get Dean." I was like, okay, everyone is entitled to an opinion or three, and it's great that fans are so possessive of the show, but that's officially ridiculous. He created the character. At a certain point, if a character is going a direction the creator has always intended and it makes you say 'that guy doesn't get it', I think you gotta ask yourself if maybe you just disagree, and if it was your show you'd do it differently. I'm not the ultimate authority, but I hope I'm one authority. I've certainly invested a tremendous amount of time and effort in them. And there are aspects of these characters that I suggested and shaped over many episodes, so I've contributed to their DNA. I can't control audience interpretation, and I don't want to. If I wanted to control my audience I'd quit writing for Hollywood and start writing for Washington. …. Sometimes things don't translate to an audience for reasons you couldn't have foreseen…and sometimes you just don't write them clearly enough. I've made a few forays into suckland. At which point, audience interpretation that it sucked does trump authorial intent for it not to suck. Such is life, and also it may explain why writers are famously depressive.

A discussion of authorial intent and audience interpretation is beyond the scope of this book, and has been widely debated elsewhere, but with the perception of a close relationship between creator and fans comes the assumption that fans will "get it", much as we tend to assume in any intimate relationship. Because the reciprocal relationship, however, is often mediated by third parties and especially when communication occurs in print, that assumption can backfire.

Kripke: I did an interview where we were joking and I said Jensen wouldn't give me his salary kickback and so we fired him and we're going to bring in Chad Michael Murray, and fans flipped out like it was a real thing and I had to release statements saying I was kidding. I thought in some unspoken way that everyone would know, there are only two leads….I think the majority knew it was a cliffhanger and we'd bring him back.

On the other hand, too much openness, both fans and creators appear to realize, can do damage to the balance the two sides maintain between sharing information and maintaining boundaries. The question of what and who to pay attention to, and how much openness is too much, is one that the creative side—showrunners, writers, and actors alike—struggle with. In a variety of ways, not putting too much out there is a way of sustaining interest in the Show and allowing the continuation of the fantasy free from too much intrusion of reality. In the simplest example, as *Supernatural* has become more popular and fans have actively scoured the internet (and

Vancouver) for information, Kripke was aware that to maintain suspense, they have to play some things close to the vest.

> Kripke: It's very hard to do, we have a couple of secrets coming up in Season four and have been trying to keep them under wraps. So my assistant has been rewriting sides to hide details, changing names and making fans try to decipher details. To be honest, sometimes they're right and sometimes they're wrong, but it's kind of a treasure hunt for them to figure out what it all means. The major plot points we try to hide because it takes the fun out of it.

In addition to the boundary which constrains how much is put "out there", there are boundaries on both sides which limit how much gets in as well. Gamble was aware of the lure of instant feedback and the need to avoid it in order to keep the show on track when we spoke to her during season three.

> Gamble: I'm aware of the message boards and webrings, and a few conventions. I went to Comic Con this year and the fan presence was pretty intense. Most of the writers check in on the message boards. I think this is true of most tv shows. It's instant feedback, which is hard to resist. I think it takes discipline not to check in, even though for the most part we agree it's not always helpful to read pages and pages of ranting and nitpicks from the most passionate or obsessed watchers. It's kind of crazy-making. I do occasionally google myself – my friend calls it masturgoogling – which sometimes leads me to Live Journal discussions. But I haven't delved too deep. Honestly it usually feels beside the point. I'm under pressure to come up with the next idea, and the train is moving fast. The fans are discussing stuff we finished months ago. What actually impacts my career is that I do a god job in the eyes of my bosses and studio and network. And nothing will stop a conversation about fan reaction quicker than an assistant coming in with the ratings for the week.

As a writer, Gamble avoids reading fanfiction for practical reasons. Not only would she not want to inadvertently incorporate fanfic plots into canon, but her investment in the characters she's been writing for years results in irritation when fanfic writers get it "wrong". Fans, of course, often explode in similar irritation when Sam or Dean or Castiel do something they perceive as OOC (out of character), whether onscreen or in fanfiction.

> Gamble: I never read the fanfic, sexy or G-rated. It feels weird. Partially because I've been so deep into the mythology of these two characters and this world for three seasons now, so I get really annoyed when something

isn't right; neurotic, I know, but I can't help it. And also, I would hate to accidentally steal someone's story idea.

When we first spoke to Gamble, she was already struggling with finding a balance in Show's reciprocal relationship with fans, three years before she became the showrunner herself. At the time, Sam and Dean weren't exactly on the same page, and fans were reacting strongly—and negatively—to the lack of brotherly love. Gamble was aware of fans' response, and defended the creative team's decision to go against it, setting a boundary in maintaining creative control over the characters even as she could relate to fans' feelings.

> Gamble: It's a balance, giving fans what they like and have grown accustomed to and focusing on telling a fresh, compelling story over 22 episodes. We can't get to where we're going this season without separating the boys sometimes in the short term. Our fans react in real time to episodes, but we write episodes with an eye on the last several and the next several. So sometimes there's an immediate outcry – "where are the scenes with Sam and Dean eyeball to eyeball, being all brothery?!" Well, there are so many other things going on for each of them right now, and we need them to talk to each other a little less for the moment. It's important to the story – the story of their relationship. And their relationship is growing and shifting and maturing under the intense pressures they're facing. We're doing these things to make them grow. That's one of the cool things about doing TV – you're with a couple for years and years. (Yes, I just called them a couple – but no, not like that!) You get to see what happens to the relationship over time; you earn this very intimate experience of the characters because you've invested so many hours watching them. And – this is also one of the least cool things about doing Tv. A lot of people tune in to feel that familiar feeling every single episode for 100 episodes. And they are very resistant to change. I can understand that -- I've been like that myself on occasion. But as a writer it makes me crazy.

Nevertheless, the boundary cannot be so impermeable that the reciprocal relationship isn't sustained. In a 2008 interview with *Eclipse Magazine*, Eric Kripke recognized the value of fan input.

> Kripke: You guys drive me crazy, but I love you! You force me to make the show better, so how could I not love you? It's a very smart fan base, you guys are kicking ass, so thank you. It (SPN) has been a dream come true. It is, by far, the single most satisfying thing I've ever done….this is the first show that was personal to me and that I was passionate about….It was a subject I was interested in, my obsessions….And for this to be the one that has gone the distance and for people to connect with means more

to me than you could ever know. I never take it for granted (Bekakos
2008).

Playing a Role: Boundaries from the Actors' Perspective

Supernatural's lead actors have more face-to-face interaction with
fans, and thus a different—and perhaps more boundaried—relationship
than the Show's writers and showrunners. They also have a different
understanding of who fans are and what they want from fandom, since
they tend to share different fan spaces with fans than the Show's creators,
at conventions and other in-person spaces instead of online communities
and message boards. As part of the creative team who interprets the
writers' vision and brings the characters to life, the actors must also
construct boundaries that achieve a balance between listening to fans too
much and not enough. We asked Jared Padalecki how he negotiates those
boundaries. Like Kripke and Gamble, he had already defined for himself
just how reciprocal his relationship with fandom should be in order to
allow him to do his job, and where to establish the balance between fan
service and keeping creative control over the character of Sam.

> Padalecki: Pleasing the fans, luckily, is—I hope this doesn't sound bad, I
> should preface it by saying that I love my fans, but I do not care in the
> slightest about it. It's my job not to care. If I start trying to please the fans,
> then it would backfire and I'd end up not pleasing the fans. It's my job to
> take what is given to me and plug myself into it. Like fans plug themselves
> into Supernatural, and into that world, in my world I have to plug myself
> into Sam. There are a lot of actors that could play this character, Sam
> Winchester, I could name a thousand, and I only say thousands because I
> can think of thousands, but millions that can play this character. Taller,
> shorter, better looking, less good looking, blacker, whiter, the only thing
> that I can bring to Sam that none of them can is my own experience. And
> that's it. It's not that I'm the best actor or that I look like Sam should look,
> it's just whatever I can pull from or draw from my past. So if I start to
> ignore that and try to please the fans, then I completely destroy Sam
> Winchester..... Even if it says he looks hot, he looks better than he used to,
> even that's bad, because you get cocky or you get the false confidence or
> arrogance and you just start focusing on vanity, which I don't want to do.
> My job is to flesh out Sam Winchester however I can, not to take from a
> billion people, but to play it my way, otherwise all these shows would be
> CGI.

Padalecki, like Kripke and Gamble, recognized the need to place limits
on fans' input in order to sustain his vision of Sam, the character that fans
fell in love with in the first place. His costar agreed.

Ackles: To be honest, I actually try not to read a lot of it. I've never read any fan fiction, for two reasons. One, it may just creep me out and two, I don't want to be influenced by how I play Dean by what the fans would want. If they start fan fictioning me, like Dean, in a certain way they want me to play Dean, I don't want them influencing me. If they want me to play it a little more somber, I'm like wait, no!

Many of the SPN guest actors felt the same about fans' input on their characters, but some were more open to input than others. Unlike some of the other actors, Matt Cohen (young John Winchester/Archangel Michael) sees his creation of a character as a joint construction of his own acting skills and the desires of his fans to see what they want to see.

Cohen: I want to make the movies they want to see, I want my career to be a conjunction of what I love and what they love. If they say "You should play this character" I want to look to get cast in that kind of role. It's such a small percentage of my energy to do that. If I can make 10,000 people happy, if someone asks me something and it's within my power [I'll do it].

Sometimes actors can't avoid a bit of fan influence. Gabriel Tigerman, who played Andy Gallagher on Season 1 and 2, discovered slash fanfiction written about his character and actor Chad Lindberg's character Ash when a friend emailed him a link. Meeting Lindberg in person for the first time at a fan convention, Tigerman said, was awkward—a different type of reciprocal relationship, as fanfiction influenced real life actor relationships.

Tigerman: I had vaguely heard about this genre, but I never anticipated being written in it! My buddy emailed me a link, and I was on my laptop at my parents' house, which is not the ideal way to discover that. My mom was like, what's that, and I was like, "Nothing!" It was hilarious meeting Chad… It was like "Hey, nice to…… ohhh, you're the guy…." It felt like meeting a one-night stand again. I felt like we knew each other. So 99% of it is hilarious and whatever, but there is that weird part too like huh, I never pictured that, and now…. (laughs).

Unlike showrunners and writers, the actors must also negotiate an additional aspect of openness—how thickly to draw a boundary around their entertainer personas as they interact with fans. Padalecki has been effusive in his appreciation of fans, often referring to them as "part of my *Supernatural* family." When we sat down to hear his thoughts on fandom, the first thing he said was "the fans are awesome." However, he also immediately articulated the need for boundaries. We shared SPN guest actor Jim Beaver's story of being in a parade for his former television series, *Deadwood*, when he was cheered by the crowd one minute and then unrecognized and ignored by the very same people as soon as the parade was over and he was just some guy walking back to his hotel. How does Padalecki handle this sort of disconnect?

> Padalecki: There is a buddy of mine who is also an actor, and he was saying there are so many sides of a person, and especially the sides of an actor. There is the side of Jared that I know, the side that my brother, my girlfriend, my parents know, and the side that the people at work know. There are so many different sides and aspects and I think the fans are fans of the Jared that's in the parade, in the Sam costume, the Jared that is playing Sam. I have been an actor for a while, and it's funny, I think this show specifically, being a genre show and a cult hit, people just link so much to the characters and their plight and it's the whole archetype. You know, why the *Lion King* was so successful, and the *Matrix* and *Lord of the Rings*. That story (of Jim's) is funny to hear because I have had a similar experience. Never when in a parade, but say I'm at a restaurant, and kind of make eye contact with a bunch of people, nothing huge, then once that one person comes up saying hey, can I take a picture, then everyone comes out of the wood work, and now it's like, hey it's Jared the celebrity. I think I have been very lucky, I've been in the business for 9 years, and have been very successful, but not too – It's not like I step outside my door and photographers are in the bushes. You feel for the Britney Spears, that level of fame, and not to say they are without their problems, and they are saints, but that can't be fun. I love my anonymity, and I love being able to walk around after I work out sweaty and smelly and not worry about someone seeing and writing about it on line.

Both lead actors explicitly recognized that too much openness and transparency could interfere with fans' constructions of who the actors are –constructions that fans have created and are invested in maintaining. Just as too much openness might threaten the fantasy of the canon SPN world, fans knowing too much about the real Jared or Jensen might threaten the fantasy fans have constructed of the "real people". Padalecki recognized the strength of that investment in fantasy, especially when it comes to his relationship with his costar, drawing a parallel to fanfiction. Fans interpret and co-construct their story of "J2" just as they interpret the characters on the show itself.

> Padalecki: And of course (the fans love that Jensen and I live together) because, in my opinion, every single thing we do is going to be exactly what the fans want us to do. If it got in USA Today tomorrow that he and I got in a huge fist fight and I broke his nose and he busted my eye, then they'd be like oh, look how passionate they are and they're friendly enough that they could fight. And I could go on and say I hate him, I shot him with a gun and wish he died, they'd be like man, it's so intense what

they do on camera that it's bled into real life. It has nothing to do with reality. What they think of our situation is exactly what they want it to be and it always will be. You sort of accept that or you don't. It's how I feel about fan fiction.

The boundary goes both ways; Jared believes the reciprocal relationship between fans and their fannish objects, himself included, works best when there's not too much reality imposed on either side.

> Padalecki: Just like the fans feel like they have a grasp of me, I feel like I have a grasp of the fans. But in the same way they are delusional about who I am, and don't really want to know about me, I don't really want to know about who they are. It's almost like I don't want to know any more or any less. It's flattering, they're supportive, so where they pigeon holed me, with mutual appreciation, I have pigeon holed them as thank you so much, just as you're naïve about me, I'm naïve about y'all, that's how I can still come to work and stay sane. And there certainly is not a lack of appreciation, on either end.

Padalecki keeps his own boundaries relatively tight, despite the fact that fans often perceive him as an open book. The juggling act is something he has thought a lot about.

> Padalecki: I sort of have a theory that my fans are supportive of me, but I think my fans are not interested in the Jared that my brother, my friends, my parents, my best friend or girlfriend at the time are. They are interested in the Jared they know, that Jared that is Sam Winchester. They know me as an entertainer. I mean most people I see every day, I have fantastic relationships with them. But they do not know the real Jared….. And not only do I accept that, but it's kind of the way I would prefer it. I've been told, maybe because I'm a Cancer, but the people who are truly close to me are very few and it takes a very very long time for me to let them in. I love people, but to actually know me, there are a handful. If fans think I'm an open book, then I will always be an open book. It doesn't matter if some skeletons come out of my closet. Strangely enough my true fans, the actual fans of the show, do not want to know me. I've thought about it a lot because it's intense and it's my job and it's unusual. Not unusual bad, just different.

The actor recognizes the need to keep some sense of mystery around "Jared" in order to allow him to play a believable "Sam".

Fig. 7-1. Ackles and Padalecki have each other's backs

Fig. 7-2: I see you, you see me (sort of). Padalecki greets a fan.

Padalecki: I love acting. I don't love—funny, we're talking about fame and fandom—I don't love that aspect of fame or fandom because I still love to

slum it. It's flattering and that's great but I love being Jared that very few
of my friends know. That my family knows. And as long as entertainer
Jared is out there, it is unfortunately my job even when not on set to be
entertainer Jared every now and again. Also, frankly, I think Russell
Crowe said, the more people know about me, the less people will believe
the character I play. So it is truly my job to keep Jared protected and put
entertainer Jared out there whenever, and if they are going to believe me, I
don't need to let them in. They're allowing me to do what I want, enabling
me to do what I want , so I'll enable them through what they want.

Supernatural fandom feels a strong sense of protectiveness for Ackles,
who is often painted by fans as the shy and reserved one in contrast to his
costar, who is perceived as an open book.. How does he deal with fandom
constructing a personality for him that may or may not be accurate?

> Ackles: I kind of laugh it off. Because, to be honest, like you said, I'm not
> real shy and reserved. It's funny because when Jared gets in front of people
> he's a motor mouth. Not in a bad way, but he talks alot and he has energy,
> which is great because I can sit back and be like, go ahead man. But it's
> funny cuz I go out with my family and I'm chatting it up with the waiter.

We also shared Jim Beaver's story of the *Deadwood* parade with
Ackles, wondering how he deals with the artificiality and context-
dependence of fame, and the boundary between who he is with family and
friends and who he is as at a convention. Like his costar, Ackles is
conscious of the need to shift into an entertainer version of himself,
depending on environmental contingencies.

> Ackles: It is just that. I'd love to say that it is, like you said, that open
> book thing and Jared I guess is a little more of that as himself and I tend to
> be a little watchful of what I say or how I act or what I do. It's almost like
> you put on a coat because you know you're about to go out and be
> documented. You're gonna be photographed etc. so you kind of put on this
> professional cloak and say a couple funny anecdotes, and respond
> intelligently and don't say any off color remarks and don't cuss, and
> remember that mom could be watching this and grandma could tune in and
> see it. So I've got all that kinda going on in my head, so I censor myself,
> not that I'd be throwing curse words around like a sailor. I'm conscious of
> it, and I guess that could be seen as being reserved but it's just a protection
> mechanism, and I also have to understand that they want to see me and
> interact with me. So I have to bring a lot of my personality and a lot of
> who I am to the table but at the same time I don't bring everything because
> I always want to keep something for me. So if I'm out at a restaurant, I'm
> me, I'll be completely myself or whatever, but as soon as someone comes
> up and says hey can I have your autograph, it's like a button gets pushed

and I flip into a different mode. Not like Jekyll and Hyde, but it's just like oh yeah, absolutely, how are you doing. I could be in a fight with Danneel at dinner and we can be like arguing over something completely mundane, and then if someone comes up its like hey, are you that guy from *Supernatural*? And it's like oh yeah, hey nice to meet you!

Does he feel pressured to snap into that mode sometimes on the spot?

Ackles: One time it's gotten back to me that somebody met me and said I was an asshole, a girl came up to me in a bar and said I know you, my friend came up to you and you were an asshole. But luckily I was with a bunch of my buddies and they were like, are you kidding me, he's like the nicest guy in the world, what are you talking about? But it was like a slap in the face. I can't be candid with everyone I meet, especially with people I know in that world. I guess it's pressure if you let it, but here's the great thing of the balance of that, I don't see it a lot. At the conventions I know it's coming and I can prepare myself, I know I'm going to go through 5 hours of that, and I'll put it on and it's like putting on a show. But I'm here (on set) 16 hours a day, 5 days a week, 9 months of the year and these guys are my family. So I'm like, you can see me on set joking around, laughing, playing and Action! (pops into role)

Ackles does in fact demonstrate that ability repeatedly while filming, teasing with Padalecki up until the last second and then suddenly turning into a pissed off Dean Winchester when the cameras roll. As comfortable as he is on set, however, Jensen struggles with navigating the middle ground of being "a little famous". For SPN fans, Ackles and Padalecki are true celebrities; for much of the rest of the world, they're two good looking guys who might look vaguely familiar. There is a sense of shame at being an object being watched, which Ackles compares to being a zoo exhibit.

Ackles: So I think that, and you know, we're not talking Tom Cruise, Johnny Depp, Brad Pitt type fame here, but when we're walking down the street, you might catch one out of maybe ten people that are like, you're that guy. The real weird stuff was when you're at a grocery store or somewhere well-lit and public, or an airport, urgh, god forbid an airport, and one person comes up to you in the terminal and is like (girly voice) 'omg omg omg', and then you have like 30 people jostling to see who you are and then you hear this: "Who's that?" Meanwhile, you're just going, argh. Some people are like hey, can I take a picture with you? And I'm like (whispers) yeah, just walk around the corner so it doesn't cause a scene, so people don't see, because then they're staring at me the rest of the whole flight. I'm not a household name across the country, but if a few recognize me and make a scene, then I have 30-50 people trying to figure out who I am, and then someone's like oh, go ask him who he is, and then I have this old redneck guy coming up to me saying "Hey man, who are you? Hey man, my daughter wants me to ask who you are." And I'm like uhh, not really anyone. And then he's like "No, come on man, tell me, who are you?" So then I have to run down the resume, which is completely embarrassing. I've gone through that multiple times, and it's embarrassing. So when people kind of wear hats or try to stay hidden, for me I do it not to hide from fans—I have no problem talking to somebody who likes the show or wants to ask about the show or is a fan. It's just those other people that's uncomfortable, like if someone makes a scene and everyone is looking at you, and I just want to hide. It's like all of a sudden I'm a zoo exhibit. Which is a really kind of odd feeling.

Fig. 7-3: Papparazzi! Ackles turns the tables on Padalecki and photographer Chris Schmelke

The (idealized) persona that fans want to see up close and personal sometimes collapses in the carnival space of conventions, when fans and fanned are in close quarters for extended periods of time. One of the most jarring collapses we experienced in our research came at the Eyecon *Supernatural* convention in Orlando in 2008. The convention screened a powerful indie film called *My Big Break*, a cautionary tale about the lure and danger of Hollywood starring four up and coming young actors. One of them was Chad Lindberg (Ash on SPN), who was appearing at Eyecon that weekend. *My Big Break* pulls no punches, exposing the painful consequences of gaining and losing fame and the very real financial problems that Lindberg and his housemates eventually experienced. *Supernatural* fans were shocked to see the actor they had just cheered for onstage and waited in line for photo ops, as a regular human being, temporarily broke and living on a friend's couch.

> Lindberg: I think it took them out of the *Supernatural* perspective they were in and I even had a few people change their perspective as far as us (the actors), and how they react to us at the conventions. I think it affected some people and it bothered some people because they want to know, and (yet) they don't want to know that there is all this crap because it kind of ruins it for the fans almost. They don't want to know actors are broke, they just want to see all the fun.

SPN guest actor Gabe Tigerman also spoke about the struggle to figure out who you really are when others' perception of you changes dramatically depending on what space you're in. Convention spaces change the rules for celebrities as well as for fans.

> Tigerman: In this hotel, in these certain few hundred square feet, I am Tom Cruise. I could walk around Los Angeles and no one would know me and all of a sudden I'm in this concentrated area and I'm Tom Cruise. It was very weird at Eyecon because it was connected to a mall, so when I walked out there I was no longer anybody important. I walked past somebody and I make eye contact because I'm sure they want to say hi, and then I'm like, Oh you don't care! You don't care at all. I'm just the asshole. When we were in Orlando, somebody bid on breakfast with me. I remember hearing how much they bid and I was thinking I hope this is the best breakfast anyone could ever have.

Just as fans police the boundaries, the actors are aware of the necessity to define and defend their own.

> Lindberg: I definitely have my boundaries. There are certain things I won't do … (times) when it's not okay, when they are invading my personal space. (Being accosted in the rest room, for example).

> Fred Lehne (*Supernatural*'s original big bad, the Yellow Eyed Demon): I have found that one has to be a little more vigilant as to how open you are. How accessible you are, because some people can take advantage of that. Some people go straight to way too personal.

All of the SPN actors we interviewed felt that the rewards of having fans outweighed the occasional boundary violations.

Padalecki: I think as much as sometimes it seems like fans can be a little disrespectful when they disrespect your privacy when you want to just be a person, they know when it's right. I have many times had dinner, and had someone after I got the bill say, I didn't want to interrupt you while you were eating, but my cousin is a huge fan, and lives in Houston, can I get your autograph? So it's like wow - you know, at least for me, and my fans, it's not just hey I've seen you on tv, I own you. Of course it is sometimes. And there is that group of superfans that are like you are Sam and not Jared and just don't get it, and I don't blame them or fault them - that's what your brain does, it's the first impression and that's what they've got of me. And I personally love my fans, they're the reason I get to do what I do and make money and have fun and do what I'm passionate about doing for a living and I am certainly grateful, and I haven't had any bad experiences yet. I mean, I've had butt grabs and stuff like that but nothing too too funny. One of the funnier things that happened at a Supernatural convention was in Chicago, when that sweet little girl got up to ask a question, and started sobbing, and I wanted to say it's okay, I'm a fan not of any actor in particular, but if I saw Eddie Vedder for example, I'd be like uhhhh I - I - I don't even know what I'm going to say.

Rarely, in our experience of *Supernatural* fandom, do fans break physical boundaries interacting with the actors. An exception was the "flying fangirl" incident, which caused an outpouring of shame and projected rage in fandom. How did Jensen Ackles feel about being tackled, and what actually happened at the Asylum convention? According to one of the *Supernatural* fandom's unofficial musicians, Jason Manns, who was with Ackles at the time, fandom was probably more upset than Jensen.

Manns: It was a weird thing, she just popped out and came at him like a spider monkey and I think she was trying to kiss him, with her feet off the ground. When she jumped up she kicked his legs around, and cracked me in the shin, and he stumbled backwards, and it was just so quick, she was just a little girl, but it was kind of a shock, with all the people around, and security pulled her off and I don't know how but she got out of their grips and she came running towards the elevator. We were in there and it was like slow motion, the doors were closing, and it looked scripted, she got caught like halfway in so the doors stayed open and they are holding her parallel to the ground screaming and they just carried her out – so the doors closed and we are in the elevator like, what did we just get into? She was a tiny little girl, so it was only afterwards that it really seemed scary. You are sitting there thinking like, people who step outside the realm of normal society, and behave in ways that people refer to as crazy, are crazy, and that's how John Lennon got shot. We were like, it was funny at the time, but now it's kind of scary and kind of dangerous.

Apparently Ackles was not quite as traumatized by the Flying Fangirl as fandom feared.

Ackles: I laughed at that immediately as soon as I got in the elevator. And then it was after that it was like hmm, what's to stop her really jealous boyfriend from coming at me with a little knife? And then I got a little freaked out, but I was like well, I guess if I got stabbed, I'd turn around and deck him.

Clearly the actor has learned a few things from playing Dean for seven seasons.

Part of the Process: Co-Constructing *Supernatural*

The necessity for boundaries does not take away from the development of the reciprocal relationship; rather, the limits set on both sides seem to facilitate the relationship and keep the convergence from disrupting the balance of fantasy and reality necessary for putting on a television show. As Kripke, Gamble, and the SPN actors all acknowledge, the reciprocal relationship between fans and the creative side has allowed fans to become part of the process in a variety of ways. While boundaries are clearly desired and felt necessary on both sides, nevertheless the reciprocity is valued by fans and creators alike, resulting in a high level of interaction. Many of the actors who have guest starred on *Supernatural* are particularly conscious of fan power and its beneficial effects. Working actors (if they're fortunate) have the opportunity to act on many different television shows and films, and are thus in a position to compare the ways in which the creators of different shows interact with the fans.

Actor C. Malik Whitfield, who played African American detective Victor Henrickson on SPN, talked about the impact of fan accusations of racism on *Supernatural*. He noted the positive impact that *Supernatural*'s reciprocal interaction with fans has had on the Show and the broader culture, and his perception that the creative side was uniquely open to listening.

Whitfield: People were very not happy (about Henrickson's death), and I thought that's good. Any time that people express themselves, it will change the format in which tv is done. Take nothing away from the execs, but that doesn't mean they get it right all the time. What's great is when

you have that interactiveness and response because it says maybe we're
onto something, and let's listen to the response and the different
components to making a show that can stay around. I think it's so cool,
anything is possible with the SPN fans.

The guest actors have benefitted directly from the high level of
investment that *Supernatural* fans have in the Show, and their willingness
to make their opinions known. Because these actors are not accustomed to
fame, their boundaries tend to be looser when interacting with fans, both in
online fan spaces and face-to-face ones. *Supernatural*, with its uniquely
passionate fans, has allowed many of them the opportunity to experience
fame on a level they would not have otherwise, but only within the
specific boundaries of SPN fannish space. They see themselves, like the
fans, as "part of the process." Richard Speight Jr. has played the Trickster
and the archangel Gabriel across five seasons of SPN, and is a regular on
the convention circuit. He sees the reciprocal relationship with fans as
having a positive impact on the Show, and recognizes his own role as part
of the process.

> Speight: Kripke and everyone is paying attention. Fans do have a direct
> effect on the show, this show follows what you do. I don't think it's
> detrimental at all, it's not to sabotage what they love but to improve what
> they love. To increase it and see more of it. People really do their
> homework. I'm fascinated by this culture because it's so new to me. If
> people watch and like our work, it's great to have a venue like this with
> people who like and want to talk about it. It's so participatory and
> interactive, at a certain point it's going to be almost an Encyclopedia
> Brown book like do we go with Jared or Jensen. If they don't like the
> character I'm playing, if it's a hindrance to the show and the producers
> know, then I might lose a job, but that's a good thing. If they don't lose
> me and I'm driving the show down then maybe the fans lose interest and
> the show goes away. Actors are just a part of the process.

Actor Matt Cohen agreed.

> Cohen: I think *Supernatural* has created such a special thing between the
> fans and the cast and crew on set and the creators behind the scenes – this
> is really a unique show. There's really nothing like this out there. There's
> not many other shows where all the fans come, they meet each other and
> become buddies and they're hanging out, and the actors are talking and
> hanging out, we're singing together. I really act like myself. I'm this guy.
> I'm a dork, I don't care. And it's nice to be able to give that to the fans
> without them going "Oh he's not what we thought. They're like "Oh my
> god! He's like us! We're the same people."

Actress Kim Rhodes, who played Sheriff Mills, was interviewed at the start of Season 7 about her reaction to *Supernatural*'s dedicated fan base. She, like others on the creative side, found the reciprocal relationship with fans to be different than what is experienced on other television shows. Like Speight, she recognized that she—and fans—are part of the process, and viewed the creation of *Supernatural* as a communal co-production.

> Rhodes: This was the first time I saw a TV fan base as we are all "us". There are different roles within that "us" but (*Supernatural* has) really perfected and honored the art of the audience being integral to the art. Nobody is a brilliant actor in their shower. They might think they are but communication is a two way process and it's really hard to remember that when you never come in contact with your audience. And it's really easy for an actor to start thinking it really is all about them, when in fact, we are the servants…. Really, it's all about you? Let's see how well you do without electricity—"Oh! You're naked 'cause wardrobe didn't show today!!" So this is a really great symbiotic relationship and communal creation of a show. So I think that's also why it's such a passionate fan base. Because people understand that they're being honored as part of the process and not just passive observers (Kinzie 2011).

Rhodes' use of the word "honored" could be construed to mean anything from the appreciation cast and crew have expressed in interviews to the Show's incorporation of fandom into canon as it broke the fourth wall, but Rhodes feels that a sense of "we're all in this together" exists among cast, crew and fandom.

Recurring guest star Jim Beaver also explicitly recognized the creation and reception of the Show as an interpretive process—one which includes the creators, writers, actors and fans.

> Beaver: Frankly I'm dumbstruck about any of this attention to Bobby. There have been a couple of times I've googled him, and I see there's a growing base of people who are very fond of the character, and every time I look again, I'm further astonished. A lot of actors don't care what the audience thinks in a specific sense, but every once in a while I will to see what pops up, and I was struck by how many times people would get into conversations about the tiniest little details, like what does that mean. I remember there was something about the charms I gave them so they wouldn't get possessed, and somebody said, 'did you see the look on Bobby's face when he handed those charms to them? It looked like he had something he wasn't saying'. Well, what I was keeping back was I had no idea what I was talking about! It's interesting to see how invested people are, not just in the show and the characters, but in the minutia of it. Sometimes even the actors don't know – the whole thing is an interpretive process. Even the writers are interpreting Eric's vision. And the director

and the cinematographer, and then it gets handed over to the audience to do it over again. Who's to say who's right? I find it all an impressionistic experience. I love to find bits of subtext that didn't occur to me before. Subtext is great!

Fig. 7-4: Signs of affection: Fan gifts in a con green room.

Supernatural fandom would heartily agree with him--after all, as we've noted, fanfiction is often based on perceived subtext between characters. Fans and aca-fans have cited *Supernatural*'s facility with subtext as one of the reasons there is more *Supernatural* fanfiction than nearly any other media property in existence, including a vast amount of Wincest inspired by the Sam/Dean subtext fans many fans see in canon, and Destiel, inspired by similar Dean/Castiel subtext. The actors see their role in the interpretive process as connected to their ability to convey nuanced characters and emotions, some of which is based around the subtext fans love so much. Thus, subtext becomes a point of intersection that unites the actors and the fans, as both interpret the writers' vision.

Fig. 7-5: We're all in this together. Fan-made quilt hangs in the production office.

Beaver: Freud would probably go along with that. Jared and Jensen probably pick a bone with it, I'm sure they're aware of it. I'm kind of amused, but the fact is, you can draw those sorts of connections and parallels to almost any aspect of life if you pull apart at them long enough. My favorite movie in the world is John Ford's *The Searchers*. The driving force of the plot is John Wayne's love for his brother's wife and vice versa. And there is not one word of dialogue relating to that. You see the looks between the characters, you see his reaction when she dies – but nobody says a word about it. I've always thought the best actors know something you don't know. Like they've got a secret, and it may never get revealed. The best people I've ever seen act, I'm seeing all this stuff and there's something underneath too, and it makes me want to watch and figure it out. It wouldn't work if these guys weren't good actors. I think you could do an episode of *Supernatural* without a single word of dialogue with this bunch, because the crew on this show is capable of doing an awful lot of expression non-verbally, and making people really think deeply about what is being conveyed with no words. We all feed off each other pretty well. The fact we all like each other so much is helpful, but it's also the fact that Jared, Jensen and I are pretty similar actors. We all three are the kind that can be joking around, and then they say action, and we are in it. None of us are the kind of guy that has to sit in a corner for an hour to get ready. We just kind of relate to each other in ways that work well, and fit well. I mean, I did an episode of *Melrose Place* once, and I wouldn't want to do an episode with no dialogue with them!

When we first interviewed Misha Collins, he had just joined the cast and had not yet been to his first convention to meet fans in person. Nevertheless, he already had at least a passing familiarity with slash and was already aware of the power of subtext in *Supernatural*, and that the chemistry between Castiel and Dean was contributing to his character's acceptance by fans.

> Collins: The scenes we've (Jensen and I) had together, there's something that clicks, and they're easy, the way we interact with each other. I don't know why, but there's always a certain intensity, a quiet intensity that organically comes out when we're doing scenes.
> Us: Castiel is a complicated character. Is he good? Is he not good? Does he like Dean, does he hate Dean, does he want to take Dean apart?
> Collins: (deadpans) Does he want to take Dean to bed?

The reciprocal relationship between *Supernatural* fans and the creative side has developed over the course of seven seasons. As fans and creators got to know each other, the increasing openness and communication began to break down initial misconceptions on both sides, allowing points of intersection and understanding. Actor Jim Beaver was initially confused about who SPN fans were, once he found out about the breadth of fanworks they were producing.

> Beaver: I was shocked when I first started hearing about Wincest, just because it didn't jive with my idea of who the fans were. My impression is the majority of *Supernatural* fans are women between 28 and 50, and that doesn't seem to be the kind of group that would gravitate toward that interpretation. I'm not thinking about the brother part, just the homosexual part. I had no idea we had so many gay (male) fans. I would have bet the farm that romantic/erotic fanfiction for this show would have involved one or the other of the guys and a damsel in distress.

Jim's estimation of *Supernatural* fandom was, by most estimates, fairly accurate as far as gender, but his assumption that female fans only want to read traditional romance fiction wasn't. Over the past ten years, at least a dozen assessments of the gender and sexuality breakdown of fandom have been conducted by fans themselves, mostly through online polls. The results suggest that while the writers and readers of m/m slash fiction are often female, they are just as likely to be queer as straight.

Beaver: Well, that helps me understand better the reaction to Ruby and Bella. Maybe I'll jot one down myself!

Jensen Ackles was also surprised when he first learned who *Supernatural* fans were, after he finally had the opportunity to interact with them face to face. His reaction also hints at another aspect of reciprocity—just as fans are invested in the actors being who the fans want them to be, the actors are also invested in who the fans are. The more similar each side sees the other, the more comfortable both are in taking part in the co-construction of the Show, and the thinner the boundary between them needs to be.

Fig. 7-6: Ackles is a Sam fan too

Ackles compares his own investment in the Show and the character of Dean to that of the fans, drawing parallels.

Ackles: It was kind of shocking, I guess not shocking but surprising in a sense, when the show really got its feet under it in the middle of the first season and we finally started getting some feedback and some recognition, and it was kinda from unlikely characters. We came on the WB, and it was a network that was focused on a demographic that was obviously much younger. The people coming up and talking to us, or writing about the show online, and the fan mail, happened to be an older audience and a very intelligent audience. People who weren't just going, oh what side of the bed do you sleep on and do you wear boxers or briefs, they wanted to know why this character said this and what did they mean by that, because there could be double meanings, and how this character relates to that character or not. It was kind of refreshing, it was kinda nice … it wasn't just a show about two young guys who try to be sexy or hot, or play that easy card that those kind of shows or networks try to play….So it turned out to be a fan base that was surprising, and welcome and different. I enjoy the fact that people actually are interested in the story and the characters and why they do what they do and why they interact the way they do, which was my initial attraction to the show in the first place.

Resisting an awareness of sometimes being objectified by fans, Ackles instead feels a mutuality with the fans, in that the unique characteristics of *Supernatural* that attract fans are the same things that made him want to do the show.

Ackles: Initially actually they wanted me to read for Sam and when I went in I read for Sam and as soon as I was done, I made my case about Dean because he just popped off the page for me. I really liked the humor aspect of it and his arrogant air and there was just something about him, and I just wanted to play that role. I liked the chemistry between Dean and his father, Dean and his brother, so there was an attachment and a likeness that I liked that I found in Dean very early on. It wasn't just like oh it's gonna be two guys showing off their muscles as much as they can so we can get a 13 year old girl to buy our posters and lunchboxes. And I remember in the beginning, publicity was like these guys are in their mid to late 20's, we have to put them in *Tiger Beat* and *Teen Vogue*, and Eric was like no, this is not that show. It's not about the Backstreet Boys riding around in a cool car. These are two hardened brothers who come from a really rocky, dark past, and they are going to have a dark future. This isn't a show for the light hearted. So I think that's what drew a lot of people. I know McG in the beginning, and David Nutter, and myself, and Jared, we were really attracted to the grittiness, the dark sinister outlook on things.(Not black and white at all) There are a lot of levels and I think the complexity of it is what attracted a lot of us to it in the beginning and ultimately what attracted our fan base.

Ackles seems to understand, as do fans, how all three things—the complexity of the show, the family dynamics and the close relationship between Sam and Dean—allow for a greater level of fannish participation and investment than on most television series. At the same time, other (less valued) explanations for the popularity of the show, and of the actor himself, are de-emphasized.

> Ackles: And I think that was the underlying, kind of common denominator that bound everything together, the relationship between these two characters, and their love for not only for each other but for their family, and trying to grasp and hold on and protect as much as they could. We started out kind of positioning the show as a horror show that scares the hell out of you every week, but then there's this underlying storyline going on, this investment into these two characters, that fans really kind of gravitate to and why they kept coming back week after week and watching the show. Of course, the catch 22 of that is, just selfishly I wish that they'd add more characters to get some time off (laughing).

Both the creative side of the Show and the fandom have had a better understanding of the basis of *Supernatural*'s popularity than TPTB from the start, perhaps because of their closer connection.

> Ackles: We are definitely the odd step child of the CW and I think that this season (season 4) they have kind of realized it's probably best to let us do what we do. And since they've done that, look at the ratings!

Harnessing the Reciprocal Relationship

The creative side, as we've discussed thus far, construct boundaries to limit the flow of information and maintain creative control. They also must negotiate boundaries with fandom to preserve a sense of well-being and further their careers. Fans have a complicated relationship with their fannish objects; similarly, everyone we interviewed on the creative side described a complicated relationship with fandom. All expressed an awareness and appreciation of the impact fans had on their ability to continue to do the work they love doing. At the same time, all worried about their ability to remain popular with the fans, and recognized the risk of losing fans' affections. The SPN actors have all had to negotiate boundaries to maintain the integrity of their characters, as well as to insulate themselves from negative evaluation, which is especially prevalent in anonymous online spaces. Misha Collins talked thoughtfully about the difference between being on a show like 24, where there were more people watching but, as he pointed out, "no one interviewing me," and a show like *Supernatural*, where fans are not only watching but expressing their opinions.

Collins: I think it makes me take it a little more seriously. It sort of makes
it feel like a bit more of a responsibility. It's just not some junk that people
are half watching. There's a bit more devotion on the receiving end. The
other thing is, seeing how nasty fans are to the people they don't like, to
the women, it makes you conscious of that. There's a little bit of fear for
me, being new.....what if they turn on me? It would be devastating, it
would be like a divorce. I don't want to go through that.

By the time we interviewed Collins again in 2011, he had three years
of experience with fandom, and was thoughtful about the norms and
expectations on both sides of the fan/celebrity fence. He had also broken
many of them.

Collins: I think what made me do it (break the First Rule of Fandom) is
that I don't terribly like rules or conventions or being bounded by the
insidious forces of normalcy. I had a moment when I first got on
Supernatural when I was like, oh my god, people are paying attention to
me, I have fans, maybe I should cultivate an image and try to seem really
cool. I had this moment of being commercially self conscious and it took
maybe a month for me to realize no, this is not who I fucking am, and
here's a picture of me in drag, which is by the way so much more
liberating and relaxing. There's not a more sure fire way to give a stifled,
boring, empty, vapid, meaningless interview than....trying to say the right
thing.

He was also the first guest to decide not to comply with the American
conventions' customary "no cursing" rule. His refusal, and his insistence
on interacting with fans as adults instead of infantilizing them, had the
effect of reducing fan shame. The change in norms also changed the
character of the boundaries in place at conventions between fans and
celebrities, which were also challenged by Collins.

Collins: It's a strange phenomenon that happens, but there's a certain sense
of basic rules that, as an actor coming into celebrity, you almost inherently
understand, as though it's inherited. You're supposed to interact with your
fans in a certain manner—sort of distant, reserved, boundaried. But then if
you take a step back and analyze it, to what end? What is it that you're
really protecting? You don't want people showing up at your house, but
there are so many other boundaries that are kind of arbitrary that we all
subscribe to automatically without even thinking about it.

Fans also absorb the norms and expectations for how to behave—and
how not to.

Collins: Absolutely, it's on both sides. Everybody knows they're supposed
to behave in a certain way. There never was a manual, but the normative

behavior has been established somehow. It's funny, I still see myself falling into this. Why am I behaving this way? Why am I so reluctant to share information or whatever? Actually the fans are by and large so respectful of those boundaries, that you're kind of inherently safe. Like all this bullshit of five security guards every time you go to the bathroom at an event. No one is going to do anything to me. No one ever has or ever will, and yet it's something that's considered normal.

Some of the actors have learned the hard way, however, that boundaries are sometimes necessary, especially to protect themselves from reading too much online opinion.

> Padalecki: I'm lucky because I'm able to avoid the internet and opinions. I remember, when I started *Gilmore Girls*, I was 18, fresh out of Texas, just graduated high school, pretty naïve -- and the 5th episode they cut my hair and the internet was kind of new and I was like oh, weird, they write about this? Cool. And so I read about it and it was like oh, Dean has a different hairstyle and a girl was like he looks ugly, he looks like a girl, and I was like, that hurts! So for whatever reason I was able to completely stop. … I'm not a masochist, it hurts so I stay away. And it's stupid that I'm hurt, but still, I am hurt.

Padalecki is quite aware of the way in which internet anonymity makes it both easier to say hurtful things and harder for the recipients to interpret them.

> Padalecki: I'm gonna piss off a lot of people, but I think the internet can be terrible and hurtful. If I read on the internet his hair cut is horrible and he's ugly, I'd be more hurt than if I were to talk to someone who said I think you look ugly with this haircut. Because I could get where they are speaking from. I could either write it off as this person is either just an asshole, or know how to take it. I've read some pretty scathing things about myself.

The actors attempt to draw boundaries around the personas they adapt as entertainers, as a means of self-protection.

> Padalecki: I don't take it personally, it's just where they put me – they're not attacking me or my family. They're attacking a celebrity. My major issue with these things, they forget that hurtful things do hurt, we are human, and as a species, actors are emotional. Unfortunately sometimes these things sneak in and it's like ow, I thought I was protected against this, where did that come from? Some days are harder than others, and some days the real Jared is having a hard day and it's like ow, and then sometimes I'm fine, and I remember who my parents want me to be and who I am and it's like that's ok, whatever, I'm not taking offense. This is

what they need and want and as an entertainer I'm putting myself   out
there for that. If the negative about living my life and being an entertainer
and getting paid for what I'm passionate about is that some people say
some negative things about me, who cares.

The advent of Facebook, and verified accounts on Twitter, have
allowed the creative side to take some control over their relationship with
fans. Misha Collins, Jared Padalecki, Jim Beaver, and most of
Supernatural's guest actors utilize these tools regularly to communicate
with fans and mobilize the significant power of the SPN fandom to
popularize their other projects. The immediacy of Twitter has created the
perception that celebrities are more accessible, and with it the expectation
of more communication. When fan/celebrity interaction does occur, it
sometimes goes off the rails in unexpected ways, as in *Inglorious Basterds*
star Eli Roth's sexualized chats with his fangirls after someone linked him
to erotic fanfiction starring his character – and himself. Without handlers
or publicists to mediate between them, the interaction was unexpectedly
volatile.

There are benefits to celebrity/fan Twitter interaction, however, for
both individual stars and the networks they work for.   Helen Anne
Peterson blogs about the advent of Twitter and its use by celebrities in a
post titled "We're Making Our Own Paparazzi", contending that the
biggest innovation created by Twitter is the way celebrities can now
negotiate their own images as a sort of 'sanctioned PR.' Who needs gossip
blogs if stars are supplying their own paparazzi pics? (2009).

Danneel Harris was one of the first actresses connected to
Supernatural (through her relationship and now marriage to series star
Jensen Ackles) to establish a presence on Twitter. Two years before she
married Ackles, Harris already had plenty of evidence that *Supernatural*
fans didn't like her, and was struggling to stay away from online fan sites.

> Harris: It's kind of bad, I try to stay away, keep off the message boards and
> stuff. Jared punishes Sandy (Padalecki's then-girlfriend) when she looks at
> it, but Jensen is like, I'm not babying you. If you see another thing you
> don't like, well… I don't go to the fan forums because they're mean, (but)
> I have friends who go on and say hey, listen to what they say about you.

She wondered if fans were having difficulty separating the bitchiness
of Harris' current onscreen character in *One Tree Hill* from the actress'
own personality, and thought that letting the fans see who she really was
might help.

Harris: I think if I weren't an actress, they wouldn't be so mean. Because the character I play (on *One Tree Hill*) is evil and mean. And they're like, why would Jensen date someone like her? And it's like, well, because she's not like that in real life! I'm not taking any more roles like that – I've been dying not to play the bitch. The internet is helping, and all the interviews. Fans are like, oh, you're not mean. So that helps. It's like, oh, that's acting, you wouldn't really push someone off a cliff and watch them die. And it's like….no!

Harris related the story of one particular anti-fan who'd been quite vocal about her dislike of the actress on Ackles' IMDB boards. She joked about making a tee shirt professing her love for this particular fan and calling her out by name, but eventually Harris did one better.

Harris: I did an interview for *Steppin Out* magazine, and at the end of the interview, the writer asked me if there was anything I would like to say to my fans. So I asked him to print "I love you merlethepearl" as a shout out, no questions asked. Too much? She once said I had no sense of humor…. (email 4/28/08).

Harris used a similar strategy on Twitter to deal with her anti-fans, with weekly "Love the Haters" tweets. She also attempted to give fans what they want by periodically tweeting pictures of her husband, a strategy which was quite successful—and to avoid what they didn't want, by making herself scarce at *Supernatural* conventions where he was appearing.

Harris: I just kind of stay out of the way. It's awkward for me because I don't really like to be in the room when he's signing stuff, because people will look at me and wonder, or make it something about me, saying I'm uncomfortable, and they'll write on the internet, oh she's so weird. I like to stay out of the way and watch him do his thing, because he has such a great personality. I think he can do anything. When you watch the one you love being loved by all these people, it warms your heart. It's fun for me to watch. I'm a fan of Jensen's.

The more savvy SPN guest actors have utilized Twitter and Facebook to mobilize fans and encourage them to advocate for certain characters' return to the Show. Chad Lindberg told us he was fully aware, and very appreciative, when fans facilitated his return to *Supernatural* in 2010, via Twitter. The reciprocal relationship here seems skewed in the opposite direction, with fans holding the power and the celebrity investing a great deal of time and energy to facilitate the relationship and keep the lines of communication open.

Lindberg: It was a cathartic moment for me because I worked so hard to get back to that point with the show. You know, making a lot of the connections, meeting all the fans, and really sort of immersing myself with them and being in tune – on Twitter and Facebook, sort of leading an army (laughs) and responding to their letters and their videos and their love for the character and for me. I got back to the set and the general consensus was that the fans were a major part of why I was back. Basically Eric Kripke got the news somehow – I don't know if he was checking or got emails, but collectively he was [aware] that "The fans love Chad and we have to have him back." And so that was the word that I was given and that's amazing! And that's partly why I announced it on Twitter, because I felt they had a hand in helping me achieve that and I wanted to share that with them and let them take that ride with me.

Lindberg, like most of the SPN actors, is well aware that the reciprocal relationship that *Supernatural* has with its fans is stronger than most.

Lindberg: This particular fan base is, I think pretty strong. They have the power to shut down Twitter! I've seen write-ups about them in magazines as being a pretty unique and strong fan base. It's pretty awesome. Fans will get together and make it happen and I think we did and that's cool. I saw an opportunity with Twitter because every week the *Supernatural* fans were taking on Twitter with something, right? And it was just creating all this buzz about *Supernatural* online, so I jumped in there with them and I just said "Let's get me back on the show." And they were fighting for it and then there was a petition started with 1500 signatures! The fans are what's truly holding the show up in a lot of ways, so of course they would have a lot of power. That's exciting. Ten years ago, I don't think that would have been possible. Now there's that instant communication with them. So it worked for me.

That *Supernatural* fans voice their preferences in a loud and organized fashion is another aspect of the reciprocal relationship, and evidence of fans as "part of the process." Actor Todd Stashwick (Dracula in the "Monster Movie" episode) told us that fans mobilized through Twitter and Facebook to convince the organizer of the Asylum UK conventions to have Todd appear as a guest. He later successfully utilized the power of the SPN fan base to generate interest in his online comic *Devil Inside*.

Stashwick: I have heard some actors complain about Twitter; they also don't know how to use it. Like I'm not going to twitter "Um, tasty milkshake." Actors can shoot themselves in the foot with what they twitter, but they can also shoot themselves in the foot with what they say in an interview. In this technological age, why would you cut off a tool?

For the working actors who have appeared on *Supernatural*, the Show's uniquely reciprocal relationship with its fans has been a positive for their careers, which took most of them by surprise. Not only is this a fandom which interacts closely with the creative side online, but in real life as well. There are dozens of *Supernatural* fan conventions every year which bring fans and the creative side face to face, blurring the physical boundaries between fans and actors, though not erasing them. The convention circuit has brought a level of popularity that many of the working actors never anticipated, in addition to a lucrative second income. Richard Speight, Jr. was convinced that Creation Entertainment had made a mistake when they booked him for his first *Supernatural* convention.

Speight: I'm not a celebrity, I'm a working actor. My biggest fear was showing up and having nobody recognize me and just feeling like the biggest jerk! I don't know if I want to put myself out there to look like an a-hole. I had this image of me sitting under a Banner that said, 'Meet Richard Speight Jr' and people just walking by. I would be trying to hand out my autograph and people would just be like, no it's okay. So I just didn't know what to expect. And you see the internet every now and then when people say that dude sucks! So I didn't want to come here and be told how much I suck. Showing up, it has been such a different experience. The first time I saw the crowd was when I was on stage, and it was a huge crowd and I was so relieved, because my fear was -- my mom, four rows back.

Gabe Tigerman had similar fears, as did many of SPN's guest actors. All were overwhelmed by the reception they received at conventions.

Tigerman: It's flattering, totally. I remember when I got invited to the first convention, I was like, you know I only did two episodes, right?? I really thought it was a mistake.

Matt Cohen: The fans have made me feel like I'm something important to the show and that's irreplaceable, because then you go home and you say "Damn, somebody likes what I'm doing!" when you question every word that comes out of your mouth - every actor does. . It hurts my feelings if one fan dislikes me.

Tigerman: It's a little bit surprising. As an actor you go on auditions, you get the job, you watch it, and that's kind of it. Until you get to a certain level, you don't see the fan response and this was the first time I saw it. Walking into a room in Orlando with 400 screaming girls is something every man should experience. It was overwhelming. It's so great to see that something you did or were a part of affected people.

Fred Lehne: A person can't help but like walking into a room full of people who like you. I've been around long enough to keep it in perspective, I think. Some people walk up to me in a photo op and the person is trembling, and I like to settle them down and be like, I'm glad to meet you, and there's nothing special about me. I take pleasure in letting them know I'm just a person, if I can make their day a little better. I like kindness, and community, and it makes both of us better people. I'm a lucky man, and I'm grateful for it.

Samantha Ferris (Ellen on SPN): It was an absolute blast, I mean how can it not be? You get to meet people who love what you do, love your work, constantly tell you that, you're safe, you're protected, you're surrounded by people who love you. How can that not be an ego boost?

Richard Speight Jr.: The thing that is important for everyone to know who comes to these conventions is that the lion's share of actors, at least the actors that I know, love doing what they do for a living, they don't do it at home in the living room for themselves. They do it on a TV set for an audience, or in a theater for an audience. So when an audience reacts, whether it's applause the night of or reactions later on, it's awesome. So anytime you're going somewhere to be surrounded by people who like what you do, it's a great experience. I never have a hard time talking to people or answering the same question 30 times. That's what you do this stuff for, you don't do this to say leave me alone man, I don't want to talk about it. If you're into that, then you've picked the wrong industry.

Matt Cohen was so overwhelmed by the fan reaction at his first *Supernatural* convention in New Jersey in 2010 that he jumped off the stage to give a fan a hug, something not ordinarily considered appropriate within the boundaries of convention space. He was also savvy enough to realize that if he hugged one fan, he'd have to hug them all.

Cohen: I've hugged almost every fan at every convention since then. I figure it's the least I can do when these people are supporting your body of work. Without fans, without what's called "box office" in our industry, you can't work. You can make independent movies for the rest of your life but you're not going to make enough money to survive. Nobody's going to see it, you're not going to get the exposure, it's never going to progress [your career]. So you gotta have the fans.

Cohen actively works at making the relationship between himself and his fans as reciprocal as possible, out of his recognition that it's necessary for box office, but also what seems to be a genuine desire to give back to fans.

Cohen: I try to stay really active (online), answer any question I can, any Happy Birthday I can send out. I did a photoshoot on Monday and I said "Here you go" and put out two pictures online. My agent and manager don't even have those pictures yet. I give to the fans. They give to me. They let me pay my bills and have a life. It's nice to be appreciated, it's

nice to know you're appreciated and that's what I want the fans to know—
I appreciate them. It's not a joke to me. It's not like "I'm a celebrity, I'm
going to be nice to you because I'm a fucking celebrity and I have to be."
No. I need them. We need each other.

Cohen has consciously thinned the line dividing him from fans,
inviting fan input and attempting to adhere to fan influence. Cohen
accepts the responsibility of keeping up the persona that fans want to see,
including physical appearance.

> Cohen: If you're not giving back, why should people pay you so much
> money to recite lines? I know actors who can't get an agent, can't get an
> audition. So when I go on an audition I make it like a day of work. I wake
> up at six in the morning, I go to the gym, I get focused, I eat the best
> breakfast, I make it like my 9-5. . . . And I work out in the gym because it's
> a necessary thing for a guy who's my character type, I have to be fit.
> Truthfully I walk into an audition and it's me and ten dudes who look like
> Jared and Jensen.

Most of the working actors of SPN are invested in creating and
sustaining a positive and reciprocal relationship with fans, and expressed a
desire to "make it good" for the fans.

> Jim Beaver: I try really hard to be the actor I hoped my heroes would be. I
> really try to respond to fans in the way I would have wanted someone to
> respond, but with the internet, I can't keep up. It's not that I don't want to.
> Frankly my biggest concern about going to conventions is giving the false
> impression of dismissing people. When you've got a lot of people wanting
> your attention, I don't want to be somebody that even accidentally makes
> someone think he's stuck up and was ignoring me. I'd better bone up on
> the shows too, because people have a right to expect that Bobby knows
> certain things. Somebody asked me how Bobby's relationship with the
> boys differs from John's relationship, but I've never seen an episode with
> John, I've never met him, I don't know anything about his relationship!
> Maybe I'll just quote some John/Bobby slash. I know, I'll get a tee shirt
> that says I Write John/Bobby!

> Chad Lindberg: I love to make sure people have a memorable experience,
> and if I'm asked to get on the table and pose for them, I'll do it.

In fact, he did just that at the 2008 Creation *Supernatural* convention
in LA, splaying himself across the center of a round table while eight
fangirls regarded him appreciatively. As we've discussed, this is the sort
of objectification that fans often feel guilty or remain in denial about. So
we asked Lindberg whether it was weird, or freaked him out, or was sort

of fun. His answer? All of the above. Most of the guest actors relate to
SPN fans' passion, and are eager to validate it—or share it—another way
of de-emphasizing and thinning boundaries.

> Lehne: Everyone saw William Shatner on Saturday Night Live say
> "Get a life" to fans, and I think he's kind of an asshole for saying that.
> Kind of a slap in the face to your fans. What I found is that there are
> people who are passionate/obsessed about everything. They go to a hockey
> game, and get together and meet like minded folks, and they revel in it, it's
> good, there's nothing wrong with it. There are crazy people every once in a
> while, and I'm not Jared or Jensen, but mostly these people are good, it's a
> passion.
> Cohen: I'd rather be around a passionate nerd than a non-passionate
> cool person. Because if you lack passion, your obsessed about something.
> Obsessed people care. I'm passionate about so many things, it becomes an
> issue at certain points but at least you have the ability to feel that much
> about something,

Musician Jason Manns, who's a frequent musical guest at *Supernatural*
conventions because of his close friendship with Jensen Ackles, even put
the appreciation that all of the actors describe for the fans to music, writing
a song as a thank you to the SPN fans who so wholeheartedly embraced
him and his music, called "I Do It For You."

> Manns: I just wanted to write it as sort of a thank you to the fans. They
> have been unbelievable and I have a pretty unique perspective because
> most guests come to a con after they are famous, and I'm not famous yet.
> But coming here has grown into people asking me to be a part of the
> convention as a separate entity, and it's because of the fans. So to me it
> really is a symbiotic thing, I'm just thankful to the people who come out
> and support, and buy the albums, because literally without them, I
> wouldn't be able to do what I love.

David McKay, embraced by the *Supernatural* fandom as the director
of Jensen Ackles' indie film *Ten Inch Hero*, made the reciprocal
relationship between creator and fans literal with his first film. He got the
autograph of the first person who asked him for one.

Breaking Boundaries: How the Creative Side Feels about Fanworks

As we've seen, the creative side are not the only ones shoring up
boundaries when it comes to the reciprocal relationship. Fans often
attempt to draw impermeable boundaries around fan spaces and fanworks

to keep them invisible to outsiders and spend a great deal of time and energy worrying what others think of our more controversial practices.. Fans worry about actors finding racy fanfiction, or just squeeful posts about Dean Winchester's rare appearances in a tee shirt. Fans also worry about the actors and creative team discovering fan art and vids, particularly those that are not G-rated.

In this section, we break the first rule of fandom ourselves, directly asking the creative side their views on fanworks. Boundaries around fandom insulate fans from potential criticism, but also perpetuate shame,, and fans continue to worry that the reaction of the creative side would be negative, critical, and shaming. As we saw in Chapter Five, the fear of being outed is a common source of wank. In 2011, there was virulent fighting over whether fandom has a responsibility to protect the actors from reading potentially disturbing fiction about themselves online,, resulting in hurtful infighting.

So what do the creative team think of fanworks? Because the lines of communication are indirect at best, fandom does not really know. One of our first discussions about fanworks was with guest actor Gabe Tigerman, who told us that he happened to be on set when some of fandom's worst fears (or most cherished fantasies, depending on your point of view) came true—that day the SPN crew was apparently looking at J2 manips (photoshopped manipulations of Ackles and Padalecki) and Wincest fanvids.

> Tigerman: Everyone had their laptops out, and I was struck by how the scenes were edited together to make it seem very intimate. Jared and Jensen were also showing each other, like somebody had taken two naked dudes together and put their faces on there.

Sometimes real life sounds more like the beginning of a piece of fanfiction.

Predictably, the creative side is a lot less worried about fanworks than fandom is, rarely running across something they haven't gone looking for. Their mothers, on the other hand, seem to have an unfortunate propensity to find the unexpected. Quite a few of the actors we spoke to related stories of their mothers stumbling across surprising things about their offspring on the internet.

> Kripke: I look online for input about the show, but my mother looks for input about her son. Mostly how great her son is, so I get calls at least weekly and she says, you know, on this website they called you a master. It's very flattering, but very embarrassing. I'm just a guy putting out a

show, and I'm from Ohio, and the idea of being a master of anything is
very embarrassing, and I'm a little uncomfortable with the adoration.

The actors, writers and showrunners worry more about what's written
about them as individuals and presented as fact in the press, than they do
about fiction. The boundaries drawn and enforced here, in contrast to the
boundaries we've discussed so far, are largely on the fannish side.

> Tigerman: I'm not going to pretend like it's not weird to read about that,
> and it's a little violating when you see your real name. But overall it's
> creative writing. It's different than an ex-girl-friend writing a tell all!

When the audience roundly booed the fan who asked Richard Speight
Jr. about Wincest at a convention, the actor was surprised by the crowd's
reaction to the question, which he had actually approved beforehand.

> Speight: She asked me if it was fine, if she could ask that question, and I
> said okay. Again, she's not asking if I think incest should be illegal, she's
> asking about a fictional character. I get it – I understand.

Eric Kripke seemed more comfortable with fanfiction than with those
glowing comments his mother keeps uncovering online. He even had an
explanation for the existence of Wincest, and an understanding that the
level of investment that participatory fans show is an indication that the
fictional universe he created is a good place to play. The practice, Kripke
believes, keeps fans a part of the process, a collaborative effort that
doesn't necessarily influence canon, but parallels it.

> Kripke: I'm aware of fanfiction, and slash fiction between the boys
> (referring to Wincest). I think people read into the fact that there are two
> good looking guys on the road, and you can't avoid going there. I take it as
> a compliment as far as the fanfiction between the characters, because what
> we set out in the beginning to obtain is a really self contained universe in
> which fans can come and go, and the rules and progressions are consistent.
> So just as in all other good universes, you can find new ways to expand
> and explore other corners of that universe is a good sign, and the fact that
> the fans are actually doing that is a good sign. I love it and I welcome it. I
> wanted to create a universe where we welcome others to come and play,
> and it means we're developing a fresh universe successfully.

The openness of the relationship between SPN and its fans has
produced some unusual results. Kripke was surprised to learn that he had
been featured in a few pieces of RPS fanfiction, hypothesizing that the
strong reciprocal relationship the Show has with its fandom might be
responsible for incorporating the creator into the fanfic.

> Kripke: Our fans are really intelligent, they care a lot, and they seem to understand the references we're going for. We aim to create an intelligent show – I think we're the red-headed stepchild on the network. We're always joking about that, we wear it as a point of pride. But the idea of show creators being involved….what an odd development! I guess what we are probably doing on *Supernatural* is engaging in more direct dialogue with our fans, in online interviews, at conventions. We do engage in unusually strong dialogue, and maybe that's striking unusual ideas in fans.

Kripke asked to read some of the RPF he starred in, which left us with an ethical dilemma that the field of fan studies is only beginning to tackle. One was a witty piece of J2 slash, with Eric, Kim Manners and Sera Gamble as supporting players. Particularly interesting because Sera played the role of a Mary Sue in the unique way that SPN fandom writes her—in the story, she's the instigator who gets the boys together. The other was rather dark and disturbing, and definitely NC17. Kripke reacted to his own incorporation into fiction as a writer himself, understanding that once you create a character, even one based on a real person, it belongs to the writer. He also repeated one of the points often made by RPF writers—no one is actually writing about the real Eric Kripke, or Jared, or Jensen, or Misha. The characters are merely fictional creations, and the writing itself, as we explored in chapter 4, is all about the writer. Kripke was thoughtful about being on the other end of the equation.

> Kripke: I found it all very amusing. A bit strange, true, but interesting and entertaining. And illuminating. My first reaction was to laugh at how dead wrong the writers got it (beyond the obvious….) All the characterizations of me, Kim and Sera are so off the mark. (Kim and Sera barely know each other outside of conference calls, etc.) But then it occurred to me, I've written all sorts of things about real people during the course of the show (Thomas Edison, Samuel Colt, etc) and never once worried about getting my facts straight, it was all artistic license. So it's interesting to be on the "receiving end" of that artistic license. So I see how it doesn't matter whether it's accurate….even though the character is nominally "me," I have no ownership over it, it belongs to the writer. So yes, very surreal in a funhouse mirror kind of way to have a writer use you as one of their chess pieces. Or at least use a façade of you….because underneath, it's all them.

Sera Gamble also viewed her incorporation into fanfiction from a writer's point of view, finding it both odd and fascinating.

> Gamble: It feels weird. It's awfully meta. The first time I saw that someone had written me into a story, I was just confused. It's like writing the puppeteer into the puppet show or something. Which, actually, now that I've said that sounds kind of interesting in a Charlie Kaufman sort of way.

Gamble, who famously described *Supernatural* as "the epic love story of Sam and Dean", has also spent time gaining an understanding of Wincest, coming to some of the same conclusions as researchers and fans themselves about the appeal of slash. While there's a lot of joking about Sam and Dean's epic love story in the writers' room, Gamble says they don't actually sit around and "plant secret gay sex code into the scenes." She then proved herself well-tuned to fannish sensibilities (and having a sense of humor), as she added, "Sorry!"

> Gamble: We're aware of how into the boys' relationship everyone is. And of course we're aware of the subtext, or the perceived subtext. I think it happens on lots of shows with male leads who are very intimate. I grew up watching Star Trek and was vaguely aware that people liked to write stories about Kirk and Spock getting it on, so I'm not surprised. We joke a lot about it in the writers' room. There's probably a deeper insight into our culture underneath all that slash fiction. Something about men not being free to express love for one another. Plus, that which is taboo tends to enthrall and arouse people; it's one of the more interesting quirks of our species.

Many who theorize about fans' motivations in writing slash would agree with Gamble's interpretation of the practice as a cultural comment; that those who are writing the canon also have an understanding of those motivations is less theorized. SPN fandom is fond of characterizing Gamble as a fangirl. She definitely gets the appeal of one of the other controversial genres of fanfiction, hurt/comfort, as she told us when she learned about the popularity of hurt!Dean fanfiction.

> Gamble: People are writing fiction to torture Dean? I didn't know this at all! Now that I'm thinking about it, I'm not surprised. Dean is the more damaged of the two. He's had to put his own needs aside for his entire life, which tends to cook up an interestingly fucked up kind of person – and in his case, has ended up making him instinctually heroic. Selflessness is a huge part of heroism. We often say in the writers' room, when the two of them are in disagreement, that as long as they're falling all over themselves to save each other they can go pretty out there with the misguided ideas; their actions will still maintain a core of heroism. Hence Dean selling his soul – to save Sam. Also hence Sam forming an alliance with a demon – to save Dean. Anyway, yes, we torture him on purpose. It makes for good drama. And action heroes are there to be beat up – they're not nearly as heroic if they don't pay mightily for their selflessness. On our staff, no one enjoys torturing the boys more than I do. Or at least, no one else sits in the writers' room giggling their head off about it. It's because I'm turned on by the same thing those fiction writers are. I think brave, tortured heroes are sexy. Somewhere in my gooey center, underneath my eye rolling and

cynicism and my collegiate intellectualizing of story, I have a taste for the romantic. So I feel it in my gut when we get it right. Self sacrifice for the one you love is romantic. Tough guy getting beaten to shit and having a hilarious attitude about it to cover up the pain   is romantic. So it's not an intellectual process for me – my inner girly girl just lights up and goes "Tell that story! I am so not changing the channel while his lip is bleeding!"

Of course, the people most often starring in fanfiction, both in character form and "real person" fiction, are Jared and Jensen. Fans spend a significant amount of time worrying about what the actors think of this particular fannish practice, as we've seen. Padalecki was surprised by how many fans liked to think about him and his costar together in a more than friendship way, but more amused than scandalized.

Padalecki: I was not expecting that. It's so abundantly clear that we are not homosexual, not that there's anything wrong with those who are, but it's so strange to me. … Platonically, I know they enjoy that we are great friends , because we ARE great friends, and that comes across, and that I can understand. I think you can tell when someone's having fun on camera. That's why Oceans 11 did so well, because it just looked like they were having such a fun time. They're goofing around and it's fun to watch and see people really laughing and having a good time. The other part, I don't really understand so I have no theory other than, I don't know, maybe boredom?

What about the analogous stereotype that guys find the idea of two good looking women together hot?

Padalecki: Sure, oh sure. I see. I can see that, but I think the reason it's so funny is that it's so far from reality. I'm just like *what*? But sure, you know, of course, yeah—to me it might be bizarre, but whatever floats their boat. I'm glad y'all asked me about that, because it's one thing I don't really understand, and not having any experience with the human mind, or the ins and outs, it's bizarre, it's one of the things you go "alright…". I guess I will choose to take it as flattery.

It seems to be just that. After all, a significant number of SPN fans are bisexual or lesbian women, and they refer to Jared and Jensen as their 5% exception, which is a certainly a compliment.

Padalecki: I'll take it (grinning). It makes a lot of sense if there are a lot of bisexual or gay or lesbian fans that they would sort of turn it into their world.

There followed a discussion of the difference between believing something is factual versus a nice fantasy, which is how most fans enjoy their version of J-Squared—a distinction that Padalecki understood completely. For example, the fans loved that Jared and Jensen were, at the time, living together.

> Padalecki: (laughing) I guess I figured they would. And it's great, we're pretty similar guys. After a long day it's like hey man, you want to go like grab a beer, or go to sleep? He's a good buddy. When times are hard for me, or I've got something I'm going through, it's nice to be like hey man, can I just rattle with you for a little bit, rap about some stuff, and he's like sure, and vice versa.

Ackles was also amused and slightly mystified about why some fans love to imagine him and Jared as a couple. Like Padalecki, he recognized the "subtext" present in their real life friendship, and talked about the genuine affection the two have for each other.

Fig. 7-7: Real life subtext

Fig. 7-8. Brothers in real life: Jared and Jensen.

Ackles: (laughing) It's strange, because you know, being who I am and being who he is, it's like, it's just hard to kinda wrap our minds around. I mean, I've had, I need two hands to count the number of roommates I've had. Guys I've spent a lot of time with, like my best friends. I may not work with them, but we're together at home and we'll go out together, all the time and share each other's problems. It's affection, it's a friendship that, for Jared and I—God, it's a good friendship. I think with Jared and I, we knew right away it wasn't going to work if we didn't get along. The first season, I forget what episode it was, but we got heated on set and got in each other's face and I mean, we went toe to toe. There were no fists thrown or anything like that, and he ended up taking a walk down the street and cooler heads prevailed, and when we got back to our trailers, I knocked on his door and sat down and I was like listen man, that can never happen again because if that's the road we choose to go down, we are going to be living a different life. And it wasn't just me, he was like actually on the same wavelength, like I'm glad you came by, I need to get this off my chest, we need to come together if we are going to make this show work, because we're gonna be spending way too much time together to not have a friendship. And that's the last fight we've ever had. We've got each other's backs and I support him in the decisions he makes and will give him advice when he needs it, and he does the same for me. He went through a rocky thing this summer with his fiancee, and I was there for him for that. It almost turns into art imitating life, or life imitating art, we play brothers on screen but we're kinda brothers off screen as well. It's a brotherly love that he and I have.

Ackles too is well aware that fans can distinguish between fanfiction and reality, and don't necessarily believe the costars share a sexual kind of love as well as a brotherly one. Like Kripke, he understands the existence of Wincest as a consequence of the passionate investment fans have in Sam and Dean's relationship, and extends that to fans' investment in the relationship he has with Jared in real life.

Ackles: I know they don't (think it's real)—it's a hot fantasy. But I think, and you can probably help me out with this, that it might stem from their love of the two characters and how much they have invested in Sam and Dean, and there are really no other characters that they want coming into that realm. I think it's their love for these two characters, they don't want anyone to interfere. They want it to be just the two of them, all the time, and I think that's where it stems from. I don't think they really think we're gay. So I really think it's just the fact they are left with no other option when thinking of these two characters, and of course these guys are together. Though I wish that two guys can just be heterosexual males and still have a brotherly love. But that's why it's called fiction!

We asked Misha Collins about the other popular slash pairing in the fandom—the first Dean/Cas slash community was created 42 minutes after the character appeared.

Collins: (deadpans) Why do you think it took so long? Maybe the servers were down or something.

Collins is fine with the homoerotic vibe of parts of the fandom.

Collins: I certainly try not to be too homophobic in my real life and this is fiction on top of that, so it's one degree further removed, so it's easier.

Fig. 7-9: Mutual support: Ackles gets a leg up from Padalecki.

Like the other actors who negotiate the boundaries between fiction and real life on a daily basis, Collins had no trouble understanding fan fiction as *fiction*. He would, however, like to turn the tables and incorporate fans, as he and his fellow actors have been incorporated.

> Collins: I've been thinking about writing a story of my own about Dean and the fans and then I could post it out in the community.

Fig. 7-10: Misha Collins attempts angelic

Samantha Ferris, who played kickass hunter and sexy older woman Ellen Harvelle across six seasons, was impressed by the quality of *Supernatural* fanfiction. Like most of the guest actors, Ferris recognized the incorporation of Ellen into fanfiction as fandom's investment in the character, and her own portrayal as due some of the credit.

> Ferris: I've read it once or twice, and it is really provocative. It was really cute, it was about Ellen and Dean. Those are writers in the making, man, I mean they really get into it. I'm flattered if people write about me, at whatever level. Even if it is graphic. It means that your character stands out enough for someone to write about it, so it means that I've done my job, so I like it. I like it no matter what level.

Gabriel Tigerman also viewed Andy fanfic as a compliment, and an indication of fans' investment in the character and the show.

> Tigerman: I'm all for creativity and creative writing, and if what inspires people to write is characters they connect with, I think it's great practice. It's interesting to get people's take on it too….to see their minute attention to detail—it's kind of neat when people spot those little things.

Some of the guest actors seem to use their incorporation into fanfic as a yardstick of the character's importance to the *Supernatural* universe and the fans. In fact, Richard Speight Jr. had felt a bit left out, asking in an early interview why there wasn't any SPN fanfiction starring the Trickster. Once his character was revealed to be the archangel Gabriel, an integral part of *Supernatural*'s mythology, that quickly changed. Was he happy to finally be slashed?

> Speight: Yes! I am, and you know why? Because, you go to certain cultures and you go into the deepest darkest woods, and if their way of saying hello is to throw poop on your forehead, you let them throw poop on your forehead. So if their way of saying we love this guy and we love this character and embrace this character is to make him part of slash fiction? Slash away, babe!

Actor Jim Beaver suggested that fans were so good at writing *Supernatural* fanfic, that maybe they should collaborate more directly in the creation of the Show.

> Beaver: So I was reading some *Supernatural* fanfiction the other night….One of the pieces I read was really impressive. They took the idea of Dream A Little Dream of Me and had written the Bobby backstory. It was really rich and eloquently created, and I was thinking, these people could write for the show! And both in fanfiction and to a certain extent, at

the conventions, there's a kind of overlay of, or role playing kind of engagement with the characters. I think that applies to a lot of the fantasy-*slash-Supernatural-slash*-science fiction. And I don't mean "slash" in the way of fanfiction.

In 2007 this was a surprising in-joke – at the time, there were no Lev Grossman pieces in *Time Magazine* on fanfiction, after all. Beaver smirked and said, "My vocabulary is expanding."

Television is Our Campfire: Why We Watch and Write

One of the premises of this book is that there is a therapeutic potential in fandom, including the writing and sharing of fanfiction. The *Supernatural* creative side, many of them writers themselves, have a similar awareness of the healing aspects of writing—any kind of writing—which also influences their views on fanfiction. In addition to confessing to some early *Twin Peaks* fanfic writing herself, Sera Gamble understands the therapeutic potential of both writing and finding a community of acceptance that are often such large parts of fandom.   In fact, Sera emphasized that she feels very much like "one of us" with fans, especially the young creative fans.

> Gamble: There's one part of the "she's like us" that's actually quite important to me. A lot of our fans are creative teenagers, artist types, and if they're anything like me thy're having the shittieest time imaginable getting through high school. I felt so alone, so different from everybody else when I was younger. I know that's practically a universal feeling. But I was such an intense kid. I was one of those loud, bright, sensitive girls who are virtually radioactive with pain and confusion. And I wrote all the time, every day, just to get through it..... I wish I had known some successful working writer who said to me, "I have been where you are, and I can tell you that if you keep writing your way through your pain, it will save your life. It will help you create a life that is fulfilling and meaningful. And you'll even one day get to do what you love for a living." It would have felt like someone telling me, "You are at mile sixteen. Don't panic. It's not this hilly all the way through. There's a bit down the road where the terrain is a lot smoother."

Jim Beaver is also aware of the therapeutic potential of writing, which got him through the most difficult time of his life. When his wife was diagnosed with terminal lung cancer, he started an email newsletter that he sent out every night, now published as the book *Life's That Way*.

Beaver: The writing itself was not hard to do. It was hard stuff to write about, but it was very therapeutic. I think it saved my sanity, and that's one of the great gifts, discovering for myself and being able to tell other people how valuable it is to express what's going on with you in times of turmoil and prevail. Because I found it miraculously helpful. I think it applies to anyone that writes, including fanfiction.

Jim, like many of the actors, finds common ground between the fans and actors, seeing both as drawn to fantasy and creativity as a way of working through personal issues.

Beaver: I've got an actor friend who says nobody got into this business because they're healthy. It applies on both sides of the fandom fence. Any time someone grasps that persistently at something, it's filling some kind of need, and any time there is need, there is damage—or at least lack.

Several of the actors related to the therapeutic value of emotionally engaging with the Show itself, whether watching or participating.

Stashwick: Movies and television, they are safe ground for us to field test our emotions without consequence. I can go and see Rachel getting married and weep like a child without actually losing anybody in my family, and so I think that alone is an importance release valve. And the people that do that to us, become very important to us. It's powerful, and so I think fandom is gratitude. It's a way of thanking you for taking me to places that I many not let myself go to in my normal life. I may not let myself weep like a child in front of my wife, but at a movie, if I'm being moved, I'm crying like a baby or I'm laughing … laughter is such a release, too, and fear as well. It's like fear of death, and then release from that fear of death. We get to confront death in a jovial, playful way, then we get to walk out and say WHEW, it wasn't me.

Padalecki: I think the big thing that has drawn fans to the world of *Supernatural* is that each has turned it into their world. It's no longer about guys on the road or hunting demons, it's connected to some part of them that they might not even know exists. They're like oh, it's kinda like this! That's one of the great things about mythology - the point is to reflect some part of your own life. So you start going Oh, Luke Skywalker kind of doesn't know what he's supposed to be, he's kind of struggling, kind of like me, I'm having my own struggles.

The reading and writing of fanfiction as therapeutic resonated with Jared.

Padalecki: That makes plenty of sense. There's no other logical reason. I don't think any movie or show is that good to be so committed to it unless it's sparked something in you.

In fact, Padalecki identifies the same desire for some healthy escape on the part of cast and crew as within the fandom watching and participating in the Show. That's why so much laughing goes on between takes on the SPN set.

Padalecki: It's almost like the same escapism that our fans are enjoying when they are watching, we are enjoying when we are filming. So it's nice for them to call action and you just lose yourself for a minute.

The reciprocity and mutuality of the relationship between fans and the creative side bringing a show like *Supernatural* to life are recognized by both in the common elements that draw us in, and the satisfaction we get from the human tradition of storytelling—whether onscreen or in an online fanfic community. As actor Todd Stashwick eloquently put it:

Stashwick: I think everyone has had an experience of connection with a show at an emotional level—or connecting with the characters emotionally. For me, I was watching Six Feet Under at a time when my best friend passed away and it was like the episodes were speaking to me. Peel the onion, it's the hero's journey. Family and loss and demons, all that stuff that we're doing, sacrifice. This is what we used to do where the bard would take out his guitar and share his story with us, but now we've moved on to a global way of doing the same thing. Television is our campfire.

At the same time, many on the creative side recognize the same need for a safe space that fans themselves express. Thus, both sides seem content to maintain a boundary between fan spaces and the creative side— to avoid too much influence on the creative vision, sustain the fantasy, and allow fans to remain part of the process, with the freedom to play in the SPN sandbox however they want.

Gamble: I think we're all happy to have inspired people to write stuff of their own, and what they write is really none of our business.

Actor Misha Collins felt the same shortly after he joined the Show.

Collins: I have only a very vague sense of what fans are doing online. I'm not really sure, because not being a fan, or being a member of fandom, not really knowing how to negotiate the spaces, not being versed in that or even the technology , it's kind of a barrier and it just makes it all look like a foggy, confusing mess that I don't have the patience to unravel.   I imagine that makes it a little bit more protected and it feels more special, more exclusive. It's not the kind of thing that any random person is going to come in and screw things up, you have to kind of find it and log in.

When we spoke to Collins again during the filming of Season 7, he told us that what had surprised him most about fandom is the "overwhelming creative energy of the fan community."

Collins: I never imagined that creative energy would be such a strong force. And that also motivates me to try to figure out how to play with that or use that. It's such a fascinating social experiment, like what can be done with this? I'm interested in doing massive art projects with fandom for charity, because there are a lot of amazing artists.

When our interview with Samantha Ferris touched on fanfiction, she instantly related to fan shame when she asked about "real person fiction". Upon learning that those are stories written about her and another actor, usually Ackles, Samantha laughed—and asserted her boundaries.

Ferris: Interesting. That'd probably turn me on, I don't know if I'd want to read that!

Like Collins, she also perceived the boundaries around fan spaces, and fans' tendency toward shame and discomfort when the creative side crossed them. The creative side is concerned that too much input from fans would change the canon universe in a negative way; similarly, Ferris recognized the risk of change with creative side incursion into fan spaces.

Ferris: I feel a little like a voyeur. That's not meant for me, it's meant for them, and if they knew that the character would be reading it, that would change their response, and I don't want to do that, I don't want to change that for them. That's their forum, and I don't want to step in and change that. That's there for them to get their ya ya's from, and I wouldn't want them to feel ashamed or uncomfortable. If they knew, they would start writing differently. We have our outlet, let them have theirs.

The boundary between fans and the creative side is thus shored up from both sides, with too much fluidity a threat to fannish expression and fantasy investment on one side and creative control on the other. The balance remains precarious, and subject to constant re-negotiation, but seems essential to the reciprocal relationship.

Conclusion: Don't Ask, Don't Tell—
Power, Resistance and Shame

When we began researching fandom, we were in the first blush of new love—giddy with the exhilaration of discovering the most amazing television show in the history of ever and a community of like-minded others who wanted to celebrate its greatness along with us. We threw caution (and briefcases) to the wind and followed *Supernatural*'s actors and fans across the United States and Canada, celebrating the Show's renewal with fellow fans at conventions, making fan pilgrimages to Vancouver filming locations, and amassing an impressive collection of dvds, photos, and die-cast Impalas for our coffee tables. Our rose-colored glasses were so firmly in place that we saw fandom as a place of total acceptance, validation, and enjoyment—so compelling that we decided to research the phenomenon that had captured our imaginations completely. We began at the place where others studying fandom had also arrived, after three decades of theory which attempted to rehabilitate the image of the fan and validate fan practices. It's the Age of the Geek, baby, so stand up and fly your fan flag high!

In the course of writing this book—and, perhaps more importantly, in the past six years of being fans immersed in *Supernatural* fandom—we discovered that flying the fan flag is far from uniformly celebrated. A strong sense of internalized shame pervades many segments of fandom, especially for female fans. The word "fangirl" still carries pejorative connotations of crazy, hysterical, and stalker. There's shame about being a fan at all, shame over certain fannish practices, and as a result, fear about anyone "outside" fandom finding out. Shame projected onto the objects of fannish affection creates panic when the fourth wall is broken, as *Supernatural* has found repeatedly over the last few years. Protectiveness of the in-group leads to stringent policing of group norms within fandom, as fans use bullying, aggression and censure to keep fellow fans in line and the group's privacy intact.

Aca-fans experience a double dose of shame—shame about studying something as frivolous as fandom, and shame at taking pleasure in fandom ourselves instead of keeping a detached and rational distance. Cultural studies have traditionally been practiced from a position of authority, with little explication of the researcher's own experience. More recently, fan studies theorists have attempted a partial integration into fandom, following an ethnographic approach but still retaining a level of detachment. Autoethnographic studies went a step further, confessing the aca-fan's fannish history in a mostly rational and intellectualized fashion.

We have attempted to take a position of immersion, writing from within our chosen fandom and including the emotional, sexual, passionate aspects of our own and other fans' investment. The position turned out to be an awkward one. We struggled repeatedly to define our identities as both fans and academics, negotiating and re-negotiating boundaries as we moved between fan spaces and the "legitimate" status of researcher. The two positions differ widely in terms of power, making it difficult to move smoothly between them.

The boundaries muddied further when we attempted to fill a gap in the theorizing of fandom. As much as the increasingly "reciprocal relationship" between fans and the creative side has been discussed, no one had spoken to the individuals on the other side of the fence to hear their thoughts on fans and fan practices. Fans seemed convinced that the objects of their affection were dismissive at best and disgusted or terrified at worst. Theorists were, for the most part, unconcerned with what the creative side might be thinking about fans, although the use of the word "reciprocal relationship" makes it clear there is another side to consider. Crossing the boundary to actually speak to the creative side allowed us to add that missing viewpoint to our analysis of fandom. It also broke the First Rule of Fandom repeatedly, leaving us in the uncomfortable position of straddling the fence between "good fan" and "good researcher."

Our research eventually came full circle. After departing from our initial rose-colored view of fandom and taking a hard look at the negative impact of shame and the relational aggression that it sometimes creates, we nevertheless discovered that the benefits of fandom remained. Perhaps even more important than the transformative potential of fandom on a societal level, is the potential for individual change--the therapeutic potential of fandom in emotional expression, reworking identity, and coping with trauma and challenge. The fan community, while displaying its fair share of policing, bullying and other types of "wank", remains supportive of its members, providing the sense of validation and belongingness which facilitates change.

Attempting to write from the inside has necessitated crossing and re-crossing multiple boundaries, something we have not always managed gracefully. The perspective has, however, allowed what we hope is a deeper understanding of the ways in which fandom functions for individual fans. The challenge now is to move to a more nuanced understanding of fandom with a 360 degree perspective, acknowledging the changing modes of interaction and resulting shifts in power that are reshaping the reciprocal relationship between fans and the things they love.

BIBLIOGRAPHY

Abercrombie, Nicholas. 1998. *Audiences: A Sociological Theory of Performance and Imagination*. London; Thousand Oaks, Calif: Sage.

Abrams, D., A. Rutland, and I. Cameron. 2003. "The development of subjective group dynamics: Children's judgments of normative and deviant in-group and out-group individuals." *Child Development* 74: 1840-1856.

Ackles, Jensen. 2011. Supernatural - Jensen Ackles Interview Part 3 - Sky Living [UK] - YouTube. July 14.
http://www.youtube.com/watch?v=w5jjzRrWC_Y.

adellyna. 2008. Let's Talk Fandom to Celebrity Interaction. January 17.

Anderson, Charles M., and Marian M.MacCurdy. 2006. *Writing and Healing: Toward an Informed Practice*. Urbana, Illinois: National Council of Teachers of English.

angstbigbang. 2011. Big Bang Celebrating The Angst In Fic - **APOLOGIES**. Live Journal Community. August 2.
http://angstbigbang.livejournal.com/1458.html.

AP-MTV. 2009. 2009 AP-MTV Digital Abuse Study.
http://www.athinline.org/MTV-AP_Digital_Abuse_Study_Executive_Summary.pdf.

Armbruster, Jessica. 2010. Top 7 scariest fandoms - Minneapolis News - Dressing Room. August 30.
http://blogs.citypages.com/dressingroom/2010/08/top_7_scariest_1.php.

Arndt, Jamie, and Jamie L. Goldenberg. 2004. "From Self-awareness to Shame-proneness: Evidence of Causal Sequence Among Women." *Self & Identity* 3 (1) (January): 27-37. doi:10.1080/13576500342000022.

Bacon-Smith, Camille. 1992. *Enterprising Women. Television fandom and the creation of popular myth*. Philadelphia: University of Pennsylvania.

Balkie, K.A., and K. Wilhelm. 2005. "Emotional and physical health benefits of expressive writing." *Advances in Psychiatric Treatment* 11: 338-346.

Bartky, S. L. 1990. *Shame and gender. In Femininity and Domination*. London: Routledge.

Batson, C., M. Polycarpou, E. Harmon-Jones, H. Imhoff, E. Mitchener, L. Bednar, T. Klein, and L. Highberger. 1997. "Empathy and attitudes: Can feeling for a member of a stigmatized group improve feeligns toward the group?" *Journal of Personality and Social Psychology* 72 (1): 105-118.

Baumeister, R., and M. Leary. 1995. "The need to belong: Desire for interpersonal attachments as a fundamental human motivation." *Psychological Bulletin, 117, 497-529.* 117: 497-529.

Beecroft, Alex. Why do women write m/m romance? The Macaronis. http://historicromance.wordpress.com/2008/08/15/why-do-women-write-mm-romance/.

Bekakos, Liana. 2008. Supernatural Creator Eric Kripke Answers Fan Questions – Part I. April 23. http://eclipsemagazine.com/hollywood-insider/5626/.

Benjamin, Jessica. 1988. *The bonds of love: Psychoanalysis, feminism, and the problem of domination.* New York: Pantheon Books.

Bivona, J., and J. Critelli. 2009. "The nature of women's rape fantasies: An analysis of prevalence, frequency and contents." *Journal of Sex Research* 46 (1): 33-45.

Bizman, A., and Y. Yinon. 2002. "Engaging in distancing tactics among sport fans: Effects on self esteem and emotional responses." *Journal of Social Psychology* 142: 381-392.

Black, Rebecca W. 2008. *Adolescents and online fan fiction.* Peter Lang.

Blank, Hanne. 2011. once more into the breach. *Filling a Much-Needed Void.* July 28. http://www.hanneblank.com/blog/2011/07/28/once-more-into-the-breach/.

Boen, F., N. Vanbeselaere, and J. Feys. 2002. "Behavior consequences of fluctuating group success: An internet study of soccer team fans." *Journal of Social Psychology* 142: 781-796.

Booth, Paul. 2008. "Rereading Fandom: MySpace Character Personas and Narrative Identification." *Critical Studies in Media Communication* 25 (5) (December): 514-536. doi:10.1080/15295030802468073.

Booth, S. 2011. "Die hard fan." *Psychology Today*, February.

Borsolino, Mary. 2006. Super Women: Supernatural's Executive Story Editor. *Sequential Tart.* December 1. http://www.sequentialtart.com/article.php?id=345.

Bourdieu, Pierre. 1984. *Distinction: A Social Critique of the Judgement of Taste.* London: Routledge & Kegan Paul.

Bukatman, Scott. 1993. *Terminal Identity: The Virtual Subject in Postmodern Science Fiction.* Durham, NC: Duke University Press.

Bury, Rhiannon. 2005. *Cyberspaces of their own: female fandoms online.* Digital formations. New York: Peter Lang. http://library.georgetown.edu/search/i?=0820471186; http://www.loc.gov/catdir/toc/ecip0416/2004007400.html.

Bushman, B.J., and C. A. Anderson. 2002. "Violent video games and hostile expectations: A test of the general aggression model." *Personality and Social Psychology Bulletin* 28: 1679-1686.

Busse, Kristina. 2010. Geek Hierarchies, Boundary Policing, and the Good Fan/Bad Fan Dichotomy. *Antenna*. August 13. http://blog.commarts.wisc.edu/2010/08/13/geek-hierarchies-boundary-policing-and-the-good-fanbad-fan-dichotomy/.

Baym, Nancy. 2011. Online Fandom» Biting And Feeding The Hands That Feed: Audience-Musician Interactions Online. *Online Fandom*. September 8. http://www.onlinefandom.com/archives/biting-and-feeding -the-hands-that-feed-audience-musician-interactions-online/.

de Certeau, Michel. 1984. *The Practice of Everyday Life*. Berkeley: University of California Press.

Chan, Suzette. 2010. Tarts talk about Supernatural 5.09: The Real Ghostbusters. *Sequential Tart*. January 4. http://www.sequentialtart.com/article.php?id=1603.

Chander, Anupam, and Madhavi Sunder. 2007. Everyone's a Superhero: A Cultural Theory of "Mary Sue" Fan Fiction as Fair Use. California Law Review, April.

Cicioni, Mirna. 1998. Male pair bonds and female desire in fan slash writing. In ed. Cheryl Harris and Allison Alexander. *Theorizing Fandom: Fans, Subculture and Identity*. New Jersey: Hampton Press.

Classen, S. 1998. Redeeming values: Retail coupon and product refund fans. In , ed. Cheryl Harris and Allison Alexander. *Theorizing Fandom: Fans, Subculture and Identity*. New Jersey: Hampton Press.

Colby, Edward. 2011. *Monday Books Blog Report: The "Creative Sandbox," Pottermore, and an Author Who Did It First*. Vol. 2011. 10/19/2011. June 27.

Cooper, A., D. Delmonico, E. Griffin-Shelley, E., and R. Mathy. 2004. "Online sexual activity: An examination of potentially problematic behaviors." *Sexual Addiction and Compulsivity* 11: 129.

Corey, G., and M.S. Corey. 2006. *Groups: Process and Practice*. Belmont, CA: Thomson/BrooksCole.

Costello, V., and B. Moore. 2007. "Cultural Outlaws: An Examination of Audience Activity and Online Television Fandom." *Television and New Media* 8 (2): 124-143.

Couldry, Nick. 2007. *Media Consumption and Public Engagement: Beyond the Presumption of Attention*. Consumption and public life. Basingstoke, Hampshire: New York: Palgrave Macmillan.

cupidsbow. 2007. Women/Writing 1: The Response So Far. April 28.

Dehue, F., C. Bolman, and T. Vollink. 2008. "Cyberbullying: Youngsters' experiences and parental perception." *Cyberpsychology and Behavior* 11 (2): 217-223.

Dell, Chad. 1998. "Lookit that hunk of man!": Subversive pleasures, female fandom, and professional wrestling. In , ed. Cheryl Harris and Allison Alexander. *Theorizing Fandom: Fans, Subculture and Identity.* New Jersey: Hampton Press. New Jersey: Hampton Press.

Dodge, K.A., and J. D. Coie. 1987. "Social information processing factors in reactive and proactive aggression in children's peer groups." *Journal of Personality and Social Psychology* 53: 1146-1158.

dodger_winslow. 2011. I Digress; Therefore, I Am. - True Love Letters are Never a Mistake. Live Journal. February 26.

Doty, Alexander. 2000. *Flaming Classics: Queering the Film Canon.* New York: Routledge.

Driscoll, Catherine. 2006. One true pairing: The romance of pornography and the pornography of romance. In , ed. Karen Hellekson and Kristina Busse. *Fan Fiction and Fan Communities in the Age of the Internet.* Jefferson, North Carolina: McFarland.

Dunlap, K., and C. Wolf. 2010. "Fans behaving badly: Anime metafandom, brutal criticism, and the intellectual fan." *Mechademia* 5: 267-283.

Ehrenreich, Barbara, Elizabeth Hess, and Gloria Jacobs. 1992. Beatlemania: Girls just want to have fun. In , ed. Lisa Lewis. *The Adoring Audience: Fan Culture and Popular Media.* New York: Routledge.

Eidelman, S., and M. Biernat. 2002. "Derogating black sheep: Individual or group protection?" *Journal of Experimental Social Psychology* 39: 601-609.

ellen_fremedon. 2004. Slash shock, shamelessness, and a rec. Live Journal. December 2.

End, C. M. 2001. "An examination of NFL fans' computer mediated BIRGing." *Journal of Sport Behavior* 24: 162-181.

End, Christian M, and Natalie J. Foster. 2010. "The effects of seat location, ticket cost, and team identification on sport fans' instrumental and hostile aggression." *North American Journal of Psychology* 12 (3) (December): 421-432.

fanficrants. 2010. It's a HOBBY! Live Journal community. *fanficrants.* August 16. http://fanficrants.livejournal.com/9787994.html.

Fine, Michelle. 1988. "Sexuality, schooling and adolescent females: The missing discourse of desire." *Harvard Educational Review* 58 (1): 29-53.

Finn, J., and M. Banach. 2000. "Victimization online: the down side of seeking human services for women on the internet." *Cyberpsychology and Behavior,* 3: 243-254.

Fiske, J. 1992. The cultural economy of fandom. In , ed. Lisa Lewis. *The Adoring Audience: Fan Culture and Popular Media.* New York: Routledge.

Ford, Anne. 2005. To Mordor and Back. *Chicago Reader.* October 6. http://www.chicagoreader.com/chicago/to-mordor-and-back/Content?oid=920098.

Francis, M.E., and J.W. Pennebaker. 1992. "Putting stress into words: The impact of writing on physiological, absentee and self-reported emotional well being measures." *American Journal of Health Promotion* 6: 280-287.

GarlandGrey. 2011. Sexual Inadequacy: Ambiguously Gay Wizards. *Bitch Media.* August 2. http://bitchmagazine.org/post/sexual-inadequacy-ambiguously-gay-wizards.

Garrison, Lindsay. 2010. "Crying for Justin Bieber" and Negotiating Affective Fan Performance | In Media Res. *In Media Res.* June 15. http://mediacommons.futureofthebook.org/imr/2010/06/14/crying-justin-bieber-and-negotiating-affective-fan-performance.

Gilligan, Carol. 1993. *In A Different Voice: Psychological Theory and Women's Development.* Cambridge, Massachusetts: Harvard University Press.

Gimlin, D. 2010. "Uncivil attention and the public runner." *Sociology of Sport Journal* 27 (3): 268-284.

Goffman, E. 1963. *Behavior in Public Places: Notes on the Social Organization of Gatherings.* London: Collier-Macmillan Ltd.

Gray, Jonathan, Cornel Sandvoss, and C. Lee Harrington. 2007. *Fandom: Identities and Communities in a Mediated World.* New York: New York University Press.

Green, S., C. Jenkins, and H. Jenkins. 1998. Normal female interest in men bonking: Selections from The Terra Nostra Underground and Strange Bedfellows. In , ed. Cheryl Harris and Allison Alexander. *Theorizing Fandom: Fans, Subculture and Identity.* New Jersey: Hampton Press.

Greenberg, M.A., C. B. Wortman, and A.A. Stone. 1996. "Emotional expression and physical health: Revising traumatic memories or fostering self-regulation?" *Journal of Personality and Social Psychology* 71 (3): 588-603.

Grossman, Lev. 2011. *The Boy Who Lived Forever.* July 7. http://www.time.com/time/arts/article/0,8599,2081784,00.html.

Grunert, Jeanne R. 2008. *Why I Write Fan Fiction.* Vol. 2011. 10/19/2011.

Hariton, E. Barbara, and Jerome L. Singer. 1974. "Women's fantasies during sexual intercourse: Normative and theoretical implications." *Journal of Consulting and Clinical Psychology* 42 (3) (June): 313-322. doi:10.1037/h0036669.

Hellekson, Karen, and Kristina Busse. 2006. *Fan Fiction and Fan Communities in the Age of the Internet: New Essays.* Jefferson, N.C: McFarland & Co.

Herman, Judith. 1992. *Trauma and Recovery.* New York: Basic.

Hills, Matt. 2002. *Fan Cultures.* Sussex studies in culture and communication. London; New York: Routledge.

Hills, Matt, and Henry Jenkins. 2001. "Intensities interviews Henry Jenkins." *Intensities* 2 (July 7). http://intensities.org/Essays/Jenkins.pdf.

Hinerman, S. 1992. "I'll be here with you': Fans, fantasy and the figure of Elvis. In ed. Lisa Lewis. *The Adoring Audience: Fan Culture and Popular Media.* New York: Routledge.

Holmes, Su, and Sean Redmond. 2010. "A journal in Celebrity Studies - Celebrity Studies" 1: 1-10.

Jenkins. 2011. Acafandom and Beyond: Week Three, Part Two (Kristina Busse, Flourish Klink, and Nancy Baym). June 29.

Jenkins, Henry. 1988. "Star Trek rerun, reread, rewritten: Fan writing as textual poaching." *Critical Studies in Mass Communication* 5 (2): 85-107.

—. 1992. *Textual Poachers: television fans & participatory culture.* Studies in culture and communication. New York: Routledge.

—. 2006. *Convergence Culture.* New York: New York University Press. http://hdl.handle.net/2027/heb.05936.

—. 2007a. Supernatural: First Impressions. Blog. *Confessions of an Aca/Fan.* January 15. http://henryjenkins.org/2007/01/supernatural.html.

—. 2007b. *The Wow Climax: Tracing the Emotional Impact of Popular Culture.* New York: New York University Press.

—. 2007c. Gender and Fan Culture (Round Fifteen, Part One): Bob Rehak and Suzanne Scott. *Confessions of an Aca/Fan: Archives.* September 14. http://www.henryjenkins.org/2007/09/gender_and_fan_culture_round_f_3.html.

Jenson, Joli. 1992. Fandom As Pathology. In *The Adoring audience: fan culture and popular media*, ed. Lewis. Psychology Press.

Jetten, J., R. Spears, and A. Manstead. 1996. "Intergroup norms and intergroup discriminatin: Distinctive self-categorization and social identity effects." *Journal of Personality and Social Psychology* 71: 1222-1233.

Jung, Susanne. 2004. Queering Popular Culture: Female Spectators and the Appeal of Writing Slash Fan Fiction. *Gender Forum:* http://www.genderforum.org/issues/gender-queeries/queering-popular-culture-female-spectators-and-the-appeal-of-writing-slash-fan-fiction/.

kalichan. 2010. what's love got to do with it: my thoughts on *fail. Live Journal. November 23.

Karp, M., and D.W. Stoller. 1999. *The Bust Guide to the New Girl Order.* New York: Penguin Books.

Kinzie, Charlotte. 2011. The "Supernatural" Sheriff is Back In Town. *Affairs Magazine.* http://affairsmagazine.com/wordpress2/2011/08/10/the-Supernatural-sheriff-is-back-in-town/.

Klein, K., and A. Boals. 2001. "Expressive writing can increase working memory capacity." *Journal of Experimental Psychology: General* 130: 520-533.

Krustritz, A. 2003. "Slashing The Romance Narrative." *The Journal of American Culture* 26 (3): 371-384.

Kubicek, John. 2011. This is a Meta Slideshow: TV's 20 Most Self-Referential Shows. *BuddyTV.* February 22. http://www.buddytv.com/slideshows/supernatural/this-is-a-meta-slideshow-tvs-20-most-selfreferential-shows-9923.aspx.

Lancaster, Kurt. 2001. *Interacting with Babylon 5: Fan Performance in a Media Universe.* 1st ed. Austin: University of Texas Press.

Lange, A., J. Van de Ven, and B.A. Schrieken. 2000. "Internet mediated, protocol-driven treatment of psychological dysfunction." *Journal of Telemedicine and Telecare* 6: 15-21.

laurenist. 2010. Misha Collins or: How I Learned to Start Worrying and Hate Sean Penn. Blog. *International Withouth Pity.* August 23. http://laurenist.wordpress.com/2010/08/23/misha-collins-or-how-i-learned-to-start-worrying-and-hate-sean-penn/.

Leiblum, S. R. 2001. "Women, sex and the internet." *Sexual and Relationship Therapy* 16 (4): 289-405.

Leitenberg, Harold, and Kris Henning. 1995. "Sexual fantasy." *Psychological Bulletin* 117 (May): 469-496.

Lynn, Euros. 2006. The Runaway Bride. *Doctor Who.* BBC, December 25.

Macleod, Allison. 2009. The curious case of the game show neuroscientists, or how NOT to research an online community. The Human Element. September 3.

http://mackle.wordpress.com/2009/09/03/the-curious-case-of-the-game-show-neuroscientists-or-how-not-to-research-an-online-community/.

Markus, H., and P. Nurius. 1986. "Possible Selves." *American Psychologist,* 41: 954-969.

Marques, J., D. Adams, and R. Serodio. 2001. "Being better by being right: Subjective group dynamics and derogation of ingroup deviants when generic norms are undermined." *Journal of Personality and Social Psychology* 81: 436-447.

Meekums, Bonnie. 2005. "Creative writing as a tool for assessment: Implications for embodied working." *The Arts in Psychotherapy* 32: 95-105.

Meerkerk, G., R. Van Den Eijnden, and H. Garretsen. 2006. "Predicting compulsive internet use: It's all about sex!" *Cyberpsychology and Behavior* 9 (1): 95-103.

Meggers, Heather. 2012. "Discovering the Authentic Sexual Self: The Role of Fandom in the Transformation of Fans' Sexual Attitudes." In *Fan Culture: Theory/Practice*, ed. Katherine Larsen and Lynn Zubernis. Newcastle-upon-Tyne: Cambridge Scholars.

missyjack. 2010. A box of mirrors, a unicorn, and a pony. Live Journal. *a queer and pleasant danger.* March 17.

Monaghan, John, and Peter Just. 2000. *Sociological and Cultural Anthropology: A Very Short Introduction.* Oxford: Oxford University Press.

my_daroga. 2010. Hollywood RPF. Dreamwidth. May 25.

mystifyingbliss. 2007. Naruto-fandom. Live Journal Community. *fanficrants.* September 18. http://fanficrants.livejournal.com/5494269.html.

Nachbar, John G, and Kevin Lausé. 1992. *Popular Culture: An Introductory Text.* Bowling Green, OH: Bowling Green State University Popular Press.

Neuhauser, Lance. 2010. PHD Perspectives: Want to Know the Value of a "Fan?" Ask the Late 90s -. *PHD Perspectives.* May 4. http://www.mediabizbloggers.com/phd-perspectives/92801364.html.

Noonan, R. 1998. The psychology of sex: A mirror from the internet. In, ed. Jayne Gackenbach, 143-168. *Psychology and the Internet: Intrapersonal, Interpersonal and Transpersonal Implications.* San Diego: Academic Press.

Ohanesian, Liz. 2009. Comic-Con's Twilight Protests: Is There a Gender War Brewing? - Los Angeles Art - Style Council. Blog. *LAWeekly.* July 28.

http://blogs.laweekly.com/stylecouncil/2009/07/twilight_protests.php.
Ojala, K., and D. Nesdale. 2004. "Bullying and social identity: The effects of group norms and distinctiveness threat on attitudes towards bullying." *British Journal of Developmental Psychology* 22: 19-35.
Park, C.L., and C.J. Bloomberg. 2002. "Disclosing trauma through writing: Testing the meaning-making hypothesis." *Cognitive Therapy and Research* 26: 597-616.
Pediatrics, American Academy of. 2011. *Social Media and Kids: Some Benefits, Some Worries*. Vol. 2011. March 28.
Penley, Constance. 1997. *NASA/Trek: Popular Science and Sex in America*. New York:: Verso.
Pennebaker, J. W. 1985. "Trauma experience and psychosomatic disease: Exploring the roles of behavioral inhibition, obsession and confiding." *Canadian Psychologist* 26: 82-95.
Pennebaker, J.W., and S.K. Beall. 1986. "Confronting a traumatic event: Toward an understanding of inhibition and disease." *Journal of Abnormal Psychology* 95 (3): 274-281.
Pennebaker, J.W., and A. Graybeal. 2001. "Patterns of natural language use: Disclosure, personality and social integration." *Current Directions in Psychological Science* 10: 90-93.
Peterson, Helen A. 2009. *"We"re Making Our Own Paparazzi': Twitter and the Construction of Star Authenticity*. Vol. 2011. 10/19/2011. May 28.
Poulin, F., and M. Boivin. 2000. "Reactive and proactive aggression: Evidence of a two-factor model." *Psychological Assessment* 12: 115-122.
Prudom, Laura. 2011. *Supernatural' Preview: 5 Reasons Why You Can't Miss Friday's Meta-Filled Episode*. Vol. 2011. 10/19/2011. February 23.
Radway, Janice. 1984. *Reading The Romance: Women, Patriarchy and Popular Culture*. Chapel Hill: University of North Carolina Press.
Reysen, S., and N. Branscombe. 2009. "Fanship and fandom: Comparisons between sport and non-sport fans." *Journal of Sport Behavior* 33 (2): 176-193.
rivers_bend. 2011. On tinhatting. Live Journal. *Writ Large*. February 5.
ROFL RAZZI. Boo! For Pedophilia Double-Standards - Celebrity Pictures, Lol Celebs and Funny Actor and Actress Photos - ROFLrazzi. *ROFL RAZZI*.
Rogers, Carl. 1961. *On Becoming A Person:A Therapist's View of Therapy*. Boston: Houghton.

http://celebs.icanhascheezburger.com/2010/04/04/celebrity-pictures-twilight-moms-cheering-cops/.

Russ, Joanna. 1983. *How To Suppress Women's Writing*. Austin, Texas: University of Texas Press.

Sandvoss, Cornel. 2005. *Fans: The Mirror of Consumption*. Cambridge, UK: Polity Press.

Scheff, T. J. 1979. *Catharsis in Healing, Ritual and Drama*. Berkeley: University of California Press.

Sedgwick, Eve K. 1985. *Between Men: English Literature and Male Homosocial Desire*. New York: Columbia University Press.

Seu, Bruna I. 2006. "Shameful selves: Women's feelings of inadequacy and constructed facades." *European Journal of Psychotherapy and Counselling* 8 (3): 285-303.

Sharp, S., D. Thompson, and T. Arora. 2000. "How long before it hurts? An investigation into long-term bullying." *School Psychology International* 21: 37-46.

Sheese, B.E., E. L. Brown, and W.G. Graziano. 2004. "Emotional expression in cyberspace: Searching for moderators of the Pennebaker disclosure effect via email." *Health Psychology* 23: 457-464.

Shirky, Clay. 2003. A Group Is Its Own Worst Enemy. July 1. http://www.shirky.com/writings/group_enemy.html.

silver_spotted. 2010. writingthewall | RPF: An Aggressive Act? Dreamwidth. *writingthewall*. May 25. http://writingthewall.dreamwidth.org/5993.html.

Sloane, D., and B. P. Marx. 2004. "Taking pen to hand: Evaluating theories underlying the written disclosure paradigm." *Clinical Psychology: Science and Practice* 11 (2): 121-137.

Smucker, M.R., and J. Niederee. 1995. "Treating incest-related PTSD and pathogenic schemas through imaginal rescripting." *Cognitive and Behavioral Practice* 2: 63-93.

Stern, Teresa. 2011. "Fandom: What can it teach social workers about social networking?" Unpublished paper written for course at MSW program at Hunter College School of Social Work.

Stewart, Alan, and Robert Neimeyer. 2001. "Emplotting the traumatic self: Narrative revision and the construction of coherence." *The Humanistic Psychologist* 29: 8-39.

Straw, Amanda. 2009. Squeeing, Flailing, and the "Post-Jared-andJensen Glow": An Ethnography of Creation Entertainment's March 2009 "Salute to Supernatural" Conventions. http://www.personal.psu.edu/als595/blogs/amandalynn125/papers/ethnography.pdf.

strina. 2010. Terrible, Horrible, Motherfucking Amazing Stories I Have Loved. May 4.

sweetestdrain. 2010. The True Story of Matilda Sweetfuck - The Making of "On the Prowl". August 12.

Tajfel, H., and J. Turner. 1986. An integrative theory of intergroup conflict. In , ed. William G. Austin and Stephen Worchel. *The Social Psychology of Intergroup Relations.* Monterey CA: Brooks Cole.

Tankel, J.D., and K. Murphy. 1998. Collecting comic books: A study of the fan and curatorial consumption. In , ed. Cheryl Harris and Allison Alexander. *Theorizing Fandom: Fans, Subculture and Identity.* New Jersey: Hampton Press.

the_slash_pile. 2010. Discussion: Do meatspace people know what a kinky freak you are? Live Journal Community. *the_slash_pile.* November 4.

Thomas, Angela. 2004. Blurring and breaking through the boundaries of narrative, literacy, and identity in adolescent fan fiction. In ed. Michele Knobel and Colin Lankshear. *A New Literacies Sampler.* Cambridge: Peter Lang Publishing.

Thompson, John B. 1995. *The Media and Modernity: A Social Theory of the Media.* Stanford, CA: Stanford University Press.

Thornton, S. 1995. *Club Cultures: Music, Media and Subcultural Capital.* Cambridge U.K.: Polity Press.

toft. 2010. links, and hc_bingo. Dreamwidth. June 14.

Tosenberger, Catherine. 2008. "The epic love story of Sam and Dean": "Supernatural," queer readings, and the romance of incestuous fan fiction. *Transformative Works and Cultures.* http://journal.trans formativeworks.org/index.php/TWC/article/view/30/36.

—. 2010. "Love! Valor! 'Supernatural'!" *Transformative Works and Cultures* 4.

Tulloch, John. 2000. *Watching Television Audiences: Cultural Theories and Methods.* London: New York: Arnold; Co-published in the United States of America by Oxford University Press.

TWOP 4-18. 2009. 4-18: "The Monster At The End Of This Book" 2009.04.02 - TWoP Forums. *Television Without Pity.* April 2. http://forums.televisionwithoutpity.com/index.php?showtopic=318401 7&st=15.

TWOP 5-1. 2009. 5-1: "Sympathy for the Devil." *Television Without Pity.* September 10. http://forums.televisionwithoutpity.com/index.php?showtopic=318889 6&st=60.

Vermorel, F., and J. Vermorel. 1992. A glimpse of the fan factory. In , ed.
  Lisa Lewis. *The Adoring Audience: Fan Culture and Popular Media.*
  New York.: Routledge.
Voci, A. 2006. "Relevance of social categories, depersonalization and
  group processes: Two field studies of self categorization theory."
  European Journal of Social Psychology 36: 73-90.
Wakefield, K.L., and Daniel L. Wann. 2006. "An examination of
  dysfunctional sport fans: Method of classification and relationships
  with problem behaviors." *Journal of Leisure Research* 38: 168-186.
Walkerdine, V. 1990. *School girl fictions.* London: Verso.
Wann, Daniel, M. Melnick, G.Russell, G, and D D. Pease. 2001. *Sports
  fans: The psychology and social impact of spectators.* New York:
  Routledge.
Weldon, Estella V. 2002. *Ideas in Psychoanalysis: Sadomasochism.*
  Cambridge, UK: Icon Books.
Wheat, Alynda. 2009. "Supernatural": Sexy. Scary. Over? *Entertainment
  Weekly.* April 8. http://www.ew.com/ew/article/0,,20270843,00.html.
Wilkinson, Jules. 2010. "A box of mirrors, a unicorn, and a pony."
  Transformative Works and Cultures 4.
  http://journal.transformativeworks.org/index.php/twc/article/view/159/
  138.
Wilson, Tracy. 2011. FanStuff Guide to Fan Etiquette No. 8: Stop Doing It
  Wrong. Blog. *The Blogs at HowStuffWorks.* March 18.
  http://blogs.howstuffworks.com/2011/03/18/fanstuff-guide-to-fan-
  etiquette-no-8-stop-doing-it-wrong/.
Winans, Spencer. 2010. You Sethsy Thing: One of our favorite
  pornographer's Seth Rogen-inspired nudie drawings hit the market.
  Staff Blog. *New York Press.* February 25.
  http://www.nypress.com/blog-8358-you-sethsy-thing.html.
Yalom, I. D. 1998. *The Yalom Reader: Selections from the Work of a
  Master Therapist and Storyteller.* New York: Basic Books.
yourlibrarian: 2011. Whither the Squick. Live Journal. February 26.
Zurbriggen, Eileen L., and Megan R. Yost. 2004. "Power, Desire, and
  Pleasure in Sexual Fantasies." *Journal of Sex Research* 41 (3): 288-
  300.

INDEX

A

Abercrombie, Nicholas · 17
Abrams, J. J. · 143
aca-fans · 7, 9, 11, 13, 36, 41, 44,
  45, 46, 47, 48, 51, 53, 58, 149,
  198, 228
Ackles, Jensen · 2, 33, 40, 53, 54,
  57, 58, 60, 64, 65, 66, 71, 116,
  117, 127, 153, 154, 155, 156,
  169, 172, 175, 178, 185, 190,
  191, 194, 195, 201, 202, 203,
  206, 207, 212, 218
aggression · 13, 118, 119, 121, 124,
  129, 130, 228
  reactive · 119, 127, 130, 131,
    136
  relational · 66, 115, 121, 229
Anderson, Charles · 114
anonmeme · 120
anonymity · 13, 106, 120, 121, 186,
  205
  aggression · 82
  self expression · 67
Archive Of Our Own (AO3) · 19,
  20
Arndt, Jamie · 66
authorial intent · 179, 181, 215
authorized discourse · 11, 66, 67,
  68, 69, 80
autoethnography · 59, 228

B

Bacon-Smith, Camille · 12, 100,
  152
Balkie, K.A. · 103
Bartky, Sandra · 61, 62, 74, 80
Baumeister, Roy · 113
Baym, Nancy · 37, 38, 47, 48, 149,
  150, 153
Beatlemania · 12, 60, 64
Beaver, Jim · 21, 150, 156, 185,
  190, 197, 199, 200, 201, 206,
  211, 223, 224, 225
Beecroft, Alex · 80, 81
Benjamin, Jessica · 63
Bieber, Justin · 59, 60, 61
Big Name Fan (BNF) · 22, 30, 122
Bivona, Jenny · 137
Black, Rebecca · 36
Blank, Hanne · 36
Boen, F. · 124
Bogost, Ian · 47, 59
Booth, Paul · 36
Booth, Stephanie · 128, 130
Bourdieu, Pierre · 47
bromance · 2, 151, 152, 171
Bukatman, Scott · 59
bullying · 13, 90, 108, 115, 118,
  119, 120, 121, 124, 228, 229
Bury, Rhiannon · 38, 45, 64, 68
Busse, Kristina · 7, 37, 45, 47, 60,
  64, 84, 149, 150

C

canon · 3, 20, 92, 96, 100, 132, 141, 151, 152, 153, 155, 157, 162, 164, 167, 170, 176, 182, 186, 197, 198, 214, 216, 227
carnival · 21, 145, 155, 192
Castiel · 124, 131, 152, 200
catharsis · 86, 102, 114
celebrity · 29, 43, 211
    fan/celebrity interaction · 14, 145, 206
censorship · 10, 19, 20, 136, 140
Chander, Anupam · 30
Cicioni, Mirna · 85
Classen, Steven · 86
Cohen, Matt · 58, 176, 185, 196, 209, 210, 211, 212
Collins, Misha · 84, 130, 131, 153, 154, 155, 156, 172, 177, 200, 203, 204, 206, 220, 221, 222, 226, 227
Comic Con · 3, 11, 31, 59, 126, 128, 129, 130, 182
community · 12, 20, 21, 30, 34, 49, 67, 84, 85, 86, 89, 92, 94, 96, 97, 105, 112, 113, 114, 124, 125, 127, 224, 227, 229
conventions · 14, 15, 16, 17, 21, 22, 25, 33, 53, 77, 130, 144, 145, 155, 182, 184, 191, 192, 193, 207, 208, 209, 210, 211, 212, 215, 224, 228
    Asylum · 57, 116, 156, 194, 208
    Creation · 32, 33, 127, 145, 155, 157, 211
Cooper, Al · 135
Cooper, Chris · 32, 175
Corey, Gerald · 114
cosplay · 15

Costello, Victor · 143
Couldry, Nick · 36
Creation Entertainment · 1, 21, 209

D

Davies, Russell T. · 143, 177
de Certeau, Michel · 6
Dell, Chad · 64
displacement · 101, 102, 104, 106, 107, 111
Doctor Who · 43, 45
Dodge, K.A. · 119
Doty, Alex · 10, 46
Dreamwidth · 20, 95
Driscoll, Catherine · 86
Dunlap, Kathryn · 125, 142
Dyer, Richard · 43

E

Ehrenreich, Barbara · 64
emotionality · 38, 40, 59, 66, 101
empowerment · 100, 101, 104, 107
expressive writing · 12, 85, 86, 101, 102, 103, 104, 106

F

Facebook · 14, 16, 118, 150, 178, 206, 207, 208
fame · 8, 43, 50, 186, 190, 191, 193, 196
fan pilgrimage · 40
Fandom Wank · 12, 13, 118, 123, 125, 130, 142
fandomsecrets · 75, 98, 99

fanfiction
   gen · 94, 123, 131
   hurt/comfort (H/C) · 73, 75, 76,
     90, 92, 93, 94, 97, 101, 109,
     110, 111, 112, 164, 216
   mpreg · 20, 76, 83, 94
   real person fiction · 19, 47, 124,
     131, 134, 140, 146, 147, 148,
     150, 160, 161, 162, 215, 227
   slash · 12, 15, 40, 45, 49, 67, 73,
     74, 75, 76, 77, 79, 80, 82, 85,
     87, 90, 92, 93, 97, 98, 100,
     101, 106, 107, 109, 111, 112,
     123, 124, 131, 141, 151, 152,
     155, 156, 161, 162, 164, 166,
     169, 185, 200, 211, 214, 215,
     216, 220, 223, 224
   Wincest · 20, 80, 90, 110, 117,
     123, 131, 144, 145, 152, 156,
     162, 163, 164, 167, 170, 198,
     200, 213, 214, 216, 220
FanFiction.net · 19, 20, 78
fantasy · 13, 59, 60, 64, 66, 67, 68,
   78, 81, 85, 86, 91, 92, 132, 135,
   137, 151, 164, 170, 176, 181,
   186, 195, 218, 220, 224, 225,
   226, 227
fanvid · 73, 90
Ferris, Samantha · 210, 223, 227
Fine, Michelle · 66, 80
first rule of fandom · 1, 12, 13, 62,
   78, 79, 117, 144, 147, 150, 156,
   168, 204, 213, 229
fourth wall · 13, 14, 122, 144, 146,
   147, 150, 154, 155, 156, 157,
   158, 161, 162, 167, 168, 171,
   172, 173, 177, 197, 228
Freud, Sigmund · 59, 61, 113, 199

G

Gamble, Sera · 123, 152, 154, 159,
   162, 172, 177, 180, 181, 182,
   183, 184, 195, 215, 216, 224,
   226
Garrison, Lindsay · 59, 60
gift economy · 88
Gilligan, Carol · 62
Goffman, Erving · 124, 128
Gray, Jonathan · 45
Greenberg, M.A. · 102
Grossman, Lev · 148, 224
Grunert, Jeanne · 108

H

Hanson, Rae · 34, 35
Harris, Cheryl · 45
Harris, Danneel · 53, 71, 206, 207
Harris, M.G. · 148
Harry Potter · 9, 57, 149, 151
Hellekson, Karen · 7, 45, 84
Herman, Judith · 104, 105
hierarchy · 13, 25, 121, 129
Hills, Matt · 7, 8, 10, 45, 46, 47, 49,
   84, 142
Hinerman, Stephen · 84, 85
Holmes, Su · 43

I

icons · 7, 67, 68, 71, 90, 131

identity · 7, 11, 32, 33, 34, 52, 61,
   62, 84, 85, 86, 87, 88, 102, 103,
   104, 106, 107, 108, 109, 112,
   117, 123, 124, 125, 128, 129,
   152, 163, 203, 229
idfic · 95
immediacy · 3, 150, 206
immersion · 7, 38, 48, 229

J

Jacobs, Gloria · 64
Jenkins, Henry · 2, 8, 12, 45, 47, 48,
   49, 53, 59, 67, 86, 100, 101, 107,
   109, 149, 150, 176
   Confessions of An Aca-Fan · 37,
      47, 149
   Convergence Culture · 3, 14, 84,
      143
   The Wow Climax, 7
Jenson, Joli · 44, 45
Jetten, J. · 124
Journal of Celebrity Studies · 43
Jsquared · 90, 131, 155, 170, 186,
   213, 215
Jung, Suzanne · 106, 107

K

Karp, Marcelle · 63
kink · 49, 50, 66, 78, 81, 91, 93,
   135, 136, 137, 138
Klink, Flourish · 37, 47, 149
Kripke, Eric · 2, 122, 123, 129, 154,
   157, 159, 160, 161, 162, 163,
   164, 165, 167, 168, 169, 170,
   171, 172, 177, 178, 179, 180,

   181, 182, 183, 184, 195, 196,
   208, 214, 215, 220
Krustritz, Anne · 100, 101
Kubicek, John · 157

L

Lancaster, Kurt · 7
Lause, Kevin · 42
Leary, Mark · 113, 123
Lehne, Fred · 193, 209, 212
Leiblum, Sandra · 66, 136
Leitenberg, Harold · 66
Lindberg, Chad · 185, 193, 207,
   208, 211
Live Journal · 3, 17, 20, 36, 49, 110,
   178, 182
Longhurst, Brian · 17
Lord of the Rings · 52, 151, 186
lovemaps · 135, 136, 139, 140

M

MacCurdy, Marian · 114
Malin, Adam · 21, 22, 54
Manners, Kim · 144, 172, 215
Manns, Jason · 33, 194, 212
Markus, Hazel Rose · 103
Marques, J. · 124
Mary Sue · 30, 97, 125, 162, 215
Maxwell, Sarz · 111, 112
McKay, David · 212
Meekums, Bonnie · 103, 104, 109,
   110
Meggers, Heather · 66
meta · 14, 73, 83, 86, 90, 91, 93, 97,
   108, 118, 134, 146, 157, 163,
   164, 169, 172, 173, 215

metafandom · 78, 91, 92, 94, 105, 109, 142
Monaghan, John · 36
Moore, Barbara · 143
Moore, Ronald D. · 177
Murphy, Keith · 86
My Big Break · 193

N

Nachbar, John · 42
narrative therapy · 12, 86, 101, 103, 104, 107, 109, 110
Neuhauser, Lance · 6
niche-seeking · 9
Niederee, Claudia · 104
Noonan, Ray · 136

O

objectification · 64, 68, 73, 74, 160, 165, 202, 211
Ogas, Ogi · 49, 85
Ojala, K. · 124
One True Pairing (OTP) · 131, 132, 135
online sexual activity · 135
Organization for Transformative Works · 19, 50
Orwell, George · 42
outing · 52, 123, 127, 157, 165, 167

P

Padalecki, Jared · 2, 40, 59, 73, 129, 130, 144, 153, 154, 155, 170, 172, 175, 184, 185, 186, 187,

190, 191, 194, 205, 206, 217, 218, 225, 226
participatory fandom · 9, 16
Penley, Constance · 86
Pennebaker, James · 101, 102, 103
Peterson, Helen Anne · 60, 206
picspam · 59, 90
Plastic Winchester Theater · 30, 32, 33
pleasure · 1, 10, 11, 30, 41, 47, 63, 67, 78, 93, 95, 130, 135, 167, 210, 228
Postman, Neil · 42
Poulin, F. · 119
Presley, Elvis · 84, 86
projection · 12, 13, 14, 70, 85, 135, 146

R

Race!Fail · 127, 141
Radway, Janice · 12, 64, 167
reciprocal relationship · 8, 13, 14, 143, 144, 159, 173, 176, 177, 178, 179, 181, 183, 185, 187, 195, 196, 197, 200, 207, 208, 209, 211, 212, 214, 227, 229
Rehak. Bob · 45
Reysen, S · 128
Rhodes, Kim · 197
Rogers, Carl · 103
role playing games · 9, 16, 144
Rudski, Jeff · 128
Russ, Joanna · 74, 88

S

Sandvoss, Cornel · 7, 8, 10, 45, 48,
    84, 85, 112, 123
Scheff, Thomas · 102
Sedgwick, Eve · 100
Sequential Tart · 173
Seu, Irene Bruna · 61, 62
shame · 9, 57
    academic · 1, 42–48
    and gender · 59–66
    fan shame · 58
    internalized shame · 12, 13, 67,
        69, 73, 105, 134, 146, 228
Sharp, S. · 118
shipping · 132, 134, 135
Shirky, Clay · 121, 122, 123
slash · *See* fanfiction
Sloane, D. · 101, 103
Smucker, Mervin · 104
soap opera · 48
social identity · 123, 124, 129
sockpuppet · 82
Speight Jr., Richard · 145, 196, 197,
    209, 210, 214, 223
sports fans · 130, 131
Star Trek · 12, 21, 100, 126, 216,
    235
Star Wars · 9, 59, 126, 128
Stashwick, Todd · 208, 225, 226
Stern, Teresa · 87
Stewart, Alan · 103
stigma · 44, 71, 112
Stoller, Debbie · 63
Straw, Amanda · 145, 155
StrikeThrough · 20
subtext · 83, 141, 151, 152, 153,
    162, 170, 198, 216, 218
Superwiki · 122, 146
Survey!Fail · 50, 127

T

Tajfel, Henry · 123
Tankel, Jonathan · 86
Television Without Pity · 17, 36,
    122, 161
Ten Inch Hero · 40, 212
Thomas, Angela · 106, 107
Thompson, John · 14
Thornton, Sarah · 7, 84
Tigerman, Gabriel · 185, 193, 209,
    213, 214, 223
tinhat · 83, 131, 132, 155
Tosenberger, Catherine · 152, 170
Transformative Works and Cultures
    · 50, 158
trauma · 86, 91, 101, 102, 103, 104,
    106, 109, 110, 111, 113, 114,
    115, 135, 136, 138, 229
trolling · 115, 136, 177
Tulloch, John · 10, 48
Tumblr · 9, 16, 151
Turner, John · 123, 129
Twilight · 16, 60, 126, 128
Twitter · 6, 14, 16, 84, 134, 150,
    153, 154, 206, 207, 208

U

universality · 86, 96, 114

V

validation · 9, 16, 30, 32, 33, 62, 68,
    73, 80, 98, 130, 228, 229
Vancouver · 32, 40, 57, 175, 182,
    228

Vermorel, Fred · 48, 84
Vermorel, Judy · 48, 84
vidding · 15, 37, 83
Voci, A · 123
voyeurism · 66, 112

W

Wakefield, K. · 130
Walkerdine, Valerie · 62
wank · 13, 49, 92, 115, 116, 122,
    123, 124, 125, 127, 128, 131,
    132, 134, 135, 136, 137, 140,
    141, 142, 146, 156, 164, 213,
    229
Wann, Daniel · 129, 130
Warner Brothers · 92
Warner, Kristen · 60
Weldon, Estrella · 113
Whedon, Joss · 144, 154

Whitfield, C. Malik · 195
Wilkinson, Jules · 158, 170, 171
Wincest · *See* fanfiction
Winchester, Dean · 2, 20, 71, 82,
    109, 167, 191, 213
Winchester, John · 2, 58, 83
Winchester, Sam · 2, 20, 165, 184,
    187
WinCon · 82, 83, 84, 97
Wolf, Carissa · 125, 142

Y

Yalom, Irving · 113, 114
Yost, Meggan · 66

Z

Zurbriggen, Eileen · 66